PARAJA

PARAJA

PARAJA

GOPINATH MOHANTY

Translated from Oriya by
Bikram K. Das

OXFORD
UNIVERSITY PRESS

OXFORD
UNIVERSITY PRESS

Oxford University Press is a department of the University of Oxford.
It furthers the University's objective of excellence in research, scholarship,
and education by publishing worldwide. Oxford is a registered trademark of
Oxford University Press in the UK and in certain other countries

Published in India by
Oxford University Press
22 Workspace, 2nd Floor, 1/22 Asaf Ali Road, New Delhi 110002, India

First Edition published in 1987
Oxford India Paperbacks 1989

ISBN-13: 978-0-19-562391-8
ISBN-10: 0-19-562391-6

Typeset by Taj Services Ltd., Noida U.P.
Printed in India by Replika Press Pvt. Ltd.

Translator's Introduction

This novel takes its name from the aboriginal Paraja tribe which has its home among the rugged mountains and forests of Koraput in Orissa. The protagonist of the novel, Sukru Jani, is a patriarch of the Paraja tribe; his story is the story of the tribe—in fact of *all* the tribes to whom these mountains and forests once belonged. The mountains are being levelled now and the forests were cut down long ago; the tribes are disinherited. Soon, perhaps, they will be only a memory. Their tale is a sad one but possesses immense charm. Gopinath Mohanty, who has spent a lifetime trying to understand these tribals of the mountains and forests, attempts to tell their story in several of his major novels. *Paraja*, perhaps the most poignant and lyrical of these, is a remarkable work by any standard and ranks among the masterpieces of Indian writing in this century.

Gopinath Mohanty belongs to a generation of writers to whom social commitment comes naturally. *Paraja*, like all his other novels, is born out of passionate social awareness, verging on anger. At a basic level his work has to be interpreted as an indictment of social oppression and abuse—a recurring theme in Mohanty's fiction. Here the exploited is a family of tribals; the exploiter, outwardly a non-tribal moneylender, is in reality the entire ethos of a materialistic civilization seeking to encroach upon and engulf a primordial and elemental way of life. Mohanty is not, however, fighting ideological battles in the manner of historians, economists and sociologists. The characters he creates are very real people set in a three-dimensional landscape. He has known the sounds and smells of the jungle he so lovingly evokes; what is more, he has obviously suffered and exulted with Sukru Jani and his tribe, drunk rice-beer with them, sung their songs, danced at their harvest festivals and starved with them when the rains failed. The author's intense personal involvement is unmistakable even if one were ignorant of this background of lived and shared experience, and it lends *Paraja* a surging power that very few Indian novels have. What is remarkable is that the novel, written in 1945, should have dated so little. Its sociological, philosophical and moral concerns remain entirely contemporary.

This is because *Paraja* is so much more than sociological or anthropological documentation. Sukru Jani is not merely the primitive tribesman ensnared by the predatory moneylender from the city; he is also quintessential *man*, waging heroic but futile war against a hostile universe, struggling ceaselessly to accept and adjust. The choice of the tribal canvas, whether by accident or design, becomes singularly appropriate to Mohanty's theme: the primeval consciousness of his tribal protagonists reflects perfectly the situation of the archetypal human being; their stark joys and interwoven anguish embody the complexity of the human condition. As was said in the citation of the Jnanpith Award, given to the author in 1974, 'in Mohanty's hands, the social is lifted to the level of the metaphysical.'

Paraja is, in one sense, a disturbingly pessimistic novel.

Mohanty seems to know that the blissful innocence of tribal existence cannot endure: it is foredoomed. There is no mistaking the nostalgia: 'it was thus', he seems to be telling us, even as we watch his Paraja men and women at work or play. Thus, even as he tells us—with complete approval—of the wild abandon of the orgiastic harvest festival, we are warned: 'The disapproving eyes of a modern society were a million miles away.' We know then that the disapproving eyes are dangerously near; the end is at hand. The gradual corrosion of innocence by a creeping, crawling, lurking evil is as maddening as any modern method of torture: it not only destroys but debases and humiliates. The contrast between natural and man-made calamity is glaring. Sukru Jani's wife, Sombari, we are told, was dragged away one day by a man-eating tiger as she collected dry twigs in the forest. Sukru Jani suffers, but for him this event is comprehensible: it is a part of his life. What he cannot comprehend, however, is the infinitely convoluted process by which he and his children are transformed from free men into *gotis* or serfs, bound to the Sahukar (moneylender) for ever. He cannot comprehend why a man should be arrested and fined for cutting down trees in the jungle. Sukru Jani and his children can only gape as the coils tighten around them, inch by painful inch. They do not even have the advantage of a complicated system of metaphysics which could explain or rationalize events for them. Their gods and goddesses are much too simple to be of much help. The saddest part of the story is perhaps the ultimate corrosion of Jili, Sukru Jani's elder and favourite daughter.

The pathos only serves, however, to highlight the symphony of existence. Flowers bloom only to droop; huts crumble and dreams are swept away like cobwebs, but all this does not invalidate the act of blossoming. Huts have to be built and dreams must be dreamt. Man is entitled to fight for the preservation of his right to dream. Life goes on.

The theme of human endurance in the face of tragedy must be universal, but what is uniquely Indian about Gopinath Mohanty's rendering is a certain compassion. He is too much in love with life to be a detached observer or critic; his sympathy flows generously and impartially to everything in creation. Ultimately, there are no oppressors or oppressed in his universe. The tyrant is as much to be pitied as the victim. Pain is transmuted into a form of cosmic laughter.

No translation can hope to capture the varied riches of Gopinath Mohanty's Oriya prose, vigorously colloquial and forthright at one moment and sublimely effervescent and lyrical at the next. Perhaps, like every translation of great literature, all that this English rendering can do is place before a wider audience something of the flavour of the original work.

Bikram K. Das

Acknowledgements

I have since 1937 written twenty-five novels in my mother tongue, Oriya. I have, besides, written some two hundred stories, published in different Oriya magazines and anthologies; of these nearly twenty-five are, in fact, short novels. But except for a few stories translated into English and published in literary magazines and collections of Indian short stories, none of my fiction has ever before appeared in English.

I am, therefore, deeply indebted to Dr Bikram K Das, Professor of English in the SEAMO Regional Language Center, Singapore, for translating *Paraja*. Working on my own original translation, and at the instance of the late Oliver Stallybrass, Dr Das prepared a condensed version which was then scrutinized and edited by Oliver Stallybrass, to whom I owe a heavy debt of gratitude.

I am also extremely grateful to Dr Sitakant Mahapatra for taking such a keen interest in seeing *Paraja* published.

The novel is dedicated to my mother.

Gopinath Mohanty

Chapter 1

Viewed from the winding road on the fearsome mountain-pass known as the Dharam-Dooar—'The Gate of Truth'—the scene below is one of violent struggle. It is a landscape of hills fighting. They stand in two rows facing each other, forty hills on one side and fifty on the other, wrestling for a foothold. In the distance, three miles to the north, a tiny hamlet crouches close to the sloping waist of a high hill. This is the hamlet of Sarsupadar in the Eastern Ghats. The road links the towns of Koraput and Rayagada and climbs up the Dharam-Dooar before dropping to the village of Lacchimpur three miles away.

The hamlet consists of two clusters of thatched huts huddled together under the shade of some trees. These are its two separate 'streets', in one of which live people of the Paraja tribe, while the Dombs live in the other.

The huts in each of the two settlements stand in parallel rows, flanked by patches of green—tiny squares of land sown with maize, chillies or tobacco and fenced in by hedges of the wild tania shrub. Beyond the hedges are fields of mandia, olsi and kandula—different kinds of millet which form the staple food of these tribes.

There are only twenty-two families living in this village.

Sukru Jani lives in 'Paraja Street'. He has his hut and his small family, and he lives in peace. His needs are simple: a bowl of mandia gruel every morning and again in the evening, and a strip of cloth four fingers wide to wrap around his loins—and these he has never lacked.

It is three years since his wife Sombari went out, early one morning, to collect edible leaves in the 'Bear Gorge', and never came back. A man-eating tiger of the big, striped Mahabala species had been lurking in the dense undergrowth in the gorge; it pounced on her and dragged her away. Since then, Sukru Jani has lived with his sons Mandia and Tikra, and his daughters Jili and Bili.

At sunset, a small fire smoulders in the narrow porch outside his hut where Jili is cooking the evening meal. She takes a little powdered mandia or mango-seed flour in an earthen pot, adds a few edible leaves, pours water into the pot and sets it on the fire to boil. Then she sits on the porch with her legs stretched out before her. Her raven-black hair is oiled and combed into a smooth, slanting bun into which she has stuck a red flower. Her sister sits by her side. She too has a red flower in her hair. They are waiting for the pot to boil. Their father and their brothers Mandia and Tikra return home after their day's work of hoeing on the hills. Each of them has an axe resting on his shoulder and each carries a hoe. They sit together on the porch.

Sukru Jani rolls a bit of tobacco leaf into a cigar and smokes. He feels restful and contented as he sits there. The thought that these four children, now grown to youth, are his, likewise the hut, though it is only a tiny, low-roofed shelter, fills him with pride and confidence. As he looks around him, he sees a bewildering mass of hills and forests and, above them, a sky so big that he cannot see where it ends. But he does not feel lost in that limitless expanse; he can still find himself whenever he wants to, and he feels that he lives.

Sukru Jani's hut has a single room divided into three compartments. Inside, it is pitch dark. The central compartment is the one that matters, for it is used both as living-room and as store, while the two compartments on either side of it are only tiny cells. In a corner of this room there is a heap of mango seeds, to be crushed into powder, boiled and eaten. In another corner of the room, seeds of the wild hedge-plant bai-gaba have been piled: these are crushed for oil. The store of food-grains in the room consists of about ten measures of mandia; a portion of this is kept in containers made of leaves sewn together, and the rest is scattered on the mud floor. The room contains three or four empty earthen pots. Hanging from the thatch are the strips of loincloth which the men wear, and the cotton saris of the two girls, as well as dozens of empty shells of dried bottle-gourd, which are used as flasks for carrying mandia gruel to the fields. Rough umbrellas, made of dried palm leaves, are scattered around the hut.

This is all that Sukru Jani's home contains; there is nothing more. The things have been piled together or thrown about in disorder; but he is familiar with this disorder and he likes it, as he likes the smoke from his hearth which lingers under the thatch and chokes him at cooking-time—for his house has no window and there is not even a chink in the walls. He loves his home, for everything in it is his own.

As the sun sets, Sukru Jani, sitting on the porch outside his hut, suddenly finds the hills buried under a shower of colour. The hilltops look a flaming red, as though their heads have been smeared with the scarlet powder which people scatter on each other at the Spring Festival. The hillsides look yellow and festive, as though sprinkled with fine turmeric powder. Below the hills, in the deep valleys covered with dense forests, the colour changes to the blue-black of the sea. Sukru Jani, as he gazes upon the scene, is filled with a sense of wonder and mystery. He shares, with all the other people of his tribe, the belief that all this has been created by invisible spirits; and now, in his peace and contentment, he sits wondering who those magical spirits might be, and which of them created the sky, the forests, the evening and the night; which spirit confers happiness and good fortune on man, and which brings storms and misery and evil days.

Facing him in the distance is a hill. From its top, down to the bottom, terraced fields have been cut all along its slope, like a stairway descending into the ravine below. The fields are full of crops. A hill stream hurries away into the ravine and he can picture the scene though he cannot see it: the water dancing over rocks and gurgling as it flows down and down. He turns round and faces the other side where before him lies a plateau, below which a narrow carpet of paddy goes winding away into the distance like a green snake. These are the paddy fields of the people of Sarsupadar. Behind the plateau are ancient mountains with their dense forests. Hills of varying heights rise tier on tier all round the valley in an unbroken ring, shutting out the rest of the world from view.

Sukru Jani feasts his eyes on the scene. Gradually, his glance comes to rest upon a low hill which has once been densely wooded, but is now almost bare, patches of cultivation having replaced the forest. Sukru Jani owns a plot of land on this hill. He remembers how, when the rain was pouring down in torrents, he joined a man named Lobo of the Kondh tribe and the two laid about them with their axes and carved out of the jungle the first clearing on that hill.

He feels happy with his life. It has been as he wanted it to be, and some kind and benevolent spirit has made everything bright and beautiful for him.

And when he thinks of his future he has no doubt that it will be brighter still. He fancies that he can even see it in the far distance, in vivid detail. A number of houses have been built for him and his sons and his grandsons. Yes, they are all there. His sons Mandia and Tikra are married and have had children. He sees even further—his grandsons are already fathers, and the chubby urchins crowding around him are his great-grandchildren. His line has multiplied. He has a big herd of cattle too: there they are—he counts sixty fine animals. And there, in front of the long row of houses which are all his, is a large cattle-shed, and this too is his. And there is the pit into which the cow-dung is thrown, to give manure for his fields. It is a very wide pit; it overflows with cow-dung, and his nostrils drink in its odour and it pleases him. Now he looks around to survey his lands which his sons and grandsons cultivate: they are all over the hills. He sees, in his fancy, that all the hills around his village have been completely cleared of forest and neatly cut into terraced fields where crops grow luxuriantly, and they are all his. Wherever he looks he sees only cultivated fields.

As Sukru Jani sits there, eyes open but sight turned inwards, he sees these visions of the future; and then, at the end of it all, he sees himself, grown old and wizened, and presently dropping down dead. But he does not quit the scene even then. He calls to mind how people of his tribe commemorate the dead. There, in a corner of the open space in the centre of the village, where the tribal dances and assemblies are held, sheltered by the shade of an old mango tree, is a memorial to all the dead of the village—a stone planted vertically for a man and laid flat for a woman. He sees his people placing a stone, erect on the ground under the mango tree, in his honour. He fancies that his spirit has entered into that stone and there it dwells, in that august company of stones which have been there down the ages. And from his dwelling in that stone he watches his race expand and flourish, and he sees the faces of his great-great-grandchildren. His eyes twinkle with pleasure. As he sits there, wrapped in his dreams, night falls and envelops the landscape.

Sukru Jani knows how strong and sturdy his limbs are. He has faith in them and he depends on nothing else. When he felled the jungle on the little hill and made it completely bald in order to raise crops, he used to work for five or six hours at a stretch, never resting his axe for a moment. Sometimes, in the past, he has carried heavy loads for officials on tour, over long distances across mountains, jungles and ravines, to their camps in the bungalows at Kakirigumma or Mankodjhulla. He has carried a hundred pounds slung from either end of a bamboo pole in nets of rope fibre and he has tramped with the pole resting on one shoulder and has earned his wages at one copper for every two miles of the journey. His body is a mass of bulging muscle; his calves are as hard as rock and his bare skin is proof against all weather. He has never known sickness or lassitude; and now he is fifty.

Mandia Jani, his elder son, looks exactly as Sukru did when he was young—strong and robust, with the face of a child. Neither hunger nor thirst can deter him from his work, and he continues to smile even when he is fatigued or in pain. But Tikra, the younger son, is different. Wide-eyed and hurried in his speech, he reminds Sukru Jani of his dead wife, Sombari.

In the evening the family crowds round the fire in a happy circle. The girls Jili and Bili, who have to fetch water from the stream, hasten up the steep ascent with earthen pots filled with water, and arrive home panting, with the water splashing to the rhythm of their movements. They chatter and laugh together, exchanging jokes and pleasantries.

Sukru Jani pulls out his half-smoked cigar from the niche between his ear and his head, lights it again and sucks the smoke in. A sense of peace and repose emanates from the quiet evening and the open hills and fills his being as he inhales.

Chapter 2

At about midday, the women bathe in the stream which flows down the hillside. The bathing-pools which the two tribes use are distinct and separate, even though they live in the same hamlet. Where the Paraja women bathe, the stream makes a bend; the place is open towards the hill while screened from the village by a patch of jungle. Just above the bathing-pool is a low waterfall, and as the stream tumbles down onto the rocks, it shines white, breaks into laughter and then goes running down into an abyss. Because of the rumbling sound that it makes, the waterfall is known as a duduma; there are several such dudumas in this land of mountains and valleys. A large banyan tree provides shade for the pool. On the banks on either side are the terraced fields of lush green mandia, leaning almost to the water's edge. A narrow trodden path crawls up the slope on the opposite banks from the banyan tree and winds away into the undergrowth above.

The sisters Jili and Bili were bathing in the sheltered pool. Jili was seventeen and her sister only fourteen. They had the pool completely to themselves. Like all women of the Paraja tribe, they had cast off their clothes and were bathing naked. Jili had her face to the stream and was washing her sari, beating it on the sheet of rock in front of her. Bili squatted in knee-deep water, cleansing her hair with a shampoo of chilli seeds. At times she would dip her head and splash water on it with her hands. On the bank was an earthen pot which she had brought with her to fill.

While the girls were bathing in the stream, two men of the Paraja tribe could be seen going up the mound that overlooked the pool. Each carried a bamboo pole on his shoulder, with a heavy load suspended from either end. They mopped the sweat off their brows as they went, and they looked neither to right nor to left. At the foot of the mound, another man could be seen loitering on the bank of the stream. He had a shot-gun on his shoulder and to outward appearance he was hunting green-pigeons among the trees on the bank. He was lurking under cover of the trees, and at times he would look up into them and then move away with halting and cautious steps. But most of the time he scanned the water with lecherous, searching eyes.

He could easily be recognized as one from the civilized world, because in those hills, where people went about half-naked, he was dressed in shirt and shorts. In the eyes of the hill folk he was a person in high authority, for he was a forest guard and it was his job to catch people felling trees in the jungle. He would bellow at them and even have them prosecuted. They knew him as the Garod or the Jaman, and, although his rank in the official hierarchy was insignificant, they stood in awe of him.

And now he was here on his rounds.

For a long time his gaze had lingered on the bathing-pool though he only seemed to be searching for birds among the leaves of a tree.

Suddenly, Jili caught sight of him. The two girls got up in confusion and, while Jili hastily wrapped herself in the sari she had been washing, Bili took cover behind her sister, backing slowly towards the bank for her own sari, which she had left hanging from a branch of the banyan tree.

Then they broke into peals of laughter.

The Forest Guard gave a brazen laugh as he hid behind the bushes.

They could no longer see him but he was eyeing them from under cover. They finished their bath hurriedly, filled their pots, clasped them to their sides and went up the slope, their wet clothes clinging to their skins and rustling as they swayed from side to side. The Forest Guard stood there, nostrils distended, and never took his eyes off them until they had disappeared. When they were gone, he whistled softly and circled back towards the village. The pigeons had flown, the weather was no longer suitable for hunting, and his gun weighed heavily on his shoulder.

The Naika, the headman of the village, needed a place where he could relax and entertain important visitors, so a special room had been provided for him outside his hut. Some of the cattle-sheds in the village had been demolished, and the bamboo mats from them used to wall up the veranda and convert it into a room. The Naika, though a Paraja himself, was an important man, for it was he who collected all rents on behalf of the Raja, and delivered them to the Revenue Inspector, known locally as the Ribini. Whenever an official of any sort came to the village, it was the Naika that he first approached.

And now that an official had come and would camp in his house, the Naika was filled with the sense of his own importance. He must be properly dressed, as befitted his rank and, at the same time, show the respect that was due to the visiting official. And so, while below the waist he wore only his loincloth, he had, in addition, put on his old coat and, on his head, a puggaree, from which his cigars, rolled out of sal leaves, could be seen peeping out. Thus attired, he went out to receive the important personage. As he approached the Forest Guard he bowed low from the waist in a gesture of deep obeisance, touching the latter's feet with outstretched hands. Then he touched his forehead and chanted solemnly:

'I bow to you, my lord, the Garod, my master! May the soles of your shoes remain cool!'

The village was still ringing with excited cries announcing the Forest Guard's arrival, and voices could be heard muttering:

'The Garod! The Garod! The Jaman! The Jaman!'

Besides the Naika there was another dignitary in the village, known as the Barik. He was a man of the Domb caste. The Barik was the village watchman, whose function was to be present always, in case the Naika wanted him. As his sign of office he carried a thick bamboo walking-stick which he now flourished as he moved round the village, bawling out to the people to assemble at once. As they arrived, they were told to fetch pulses and vegetables for the Forest Guard, and soon a handsome pile had been collected in front of the Naika's house.

No mean lord was the Forest Guard in the eyes of these people. Every villager owning a pair of bullocks had to pay a 'plough-tax' for the privilege of grazing his cattle in the forest, and the Forest Guard collected the tax. Anyone who had cleared a patch of jungle in which to grow his crops, slashing down the trees and burning them so that the ashes would enrich the soil, could be caught by the Forest Guard and fined or prosecuted. In the same way, anyone found collecting honey from the forests without a licence, or cutting down a piasal tree for timber with which to build his hut, would be answerable to the Forest Guard. And so he roamed the jungle, searching for offenders. He was the only arm of the law in a stretch of dense forest nearly thirty miles across, infested with tigers and bears, and his salary was only eight rupees a month. But those who had put him there expected him to do his duty, and the hill folk held him in mortal fear.

They brought him offerings of chickens and eggs, telling him in all humility that these were only 'vegetables'.

Many of them had some favour to ask. They placed their offerings before him and lay at his feet while they mumbled their prayers. He took their offerings and granted their boons.

Sukru Jani needed more land because his was a growing family and he wanted to get his sons married and to see grandchildren. There was a particular flat-topped mountain in the distance at which he would often look and sigh, because while two of his neighbours, Solomon and Istifan (who were of the Domb caste), had been favoured by the Forest Guard and had already cleared more than ten acres of jungle on that hill, he owned no land there. His hands itched to make a clearing there and to use the big logs to build houses for his sons; for according to tribal custom, a married son can no longer stay with his parents, he should have a house of his own.

And so, at midday, Sukru Jani went to the Forest Guard with two fat hens and three big jackfruits, which were his offerings to the 'great lord', and prostrated himself at his feet. With the humility which people of his tribe always assume on such occasions he moaned:

'Great lord, have pity on me or else I die!'

The Forest Guard made no answer. Sukru Jani got up and produced two rupees which had been tucked in the folds of his loincloth, placed the money at the feet of the Forest Guard, folded his hands and began again.

'Great lord!'

'What do you want?' the Forest Guard barked.

'Great lord, may I fell jungle on that hill over there?'

'All right, you may.'

He heard the words with great joy. His prayer had been granted. He hurried home, almost at a run.

When the Forest Guard had cooked and eaten his dinner he tied up the various offerings in neat bundles and prepared to move on to some other village where he would camp for the night. He needed men to carry his baggage, so the Barik went out and dragged four youths from the fields where they had been working. The youths carried the luggage while the Forest Guard followed at his leisure with his shot-gun on his shoulder and a crowd of villagers trailing behind. It was now late in the afternoon, and when they reached the stream there was Jili at the pool, washing some wild gurdi leaves. As the party waded through the stream the Forest Guard fell back and paused near the bank; then in a bantering tone he hailed the girl in her own dialect and asked:

'What are you doing, girl?'

'These are leaves for cooking, sir,' Jili replied.

'Will you let me have some?' he asked meaningfully.

Jili laughed.

'Didn't you take enough vegetables from our village? What do you want wild gurdi leaves for?' she said.

He could see other girls coming down the slope towards the pool and realized that it was time to go; but he felt that he had at least made a start. He turned on his heel and went.

As the girls gathered at the watering-pool, they burst into peals of laughter; joking and making fun of people was something that came naturally to them. The visit of the Forest Guard was the topic of the day, for they were not concerned with such matters as the clearing of jungle and the planting of millet; these were things which their elders would discuss.

'The beast!' one girl said. 'How he stared at me!'

'Do you know,' said another, 'he chased me!'

'Shame on him!' a third exclaimed, with a laugh. 'A fine man he is! Why, he is as thin as a dry twig! But you should have seen how eager he was!'

'How he barks!' another girl added. 'I was quite scared.'

'My father gave away our black hen to that fellow, and it was laying eggs! It's a shame!'

They discussed him for a long time and no one had a good word to say for him; but all the time they were laughing, and soon they strayed to other topics and forgot what they had been talking about.

Among these girls was Kajodi, whose father was Puri Jani. Kajodi was Jili's closest friend and was betrothed to her brother, Mandia Jani. A rumour going round the village, that Jili and Bagla, son of Rengu Paraja, had fallen in love and would marry, had reached Kajodi's ears. She splashed water at Jili, laughed and began teasing her.

'And now, Mrs Bagla?'

She splashed more water at Jili and asked: Tell me, Mrs Bagla, of whom are you thinking so deeply?'

'Oh, do be quiet!'

'No, tell me!'

Jili laughed and retorted: 'Why don't *you* tell *me* what I can do for you, my dear sister-in-law?'

'Who wants to be her sister-in-law!' Kajodi muttered.

'Who indeed!' Jili said. 'Nothing could be further from your thoughts!'

Kajodi shook her head again and again in denial, pretending to be angry; but it was only fun, like all the other banter which the two friends exchanged ten times a day.

In the centre of the village was a hut which served as a dormitory for all the unmarried girls in the village, while a little way off was the men's dormitory. It was an ancient Paraja custom for all unmarried boys and girls to sleep in their respective dormitories, rather than in their parents' homes.

But for some nights past Jili had not joined the other girls in the dormitory. Now it was Kajodi's turn to tease her about it.

'Why haven't you been coming to the dormitoiy? Are the other girls in the way?'

'Why should they be in the way? I don't worry about them.'

'No, indeed not,' said Kajodi. 'Why should one be afraid of others if one has made up one's mind? But you must come tonight, Jili. Think how your poor Bagla will suffer if you don't come. Do have pity on him. He stays awake all night and twangs his dungudunga and repeats his song: 'O my Jili, Jili, Jili, I die with Jili's name on my lips.'

Kajodi tickled Jili and sang the song over and over again. Finally she left. She paused on the ascent, turned, changed her tone to a sweet, affectionate and persuasive one and said to Jili:

'You must come tonight.'

'Yes,' said Jili simply.

Kajodi gave her a roguish smile and went on her way, while Jili turned again to the gurdi leaves she had been washing. They had been soaked too long in the water and had become slimy. The sun was setting; the sky was like a poem. The banks of the stream were deserted. A languid, abstract mood came over Jili, and she began thinking of her lover Bagla, with his powerful build and deer's eyes set in the face of a tiger. They had been playmates since early childhood and with the years Bagla had been drawn towards her more and more. They had grown up together, he like a straight and tall sal tree, and she like the siali creeper which spreads itself all over the sal tree with its clinging tendrils. Often he brought her presents of plums and flowers from the jungle as tokens of his love. Jili recalled this with pride.

In her imagination, Jili could hear the songs which Bagla sang to her, to the accompaniment of his dungudunga: songs of sorrow, and of joy, of the restless lover interminably awaiting his beloved for the appointed tryst in the forests, and the burst of tender feeling with which he welcomes her at last, when the long wait is over.

Suddenly, a deer cried out from the bushes on the other side of the stream. Jili started, realized that it was already evening, and hurried home.

Chapter 3

As the little fires began to flicker in the dark all along the streets, the hearth in Sukru Jani's house was also lit for the evening meal.

Sukru Jani was feeling very happy. Mandia, Tikra, Jili and Bili sat down by his side and he told them:

'Do you understand, my children? We start working tomorrow morning on the Mali Damaka Hill. The Forest Guard has given his permission and there should be no delay.'

He lit his cigar, and sat in the stillness of the evening, full of his own thoughts, and all his visions were of the land which he and his sons would carve out of the jungle; and of the houses that they would build, and of many grandchildren.

'Go and sleep in your dormitories tonight,' he said to his children. The announcement had put them in high spirits. They sat together chatting and bubbling with laughter. Jili sat in the dark and, unnoticed by the others, rubbed castor-oil into her hair, which she then combed neatly. Mandia drew out his dungudunga from under the thatch and retired to a corner, where he sat tuning the instrument and twanging it gently with an assumed air of absent-mindedness and indifference.

When supper was over, Jili began to make for her dormitory and Mandia for his. As they set off into the darkness, Mandia asked her teasingly:

'Where are you going?'

'Where are *you*?' Jili retorted.

The two huts stood a little way apart from each other, in the centre of the village. It was thus that the young people slept every night in their dormitories, away from their parents, with no taboos or restraints imposed upon them. Throughout Paraja history, those two huts had stood at the centre of the tribe. Here, the young men and women sang to each other across the open space that separated them. And if something went wrong, the elders would sit together in conclave next morning and the culprits would be penalized by having to offer four annas' worth of liquor to all the villagers; and then they would drink and dance and sing before the altar of the Earth Goddess, and so the matter would end. This was the only punishment for the

indiscretions of youth. Boys and girls in love had the in-
alienable right to elope, which they often did, and after
that the only thing necessary to get their relationship legal-
ized was a payment of about forty rupees by the boy to the
girl's father, as the customary 'bride-price'.

It was late at night. All was still except for the occasional
flutter of bats in the dense pipal tree that stood in the middle of the village. From the otherwise dark sky the stars
kept their silent watch over the two dormitories. Suddenly, from the men's dormitory sounds of the dungudunga
could be heard. Bagla Paraja was playing his instrument,
plucking at the single string again and again with the ring
finger of his left hand and marking time by beating on the
gourd-shell base with the fingers of his right hand, on
which he wore several rings. The wire twanged, and the
beating of rings on the gourd-shell produced a harmonious
clattering. To the accompaniment of this music, Bagla Paraja sang an ancient ballad:

> To the rhyme of the maize that is fried
> Or the maize that is boiled,
> I fashion my song;
> O my darling who keeps her word,
> Lovely is your nose-ring of gold.
> My dungudunga wears only a brass string
> But it makes exquisite music.
> Like a daughter crying out her heart
> When her widowed mother is taken away
> By another husband,
> I pine and weep for you.
> O my darling, do keep your word,
> Save me, for I die with your name on my lips,
> O Jili!

Jili held her breath as she listened to the song. By her side lay Kajodi, breathing deeply, pretending to be fast asleep. Before Bagla had finished his song, Mandia began:

> Mine is the song of three measures of mandia
> And four measures of the soft and delicate kosla.
> Come, my darling, let us play together.
> Come quickly, my darling;
> Wrap yourself round me like the pumpkin creeper,
> Let us play.
> Look; here comes my Kajodi, buxom Kajodi,
> Let us play.
> Take the true meaning of my song,
> Take its message, the pulp inside the fruit.
> Come running, come running,
> Let us play together.

Jili shook Kajodi awake and said, 'Listen, sister, listen, my brother's wife, do you hear what he sings?'

'*You* should hear the song.'

'He is calling you. Get up,' Jili said and she tickled Kajodi and pinched her hard. The two friends shook with laughter.

Then Kajodi and Jili joined voices and replied to the men's songs with another ancient Paraja ballad:

> I had cast my nets, a variety of nets;
> And I caught a fish, and caught a crab;
> But lo! I saw my mother's brother,
> And I saw my father's father.
> I was scared and I came away.
> In a village where they count sweet mangoes,
> And where they count sour ambda fruit,

This, my song of the hills, means that now
I must run.

Once again, in the other hut, Bagla played on his dungudunga; then three or four more dungudungas twanged in
unison, and, as the music grew louder, darkness slipped
from the leaves on the trees and dropped to the ground;
and a big half-moon rose on the crest of a hill while, to the
accompaniment of the dungudunga, Bagla sang:

> The garment of many colours which you wear,
> That sari woven in Lower Maliguda,
> Wash it clean again, wash it quickly.
> For my sake, beloved, come out in your very best,
> Wear your bangles around your wrists.
> Come out quickly; come, my love.
> Let us romp together, let us dance.
> In this village of our forefathers,
> The village of your mother's brother,
> The village of your grandfather.
> There is no shame,
> There is no fear;
> You have caught no fish,
> You have caught no crab.

The song set all kinds of visions floating in Jili's mind.
She lay in her bed and refused to get up, however much
Kajodi teased her. The hours rolled by and the dungudungas fell silent. Much later that night, when the moon had
flecked the pipal leaves with soft shadows, Jili sat up and
rubbed her eyes. Her head swam, her heart was pounding
and she sat still, in a trance. Then, as if restraining an impulse, she said to herself in a tone of decision:

'No, not tonight.'

Then she lay down beside Kajodi, threw her arms around her and fell asleep.

Chapter 4

Early next morning, Sukru Jani and his sons Mandia and Tikra set out for Mali Damaka Hill. They carried their axes with them.

On their way they met the Forest Guard, who was returning from his visit to the next village. A crowd of porters carried the gifts he had received. He winked at Sukru Jani and coming closer said:

'I have given you what you wanted, old man; next time I come back, will you give me what I shall ask?'

The expression on Sukru Jani's face showed how grateful he was to the Forest Guard. He raised his face to the sky and touched his forehead with folded palms in an attitude which meant 'God be my witness!'

'It must be as you wish, great lord,' he said with emotion. 'You are the ruler of the realm, the officer; you are both father and mother to me. You have but to command and I obey. Can I say "No" to anything that you want of me?'

The Forest Guard looked immensely pleased as he went on his way.

Sukru Jani and his sons reached the hill, selected a patch

of jungle and began clearing it. Their axes thudded incessantly in the stillness. It was hard work; their backs and waists ached with pain and the blood sang in their ears, but while they worked they were dead to all such sensations. Very occasionally, one of them would stop to pour out some mandia gruel from a gourd-shell flask into a cup which he would make out of a leaf, gulp the liquid down and resume work once again. The day grew hotter; the jungle wilted in the scorching noonday sun, the doves cooed in the dense coverts; at times, the dried leaves on the floor of the forest crackled as a deer scampered away; flocks of peacocks peeped at them and hid themselves; but the three men allowed nothing to distract them from their work, and while all other beings in the jungle had rest, man had none.

Day after day, the labour continued on the mountain, and at the end of a month a stretch of jungle had been cleared, while the logs which they had selected from the fellings and brought home were piled high in their courtyard. But still they continued to cut down more and more trees and to widen the clearing which they had made. At times, with the sweat streaming down his body, Sukru Jani would fold his arms across his chest and stand surveying the hills before him.

How vast the forest is! he would think, and how nice it would be if all these trees could be cut down and the ground completely cleared and made ready to raise our crops. Land! That is what we want and there would be enough land then. That patch on the hilltop over there is where I would like to grow suan, and miger and castor and kandula. They would thrive best there. Those deep valleys down below, where now the jungle is thickest, would make the best rice-lands. And surely, the banks on either side of the rivulets, where the sun never shines because the jungle is too dense, would make the best orchards of bananas and pineapples and oranges, and the orchards would stretch from end to end. How rich and black the soil is there! The trees growing there have shed their leaves down the ages; leaves have piled up on the moist ground, layer after layer, rotted and gone into the soil. And a red-gram plant grows taller there than a common guava tree elsewhere, and a castor plant throws out strong shoots. What beautiful lands they are! And all these forest lands can be reclaimed and crops raised on them! Why should there be forests, when they mean nothing to us, and not crops? After all, no one can own the forest. Land can be owned by anyone and the owner can grow crops there. God created all these lands for human beings—what a shame that man prevents his fellow men from putting them to their proper use!

Sukru Jani knew nothing of soil conservation or the danger of destroying forests. Such consideration never entered his head. He was concerned with the present and with his small personal interests. And so he wished the Forest Guard long life and prosperity because he had permitted him to cut down the forest.

'Tomorrow, my son, we move on to the other side of that flat sheet of rock,' he told his eldest son Mandia, 'that is densely wooded with sal and sahaj trees.'

As dusk fell, he could feel his dreams taking shape.

Chapter 5

Another month had passed when the Forest Guard came on his rounds again, with his gun and his bearers. The jungle lay quiet and peaceful; thin streams trickled eternally in deep ravines. But the Forest Guard had eyes only for the parade of bathing beauties under the waterfall. In that land of timid hill-dwellers he was like a king—a king to whom nobody ever said 'No'—who swelled with self-satisfaction and self-importance as he moved among his people.

In the village of Bheriki-Padara, his path led across a field of mandia, where like red flowers on a green background a row of young girls in red saris was busy picking weeds. He went past them and when he was some way off they started singing in chorus. He was charmed by their sweet voices, and the strains of the music rose and fell like mandia plants undulating in the wind.

And their song said:

> You passed through our village, O stranger,
> But spoke not a word to us;
> Go your way, we wish you well;
> But this evening, when the moon rises,
> After the barking deer has ceased to yelp,
> We shall pine for you and die.

The Forest Guard paused to listen, and the simple song touched his heart. 'Would you like to camp in this village for the night, sir?' asked one of the porters.

'No,' said the Forest Guard, 'we have work to do.'

The mountain above Sarsupadar came into view, then its girdle of forests and, finally, the village in the distance. Desire stirred in him again, as he remembered the pool where he had seen Jili bathing.

As usual, he camped on the veranda of the Naika's house. The small children who had been playing scampered away in terror at his approach. Women fled indoors and looked out with dumb eyes from the entrances of their huts, which were like fox-holes. Again the Barik went from street to street collecting the villagers, while the Naika was busy serving the Forest Guard. A goat was brought for slaughter; hens, eggs and vegetables were collected. The villagers came and made their obeisances, and the Forest Guard settled in comfortably.

In the evening, he took a solitary stroll to the bathing-pool, but was disappointed to find no one there. Perhaps, he thought, it was not yet time for Jili to come; he would wait. He hid behind some bushes and presently some girls came to the pool in small groups, and drifted away again; Jili was not among them. As dusk fell, he was still waiting. Then, at last, he caught sight of a lone figure coming down the slope, carrying a pitcher. It was Jili. With a sudden movement, he emerged from his hiding-place and stood before her, stroking his drooping moustache and smiling.

'Do you recognize me, my girl?' he began.

'Yes, indeed,' Jili replied.

'How beautiful you are!' he sighed.

'And aren't you handsome yourself,' she retorted with a smile. He took a few steps towards her and began to joke with her. She replied in the same playful vein—no girl of the hills would allow herself to be beaten by anybody in a skirmish of wit of any kind.

'May I call you my Lovely Flower, my sweet?'

'You may. But if I am to be your Lovely Flower, you will have to be my Red Sand.' These were two of the names which the Parajas—both men and women—used while courting. There were other variations on the same theme: 'Flower of the Sand', 'Fine Sand', 'Lovely Rice' and so on.

'I am staying the night,' the Forest Guard confided. 'What about a dance this evening? Will you come?'

'O yes, that would be lovely,' she replied.

'You shall sing and play on the dungudunga and I'll dance and hop.' They both laughed.

The Forest Guard sang a snatch from an old ballad in the Paraja dialect:

> Now come, my darling,
> Are you as strong as the walls of a stoutly built house?
> Are you as strong as the veranda of the brewer's house?
> Come, let me see how robust you are in your youth.

Suddenly he sprang forward, placed his hands on both her shoulders, looked into her eyes and laughed. Jili shook herself free and moved away. A girl from the hills does not mind a little flirtation, but there is a limit to such trifling; the stranger had gone beyond the limit and made a fool of himself. Jili was both surprised and shocked, but she could not express her resentment to the Forest Guard. Only her dark eyes showed her unhappiness.

A group of villagers, returning from the weekly market at Junagada, appeared on the opposite bank, talking loudly among themselves. The Forest Guard drew back. When they had gone, he approached Jili again and murmured:

'Lovely Flower.'

She did not reply.

Like a bird-catcher who raises his gum-tipped pole higher and higher towards his unsuspecting prey to smear its wings with his bird-lime, the Forest Guard continued to press his overtures and to persuade himself that she would yield. 'No one can see us,' he said in a hoarse whisper, and his eyes were burning. 'There's no one here. Why are you afraid? Come with me. We'll cross the stream and shoot green-pigeons with my gun. Come on.' He spread both his arms wide and took two eager steps forward.

Jili did not move. Her face was grave. She looked him up and down searchingly. She saw before her a stranger, tall, lanky and gaunt. His cheeks were sunken like pits and his hands and legs had been wasted thin by repeated attacks of the malignant malaria that infests the hills. He was gasping for breath and his voice was faint as he hissed through clenched teeth, 'Let's go! Let's go!'

She sized him up with perfect ease and composure. How fantastic it was, she thought, that of all persons on earth this bizarre creature should want to become her lover! For shame! She thought of Bagla, but to compare this creature with Bagla was ludicrous and insulting. She turned her back on him in annoyance and went straight home.

The Forest Guard dogged her steps till she had almost reached her house.

Then he shouted: 'Who lives here?'

'It is our house,' she replied without looking back.

'What is your father's name?'

'Sukru Jani.'

'I see.'

Jili went in. The Forest Guard found Bili at the door and asked:

'Where is your father?'

'He is up on the hill.'

'Let me see if he has kept his house neat and clean, or if it is dirty.' He entered unasked; he could always claim that he had wanted to conduct a search.

Inside it was dark. He could not see Jili but he thought he could guess where she stood.

As he stumbled around the house he kept asking: 'What's this? What's that?' Nobody answered. He continued to grope his way about, his reason blurred by lust. Bili was amazed. She too had followed him into the house. Suddenly the Forest Guard changed his mind.

'It's very dark here,' he said, and went out.

'Tell your father, when he comes home,' he added, 'that it was I, the Forest Guard, the Officer, who came here in his absence.'

Then he left.

Chapter 6

When Sukru Jani came home with his sons he heard that the Forest Guard had been inside his house while he was away. He was not surprised. He knew that visiting officials often went inside the houses of the tribesmen to inspect them. There, were some who paid such visits in order to dispense their favours, others to detect breaches of the law: contraband liquor, stolen goods, or the use of prohibited timber for constructing their huts. There could be a hundred reasons for the Forest Guard's coming to his hut.

'We are indeed fortunate that the great man visited our house,' Sukru Jani said. 'Is he not our protector, our father and our mother?'

Jili only responded with a blank 'Yes'.

'What a pity we were not there to receive him,' Sukru Jani continued, 'And that we could not offer him even a small present! There is nothing we can do about it tonight. But tomorrow we must get a bunch of plantains and go to him to pay our respects and tell him how grateful we are for the honoured visit. What do you say, my children?'

Jili was not there to answer him.

It happened that night. It was past the hour when the tribesmen have their supper of mandia gruel. All sounds of activity in the village had ceased. Sukru Jani was sauntering on the road outside his house when he saw, in the darkness, the glow of a lighted cigar coming nearer and nearer. Then he recognized the man. It was Kau Paraja; he was the headman's goti—somebody who has borrowed money and has bound himself to serve his creditor as a slave for as long as the debt remains unpaid. He called Sukru Jani aside and spoke to him in a rapid whisper. A grunt of protest broke from the lips of Sukru Jani, but Kau Paraja still persisted.

'Yes, yes,' he muttered in broken phrases, 'for Jili . . . Believe me, that's what he . . . I swear by my eyes, I'm not . . . It's she that he . . . Your daughter, Jili . . . The Forest Guard . . .'

Sukru Jani let out a roar like an infuriated animal. 'You'll get what you deserve, you rascal,' he shrieked. 'I'll break every bone in your body. Just wait, and I'll skin you alive, you scum!'

'Don't be mad at me,' Kau Paraja whined, 'I'm only here on the Forest Guard's orders. And you know very well what would happen if I disobeyed him! It can happen to you too, brother! It can happen to all of us. We just can't afford to displease our officials. When they ask us for something, it has to be produced—even if it's our wives and daughters; or else they'd have us all in handcuffs on some excuse or another in no time at all. And the whole tribe would pay for one man's obstinacy.'

'What nonsense is this?' Sukru Jani shouted. 'Yes, I know your Forest Guard is so powerful he can crush all of us. But why must that nal tree pick on my poor Jili when there are others only too willing? The Dombs would feel flattered if the Forest Guard asked for their women! Go and try your luck with them! For two rupees, he could have all the girls he wanted—they would come running from Pilemon's house and Johana's house and Alisandar's house, as they did last month when that other officer was here. Go and tell him that our Paraja women are not for sale. He can have our chickens and our millets, but nothing more.'

'I dare not tell him anything, brother,' Kau Paraja said sadly. 'Besides, he seems to be crazy about your Jili. Do you know what he told me? "I have never seen a girl like her. Her limbs must be soft as butter and her breasts are like hillocks and her complexion is the colour of lightning. Go, tell her father," he told me "that I want her." And look, Jani, he has sent ten coppers for you to buy yourself some tobacco.'

Unluckily for him, Kau Paraja could not see the expression on Sukru Jani's face. Before he could finish his speech, Sukru Jani was upon him, raining slaps and blows, with

shouts of 'Take that, you scoundrel, and that—and this—
and this—and deliver these on my behalf to your god and
master, the dirty dog of a Forest Guard; here, take this towards the forest rent that I owe him, and this towards the
plough-rent; and this for good measure. Have you had
enough, you rogue? Now get out of my sight—out, before
I kill you!'

A tribal roused to fury is like a beast of the jungle. Sukru
Jani was flushed and swollen with anger, his vision
blurred.

His hands had made quick work—hands well used to
hewing down sal trees and pounding stones into dust. Kau
Paraja was whimpering with pain as he melted away into
the darkness, as softly and mysteriously as a jackal, while
Sukru Jani continued to rage over the insult. His first impulse was to go straight to the Forest Guard and settle the
account forthwith. But then he checked himself. 'What if
the incident were to leak out?' he thought in consternation,
and gradually his throbbing head cooled down.

He stood dumbfounded, leaning against the wall and
holding his head in his arms. He recalled the scene that had
just ended, and realized he had gone too far.

'Where will it end?' he asked himself. He was puzzled
and worried.

Chapter 7

Next morning the Forest Guard left the village, seemingly unconcerned, with his gun on his shoulder and his stick in his hand. He had breathed no word of what had happened, but carried his humiliation deep within him. The villagers accompanied him some distance to see him off. Then he disappeared from view.

For Sukru Jani and his children life went on as usual, like a bullock-cart travelling along old and familiar ruts. As long as the daylight lasted, father and sons would be hard at work cutting down the jungle on Mali Damaka Hill, while the forest echoed to the thud of their axes. In the evening, the family would gather round the hearth for a gossip; and at night, the girls would go to the young women's dormitory. Presently the dungudungas would twang and songs would be exchanged. Everything continued as before, but at times Sukru Jani felt as if he had a blinding cataract in his eyes; or suddenly, in the midst of open-hearted laughter, while brimming over with a sense of well-being, he would feel the grip of an unseen hand on his throat, and a foreboding of tragedy would cloud his face like the shadow of the hills darkening a valley. He dreaded the wrath and malice of the official he had offended, and in his fear of the unknown he would press his folded hands against his forehead and cry out for help to the gods of his tribe, Lord Jhakar the All-Pervading One and Nisani Munda the Earth Goddess: 'Let no evil befall me, O Mighty Ones, and I will sacrifice pigeons and fowls before your holy altar.'

A fortnight passed and then a month, but still the Forest Guard did not return and Sukru Jani thanked his gods, thinking he would come no more. 'He may have been transferred,' he thought. He breathed freely once again and felt strong and cheerful.

They continued their work of felling trees in the jungle. At intervals, they would go down into the ravine below and join the cowherd boys who were secretly distilling liquor. And the drink set them dancing and put new vigour into them, so that all tiredness was forgotten, and each day the clearing in the forest grew wider. They never felt that the timber which they were cutting down and burning was the Raja's property, so that they were criminals in the eyes of the law; nor did they find anything wrong in secretly making liquor to drink, instead of buying it from the licensed shops. Their heads were like stone, into which such arguments and considerations could scarcely enter; in their eyes, everything that grew on the hills and in the forests was theirs to use, like the sunlight and rain and air and water, whose use no one could restrict.

As he worked, Sukru Jani could see his dreams of more land and many houses coming nearer. Mandia Jani dreamed of his beloved Kajodi, and Jili dreamed of her Bagla. It was a time for dreaming.

Then suddenly, one day, several men appeared on the crest of the hill. They were dressed in white, and one or two had hats on their heads. At the head of the group was the Forest Guard, still carrying his gun on his shoulder. Sukru Jani's axe dropped from his hand. He strained his eyes to see clearly. No, there was no mistake. It was the Forest Guard.

He tried to tell himself that he had done no wrong; but

he was filled with a nameless dread. To quieten his fears he picked up his axe again and dealt the tree which he had been cutting three or four quick blows.

It did not take the officials long to reach the spot where the trees were being felled; whereupon the Forest Guard shouted, 'Hi, you!'

Sukru Jani and his two sons came up to the officials and made a deep bow to each. They dared not ask them for particulars of their rank or office; in that land of the jungle, where no man possessed more than a rag to cover his loins, anyone dressed even in a sheet from waist to ankle could be taken for a person in high authority. He could lord it over these people, order them about and harass them, and nobody dared question his right to do so. The more outrageous his demands, the higher he rose in their estimation as an official. Sukru Jani had been brought up with these notions since childhood. He regarded it as his duty to obey anyone whom he took for a person in authority, whatever his rank.

'Who said you could fell trees here?' one of the visitors demanded.

'The Forest Guard, sir,' Sukru Jani innocently replied. 'I have his permission.'

'What! I gave you permission to cut down trees!' exclaimed the Forest Guard. 'You liar! You rogue! You misbegotten swindler! You dare to stand there and say that I gave you permission?'

'How else could we dare to touch your trees with our axes, great lord?' Sukru Jani replied. 'Did you not give me permission to clear the jungle when I asked you the other day, my lord? And then again, a second time, when I went to you, and the headman of our village was present, did you not permit me to proceed with the work? It is true and the headman has heard it. Why do you deny it, sir?'

The most senior official among them nodded, as though agreeing to something.

The Forest Guard led the officers to the spot where the Christian Dombs Istifan and Solomon had made a clear- ing. He pointed at Sukru Jani and said: 'All this is the work of that rascal, your honour. He ignores all my protests and he has cleared this entire area.'

Pilemon and Solomon came up and corroborated his statement. 'This Paraja and his two sons do not listen to anyone, your honour,' they said solemnly. 'They are des- perate rogues.'

All the patches that had been cleared were measured; the remaining stumps of trees were counted; the measure- ments were taken down on paper and the value of the loss calculated. The evidence of the other villagers was re- corded in order to pin the culprits down, and all who were asked swore that it was Sukru Jani who had felled the trees. For the tribals live under the constant threat of official persecution, and no existence in the jungle is possible un- less one learns to play hide-and-seek with the law. Every- one wanted to save his own skin, and lies were spoken with great moral conviction. Their natural simplicity and honesty had been corroded by a lifetime of fear and in- security.

Sukru Jani stood like a criminal in the dock and when he saw the officials writing, he felt as if the point of a knife was being dragged across his heart; for he had the tribes- man's instinctive dread of writings made on paper. He also heard them speak to each other in some dialect which no tribesman could understand, and this added to his terror.

Presently they nodded their heads in agreement. Sukru Jani and his sons waited in silence, swallowing the lumps that rose in their parched throats. Then came the verdict: 'Now, Sukru Jani, you are found guilty. You have caused a loss of four score of rupees to the Raja and for that you must pay.'

'I am not guilty, great lords', Sukru Jani pleaded. 'I have committed no crime. I will swear by your Book of Sections that I am innocent. I will swear by the man-eating tiger, I will stand on a tiger's skin and take the oath. Give me any oath you like and I will swear my innocence.'

'Be quiet! Are you going to pay up?'

'How can I pay such a heavy fine, great lords? Have pity, have mercy!'

'No more of your tricks. We will see about your not paying, remember that. Now you may go.'

Sukru Jani was stunned. It was as if he could see before his very eyes his tiny hut being blown away in bits by a storm which raged over the mountains as the rain came down in torrents from a black cloud.

In the same way, a single puff of wind can destroy what has taken a field-mouse a lifetime to amass.

Chapter 8

When Jili returned home from the pool she was startled to find her father and her brothers sitting broken and crumpled. They closed the door on the world outside and in the darkness of their dingy shelter father, sons and daughters hung from each other's necks and sobbed aloud while the mandia gruel remained untouched in the gourd-shell flasks. The men's axes lay outside the door; they had not even bothered to put them on the veranda.

And thus it was that in this land of hills and forests, in an unmapped corner of the wide world, luckless men and women who lived on castaway mango stones and hid their nakedness in bits of rag huddled together under the torrent of misery pouring down on their heads, and wept.

Their tears soaked the earth but were powerless to melt human hearts. And their gods laughed.

Night fell, but no one came to comfort them. It was as if they were under the scourge of a pestilence, or the curse of an evil spirit, so that all their neighbours shunned them. No one dared to tempt the anger of authority by visiting the unfortunate family.

Sukru Jani's house remained plunged in darkness. Inside, they all sat for a long time silent and motionless. Then four shadowy figures could be seen approaching the house, so stealthily that their footsteps could scarcely be heard. They hovered round the house like owls or bats, halted, paced up and down with an air of hesitation and finally brought their heads close together, talking in whispers. Then they walked up the steps of the house, stood on the veranda and called. The door opened. Sukru Jani stood in the doorway, silhouetted against the darkness.

It was Dhepu Chalan who opened the conference. He nodded his head in sympathy at Sukru Jani and said: 'Well, brother, didn't I warn you before that this might happen?' And Salingi Paraja, the headman of the village, echoed him and said: 'Yes, I knew this was coming.'

The others now took up the refrain:

'Didn't I say so? And now it has happened.'

Dhepu Chalan chanted a piece of doggerel which was often quoted by the hill folk:

> The Forest Guard's the rider,
> The tribesman is the horse,
> And always it's the rider who
> Decides upon their course.

'So you see, brother,' Dhepu Chalan said, 'that's how it is. An official is like a cloud or a tiger—and who can pit his strength against theirs?' Sukru Jani stiffened. 'I thank you for your advice,' he said drily. 'But tell me this—what is my crime? What have I been punished for? You all know that the Forest Guard gave me permission. You were all witnesses when he accepted money from me and told me that I could clear the jungle. You all heard him say so. Then how could you deny it when the officials asked you? No, you did more—you gave evidence against me and made it look as if I were the liar! You, who are my brethren, you did that to me! But I won't judge you. God will judge between you and me; he sees all. You have done your part and ruined me and now my four children will be destitute. Let it be so and let God judge.'

'Why are you blaming us, brother?' Dhepu Chalan protested. 'What harm have we done you? Just because you were in the tiger's grip, are we to go and put our heads in its mouth? You know very well that the evil eye of an official has fallen on you. Do you think anyone here is going to incur an official's vengeance? We simply dare not defy him, and you know it. We have to do as he tells us. You

are angry with us, but there's nothing we can do. We too
have our families and our children. Be sensible and try to
understand how it is with us, and then you won't blame
us.'

'But don't be afraid,' the headman consoled him. 'They
want four score of rupees, but we can settle the matter for
three.'

'*Three score!*' Sukru Jani wailed.

'But if you don't pay they'll take you to court. They'll
send you to jail *and* make you pay the fine. You understand
what that means, don't you? It's for you to decide.'

'Where can I find so much money?' Sukru Jani said in
despair. 'Do I ever see the face of money? A poor jungle
tribal like me? And what about you? You are the rich ones
of this village; but which of you has three score of rupees?'

Phaul Domb cleared his throat and said: 'Listen, I have
an idea.'

Of all the tribes dwelling among the hills, the Dombs
are known for their cunning and trickery, and Phaul was
one of the sharpest. There was always a smile playing on
his long, thin face, so like the snout of a mongoose; and his
small, crooked, expressionless eyes appeared to be seeing
and understanding everything from behind a veil, while
his shifting, wily glances darted in and out like someone
playing a game of hide-and-seek.

Phaul Domb formulated his idea: 'You won't have to go
far. Only a few miles from here, in the village of Thotaguda, near Rai-Sil, lives the money-lender Ram Bisoi. He is
always looking for gotis. There are three men in your
family, and if you were willing to serve him as gotis you
could get a loan of three hundred rupees from him, let
alone three score!'

Like all other men of the hills, Sukru Jani knew only too
well the consequences of borrowing from a money-lender.
He would have to work, almost as a slave, for a full year
and in return some five rupees would be written off. But
since he would be paying compound interest, in effect the
loan would never be repaid and he and his sons and his
grandsons would remain slaves for all eternity. He shud-
dered at the very thought of exchanging his freedom for
the miserable life of a debt-bound goti.

'No, no, no,' he cried in pain, 'It's impossible for me to
pay three score of rupees. Three score! My God! Had it
been ten rupees or even fifteen I could have tried to find the
money. I could even have risked binding myself as a goti
for that amount. But three score of rupees! It's crazy to
think of finding a sum like that. Let them rather send me to
jail.'

He sat down, spent and mute.

His stubbornness was more than they had bargained for.
The headman, Dhepu Chalan and Phaul Domb went out
and held a consultation on the road. Then they returned to
the attack.

'Now listen to me, Jani,' the headman said, 'and don't be
foolish. Listen to reason. We shall pray to the official to reduce your fine by ten rupees. You must find fifty rupees
somehow; we shall take him the money and throw
ourselves on his mercy. I'm sure the matter can be settled.
It's not difficult to get the money; you have only to go to
the money-lender.'

'Yes, that's what you should do,' Dhepu Chalan said
gravely. 'There's no other way. And if you don't pay you
will have brought about your own ruin and no one will be
able to save you. Do you know what will happen then?

Those officials are sure to arrest you. They will handcuff you and lead you away in chains and then throw you into prison. But that's not all. They will come and carry away all your belongings. They will pull your house down, dig up its foundations and remove all the timber and sell it, and recover the fine in that way. And you know what happens when you go to jail? You lose your caste and have to spend a lot of money in order to be accepted into it again. So think it over, Jani, while there's still time. Don't be rash. Get the money from the money-lender and pay up.'

Sukru Jani turned the suggestion over in his mind. He began to think that it was not so bad after all, and that the debt could be repaid in a few years if both his sons worked as gotis. 'There are many others who serve as gotis; what's the harm?' he reasoned to himself.

But this mood soon passed, and again he sank into despair. The money-lender would no doubt be only too eager to advance a loan, for he would be purchasing the services of three men, for at least five years, at a ridiculously small price. They would till the land and grow crops on the hills as before. Only they would be doing so not as free men working on their own lands for their own benefit, but on the money-lender's lands and as his slaves. They would sink far down in the eyes of the world. And what would happen to all his dreams for the future? They would never come true now—at least, not in this life, until he died and was born again. His life seemed suddenly to have been emptied of all purpose.

No, he could not exchange his shelter under the shadow of his own walls for a place among the money-lender's slaves. He could never condemn his sons to the miserable life of a goti. What crime had he committed to bring this upon himself? He had sweated in the hot sun, cutting down trees with his axe. He had hoed the hard crust of the hills, preparing the soil. He had raised crops by the labour of his own hands and had never owed anything to anybody.

It never occurred to him to question his belief in his birthright, or to reflect that one did not become the owner of something merely because one could see it every day before one's eyes. He had never worried about the legality of his actions; yet here he was, up to his neck in trouble. No amount of argument could have convinced him before, but now there was no getting away from reality. The man of the hills cannot comprehend any situation until he feels the full impact of an experience. It takes an actual blow on the back to tell him that he is in danger; and then, because he is too simple to understand cause and effect, he never knows who has beaten him and why.

And so, as Sukru Jani sat with his head bowed and his eyes on the ground, he sensed the danger hanging over him. It was like the sudden onset of the rains or of winter, or the pounce of a man-eating tiger, whose victim is aware all the time of what is happening to him as he is dragged, dazed and shaken, over rocks and thorns, and waits mutely for those terrible fangs to sink into him. Sukru Jani was now in the grip of such a nightmare. Fascinated by his own misery, he could neither speak nor distinguish good from evil, as he waited for the end.

Presently, he roused himself from his reverie and stammered in a dry, toneless voice: 'Goti! No, Naika, I can't. I have my motherless children to think of.'

'All right, Jani,' the Naika told him, 'You have the

whole night before you. Think again and give me your
answer tomorrow.'

Chapter 9

The night, as a part of the day or of human existence, had
never been important to Sukru Jani. Nights came and went
and left no mark behind. An hour after night-fall, the fire
in the hearth would die out; all sounds in the village would
cease and people would be asleep behind closed doors.

But this night was different. He was seized with an unknown fear. He thought he could hear the muffled sound
of sobbing in the dark. He was incapable of analysing his
situation objectively; instead, he kept seeing visions which,
though they appeared to him as objective, were summoned from the depths of his mind by his present agony.

He thought of his children, whom he and his wife Sombari had brought up with such difficulty. They had often
fasted in order that the children might eat. And what rows
he had had with Sombari over them! When they had built
that house together, she had worked by his side in the hot
sun like any man. Then there was the year when the rains
had been unusually heavy and a raging storm had struggled to tear away the thatch from the wall-posts, and, as
the children looked on in alarm, Sombari and he had held
on desperately to the thatch and saved it from being blown
away. Such was her concern for her children that she

would have one of them strapped to her bosom even while she worked in the field, bending down to root out weeds. She had kept her children warm in winter by the warmth of her own body.

Many were the ordeals through which she had passed in order to keep them alive and bring them up. And now that she was no more, her sons were going to be sent away to serve a money-lender as his debt-bound slaves. They would walk about with the yoke of the stranger on their shoulders; occasionally, at night, they might drop in to see him, hungry, with their empty stomachs touching their backs and their faces blanched and dry, and would then cry out, 'Father!'

And on this dark night he was alone in his misery, and Sombari was no longer by his side to help and console him. He counted the years since she was gone. Ten long years! Perhaps her spirit was roving about still, unable to find rebirth. It happened after death, they said. He fancied that Sombari's spirit was roaming all alone in the jungle, in wind and in rain, through cold winter nights.

And now he knew that Sombari was weeping. He could see her and she was weeping. He could see the tears in her wide eyes as they rolled down, drop after drop.

Sombari was weeping. He could see the never-ending rain-clouds massed in the sky and from one horizon to the other nothing but numberless shafts of rain ceaselessly falling on the tops of the greenish-blue mountains.

The vision changed. Sombari was roaming all alone in the forest, searching for something and sobbing. It seemed as if everything had been drenched in tears from a weeping sky and it was her sobbing that had caused the rain and the hurricane. And in the glimmering, tearful light everything was being carried away helter-skelter; huge trees were uprooted, mountains dug up from their bases and swept along in an advancing wave of destruction which approached nearer and nearer, tearing and drowning and driving everything before it, while intense darkness spread from east to west and blotted out his senses.

Mandia called to Tikra in the dead of night. 'Are you asleep, Tikra?' he asked.

'No, I don't feel sleepy.'

'Let's go and work as gotis, Tikra.'

'I'm willing, brother.'

They felt light-hearted, and, in the calm that utter hopelessness brings, they closed their eyes.

Sukru Jani had fallen asleep. He had a dream. He saw his land and the lands of others around it. He saw heavy crops of rice and mandia on those other lands, and the crops were swaying in the breeze. But on his land there were no crops, only tall grasses in luxuriant flower. He could see flocks of peacocks coming down the hill towards his field; they were bent on eating the flowers of the grasses, which he was trying to protect with his stick.

At dawn he woke, and the absurd dream vanished. He rose from his bed, looked around and saw that the hills and forests were already waking up from sleep. The morning revealed everything to him in vivid detail. There was no room now for doubt or hesitation. The fantasies of the previous night had disappeared. He looked at the hills, now fully awake in the morning light, and prepared himself for work. Before him lay the gnarled, rugged hills and the harsh, red soil—inescapable facts in the grim reality which faced him and had always faced him.

He took a swift decision and resigned himself to fate; he would take a loan of fifty rupees from the money-lender and he and Tikra would work for the latter as gotis until the debt was paid off. Mandia, as the elder son, would look after the house while they were away. As for Tikra, he himself would watch over him constantly and be at his side and protect him from sun and rain, as the Paraja's raincoat of palm-leaves protects his back. What did it matter if they *did* become gotis? In due time, the money-lender's debt would be cleared and they would be free to go home again.

'There's nothing unusual in being someone's goti,' he said to his children. 'What's the harm? Now, look at that Forest Guard and all those officials. What are they if not gotis? They too must have signed contracts, binding themselves to serve their masters like slaves. Do they feel unhappy? No.

'That Forest Guard, as you know, is an outsider. We do not know where he comes from. Why does he have to come so far? Why, because he serves someone as a goti and his employer has ordered him to do these things.

'I've travelled all over these hills, carrying loads for the officials until I had callouses on my shoulders. I've seen every kind when they come here on their rounds: black ones, white ones, brown ones, all speaking different dialects! Well, I've carried those officers on my own shoulders, when they came riding in their palanquins—but they too were gotis for some other master, and not free men. Their masters would give them some money every month, to buy themselves food and other things, and in return they would demand work from them. And it's no joke, you know; they are sent hundreds of miles away from their homes, to work in storm and rain and sunshine. Every man is some other man's goti. And the master for whom he works is himself driven by some unseen spirit, which rides always on his back and commands him all the things that *he* must do. And so the whole world moves.'

When he identified himself with the whole world and made a general theme of his plight, he felt comforted and refreshed.

An hour after sunrise, the Naika, Dhepu Chalan and Phaul Domb came to him, with the air of casual visitors who had just dropped in for a moment's gossip.

'What a lot of timber the poor fellow has stacked!' It was the Naika who set the ball rolling.

'And how he has laboured!' said Dhepu Chalan.

'But of course the Forest Guard and the officials are not men of our country.' Phaul Domb observed with some hesitation. 'What do they care if the tribesmen live or die?'

'Let us go to the money-lender,' Sukru Jani said quietly. 'I have decided to ask for a loan. My son and I shall be his gotis.'

They praised his judgement and his wisdom, and the Naika said: 'How could we bear to see you ruin yourself, Jani? It was our duty to tell you what was best for you. But your mind was in turmoil yesterday and so you could not reason clearly. Now come, let us go to the money-lender.'

Chapter 10

Sahukar Ramachandra Bisoi—'Sahukar' being an honorific term for any money-lender or trader in that part of the country—was a sundhi, or brewer, by caste. His father, Sahukar Janardan Bisoi, had started two large distilleries and had amassed a considerable fortune by selling liquor to the tribes in that area. The son could not continue his father's trade because the business of distillation and sale of liquor was taken over by the government, and so he had switched to money-lending.

As a token of his being a Sahukar, Ramachandra Bisoi wore a thick bangle of gold round his left wrist; and by wearing two round pendants of gold in the lobes of his ears he announced his wealth to the world. He had thick, drooping moustaches which trailed in any liquid he sipped. His deep-set eyes gleamed under bushy eyebrows and thick eyelashes with an expression of cunning, but a smile played constantly on his thick lips. He was thirty-five.

His was an easy trade. This was because he had money: money attracts money, and big money draws small money to itself. And so it was quite natural for the Sahukar's bulging money-bags, which he hung up from his thatch-eaves, to attract all the little driblets of cash which the tribals had hoarded so painfully in their miserable huts. And the Sahukar was quite indifferent as to the source from which the money trickled in, or the circumstances in which it was obtained.

A frequent reason for the tribesmen to seek loans from him was their peculiar marriage customs. A young man taking a wife would have to pay her father the jholla or bride-price, which was usually from forty to sixty rupees. No marriage could be solemnized unless the jholla had first been paid. And so all aspiring bridegrooms came to the Sahukar for loans, married the brides of their choice, and for this privilege would sweat for him year after year.

The Sahukar was a grain-lender too, lending millet needy tribals during the lean months of the rainy seasc__ and collecting back the grain—with interest—when the harvest was over. However, the interest far exceeded the principal, and the debt went on increasing from year to year.

Such was the nature of his business.

He had no business worries because the tribesmen never asked questions and never tried to cheat him. They accepted his accounts completely and delivered to him whatever sum of money or quantity of grain he demanded in repayment.

He maintained a horse, but its upkeep cost him little as it fed on weeds growing in water-logged areas. It was only slightly bigger than a donkey but it served his purpose. As the horse could barely carry his very considerable weight over the rocky ground, the Sahukar always carried a bundle of green twigs when he went riding, with which he would whip the poor animal until all the twigs were broken. And so he would ride slowly along, surveying his empire; for most of the poor tribals would have to come to him sooner or later, and he would become master of their lands and of their money and of their bodies and their souls. It was only a question of time.

Chapter 11

When the party arrived at the Sahukar's house in Thotaguda it was almost noon. The Sahukar seemed to be expecting them. His eyes gleamed. He gave each of them a swift and penetrating look before asking Sukru Jani:

'Doesn't that rice-field at the foot of the hill belong to you? Just above the stream, I mean.'

'Yes,' said Sukru Jani.

'How much do you want?'

'Fifty rupees.'

Phaul Domb explained the position, shuffling restlessly about as he did so. Three of the villagers of Thotaguda arrived. The Sahukar brought out a fat ledger and turned the pages until he came to a blank page, on which he then scribbled a deed. At the bottom he affixed a revenue-stamp, thus making the document legal. The Naika, Dhepu Chalan and Phaul Domb stood witnesses to the transaction. Then the Sahukar read out the deed:

> This agreement executed this day etc. etc. between Sahukar Ramachandra Bisoi son of etc. etc. as the First Party and
>
> Sukru Jani son of etc. etc. and Tikra Jani son of etc. etc. as the Second Party,
>
> doth hereby specify as follows:
>
> The First Party having given a loan of Rupees Fifty only to the Second Party this day etc. etc. in the presence of the witnesses to this deed named below,
>
> the members of the Second Party do hereby bind themselves jointly and severally to serve the First Par-

ty as his gotis during the tenure of the loan and thereby to be the whole-time servants and labourers of the First Party for the purpose of doing all jobs for him as he may direct, at all hours of the night and the day, and at any place where he may require them to work.

and the First Party hereby binds himself to deliver unto each member of the Second Party half a putti of mandia once a month for his food and one blanket worth one Rupee once a year in winter and the First Party further undertakes to set off against the loan on which compound interest at fifty per cent per annum shall accrue, an amount of Rupees Five only for every year of service counted from this day, rendered by every member of the Second Party as a goti under the First Party according to the terms of this deed,

in witness whereof etc. etc.

The Sahukar put his signature to the deed while the illiterate Sukru Jani, his son Tikra Jani and all the witnesses had the impressions of their left thumbs smeared with soot and oil and recorded at the foot of the deed.

The Sahukar then paid a sum of fifty rupees to Sukru Jani, and Sukru Jani returned to his village, accompanied by his son Tikra and his fellow villagers, the Naika, the Barik, Dhepu Chalan and Phaul Domb.

'And now let's go to the official,' Sukru Jani said, when they arrived at the village.

'Good heavens!' the Naika exclaimed, 'You mustn't think of such a thing! If you do that he certainly won't let you off with less than two hundred rupees. he is very angry with you.'

'Then what am I to do?' asked Sukru Jani, in some bewilderment.

'Hand over the money to us and we'll go to the official on your behalf,' said the Naika. 'Give it to me and let Dhepu Chalan and Phaul Domb come too. We shall offer him fifty rupees and prostrate ourselves on the ground at his feet. At first, he will certainly refuse to accept only fifty rupees and will fly into a rage. He may even pull off one of his shoes and threaten to use it on our heads. But we shan't budge, even if he actually beats us, until he finally accepts. But if you go, the very sight of you will make him mad. If you want to come with us you may do so at your own risk, but don't blame us afterwards if anything goes wrong.'

'But why', Sukru Jani protested, 'should he be angry with me when I count out the money before him? I don't understand. What can he do to me when I pay the money?'

'Nothing,' the Naika retorted, 'except to say that if you can pay fifty rupees you can quite obviously pay ten rupees more, or else go to jail. Well, go and try your luck! What we had in mind was different. We'd planned to approach him on your behalf, to fall at his feet and say: "Great lord, Sukru Jani is penniless; he cannot pay the fine. We, his fellow villagers, have raised a subscription to pay his fine and this is as much as we could collect. Be pleased to accept this amount and save him!" Do you hear that? Well, if you have the courage to speak to the official, go and try your luck.'

Sukru Jani thought it over; he did not reply.

'Besides,' the Naika resumed, 'there's that Forest Guard with the official. I don't know why the Forest Guard is annoyed with you, but it seems that the very mention of your name drives him mad. It is he who has prejudiced the higher officials against you. They'll never listen to you, whatever you say.'

Dhepu Chalan nodded his head sagely and said: 'It's true. That big officer has noted down things on paper. If the matter is settled to his satisfaction, well and good; otherwise you'll have to face the consequences.'

'What they say is true,' Sukru Jani thought. 'What advantage is there in my going in person? But . . . '

'So you think that I'll spoil everything if I go?' he asked.

'Why, are you afraid to let us have the money?' retorted the Naika. 'Don't you trust us? Why don't you hide behind a bush or in a tree and watch what we do? Then you can see for yourself if your money's been paid to the official or if somebody's spirited it away'

'No, no don't misunderstand me. I do trust you. You are the headman of the village—how could I not have faith in you? But I' feel easier if that official were to cross out everything that he took down yesterday, to avoid making further trouble for me. This is what worries me. After all, what do these officials care about our happiness? To them we're just tribesmen, Parajas at that—what do they care about us?'

'Is that what's troubling you, Jani? Then we shall plead with the Forest Guard and get those papers from him. Don't worry about that.'

Sukru Jani felt his throat go dry and he remained silent. He felt no conscious distrust of the headman, but he was a tribesman, and, although a tribesman easily believes all that he is told, some doubt or apprehension, however faint, will always linger in his mind and trouble him.

He handed over the entire amount to the village headman and came away.

He picked up two small bits of rope made from the bark of a creeper, held them up before Tikra and said:

'This rope, Tikra, is your document and this one here is mine; as a year of service is completed we shall tie a knot in each of these ropes. That will tell us how many years we have served the Sahukar.'

'Yes,' said Tikra.

Sukru Jani stood there, looking around him; he viewed with a loving and lingering gaze the few things he had ever owned. There stood his house. There, at the foot of the hill, lay his rice-land, the fertile land of his ancestors which was his prized heritage. Over there was the Mali Damaka Hill, on which he had found his treasure-trove of sal timber and virgin land for cultivation. Everything was in its usual place; only the sun had gone from east to west and the sunlight that lay on the hills and the jungles had wilted like the leaves of a sal tree that has been felled.

He could not think. He only knew that everything had ended for him.

'Tikra!' he called.

'Yes, father.'

'From today we are gotis, my son; we have signed the agreement and from today we are gotis!' His eyes filled with tears and his chest heaved with great sighs. The ageing father threw his arms round his son, broke into sobs and said:

'Gotis, Tikra! From today we are gotis, slaves!'

Mandia glanced at him in surprise. Jili and Bili watched in silent stupefaction. Tears rolled down their cheeks.

Tikra clasped his father in his arms—both were naked except for their loincloths—and consoled him:

'Don't worry, father. After all, it's only a few rupees. We shall repay the debt.'

Chapter 12

It was ten o'clock in the morning when the Naika thrust
five rupees into the palm of the Forest Guard, fell at his
feet, caught hold of his ankles and prayed:
'Mercy! Mercy, great lord! Pray let them off with a fine
of ten or fifteen rupees. We are poor folk, we who live in
the hills and jungles; where can we find more money?'
The other officials were with the Forest Guard, engaged
in idle chatter. A newspaper was spread out before them.
The Naika, Dhepu Chalan and the Barika prostrated
themselves at their feet and cried:
'Mercy, great lords! Mercy, your honours! We have nothing to eat—we live on mango-stones and leaves gathered
from the jungle. Have pity on Sukru Jani! The poor man
could raise only ten rupees, even though he had to become
a goti to the money-lender. Take this and save him, great
lords; you are our father and our mother, have pity!'
'Yes, I know, he is very poor,' the Forest Guard com-
mented.
Some moments passed while the senior official looked
steadily at the Naika. Then he said:
'Very well, we will reduce the fine to twenty-five.'
Some bargaining ensued. Finally the Naika paid only fifteen rupees to the official, who gave them a bit of paper on
which he had written a few words, and the matter was
closed. The Naika, Chalan and the Barika departed, singing the praises of the officials. They were in high spirits as
they retired a little way into the jungle. And while Sukru
Jani awaited his emissaries, to know the outcome of their

mission, the rest of his money was being divided between them.

Next morning, the officials struck camp and went elsewhere.

Chapter 13

A big moon rose that night, and as Jili walked slowly towards the young women's dormitory she wore a bunch of the white and fragrant flowers known as aroma-of-the-night in her hair, combed into a shining bun, which slanted to the right of her head. A cloud had passed over her life: her father and brother had narrowly escaped being sent to jail and had bound themselves to serve as gotis, and there had been sorrowing and tears at home. But, for the hill folk, sorrows were as ephemeral as the rain which poured down the slopes of the hills and was drained away in an instant; tears served only to freshen their smiles.

She had done her hair with great care and had put on her favourite red-and-blue-striped sari.

Drunk with the magic of the moonlight hills, as they rose wave upon wave, Jili flitted on into the night, her feet turning instinctively towards the young men's dormitory.

The young bucks of the tribe were celebrating the departure of the Forest Guard and the ominous group of officials. The danger was past, and life was sweet once again. Mandia Jani lay steeped in drink and the heady music of the dungudungas, all cares forgotten.

Sukru Jani and Tikra slept at home as usual, guarding the house. It was their last night of freedom.

Chapter 14

On a misty morning in November, which in the dialect of the Parajas is called 'the month of the festival of lights', Sukru Jani and his younger son Tikra went to the Sahukar's house, to begin their new lives as debt-bound labourers. The high hills sat gravely on either side of their path, and curling tresses of mist uncoiled themselves from the hill tops like loosely fitting puggarees coming unwound. In places, smaller hills overhung the narrow jungle paths like sharp-toothed money-lenders. The undulating uplands covered with the yellow flowers of the olsi crop were awakening. In the morning light it seemed to Sukru Jani, looking at the gold olsi flowers that covered the hill slopes and uplands for miles around, as if the mythical 'guardians of the ten directions' had all turned into money-lenders, and were squatting on the ground with their gold spread before them, while the whole earth belonged to them, the men with the gold. And while they sat thus, in ease and comfort, he and his son were on their way to the Sahukar's house to wear their lives away in slavery.

Thotaguda, where the money-lender Ram Bisoi lived, was eight miles away from their village of Sarsupadar, and the way led through dense jungle. The day was growing hot as they neared the village. On the outskirts, they saw large fields belonging to the money-lender, where mandia was being reaped. Sukru Jani was reminded of his own land.

'This year, we have been able to harvest our crops early, Tikra,' he said. 'But what will happen next year, my son?'

Tikra could sense the unspoken agony in his father's mind. Next year, they would both be slaving for the Sahukar, harvesting mountains of rice and mandia, milking his scores and scores of cows, building new houses for him, while their own land would lie neglected, overgrown with weeds and wild grasses.

'Don't worry about that, father,' Tikra said. 'Mandia will look after the land, and he can do more than you and I put together. We haven't land enough to keep him busy. Can our lands ever lie fallow?'

'No,' said Sukru Jani, but he was not consoled. 'What can Mandia do on his own?' he thought. 'He is only a child of yesterday.'

They walked on in silence.

Crowds of reapers were at work, swarming over the land like the worms that infest the crops. Most of them were women. They would labour for a whole day to earn a miserable three or four pice or a handful of mandia. But their clear laughter floated on the air like the long-tailed, white blossoms of the bena grass—laughter that was sparkling white and carefree. And presently they began to sing in chorus:

> Daily we labour in this field of mandia
> And pour our sweat on this land,
> And the crops grow and ripen and are harvested,

Are loaded in carts and taken away and stored.
For whom are they preserved, my love?
They are for you, darling of my heart.
For you, the maizes in my garden,
And the mandia in my fields;
When, drunk with home-brewed beer,
My eyes are flushed and unsteady,
I shall call to you, my darling,
And you must come.
But come secretly, my love,
When the moon is in the sky,
Treading softly on the shadowy patches under
    the trees;
For though I shall be waiting for you
I have my shame and fear,
In this village of my mother's brother,
In this village of my father's brother.
And if I am exposed
I shall run away in fear.
But O, my darling,
We have turned our blood into water
And coaxed the mandia to bear fruits;
It is all for you, my beloved,
It is all for you.

As Sukru Jani heard the song it tore painfully into his
heart. For him it was an empty song, without beauty or
sense. 'For whom? O, for whom?' he wailed within himself
in despair. 'For whom will the fruits of our toil be carted
away?'

It was all in vain, all blank and void, only gibes and
taunts that pierced the heart. And covering the hills and the

sky and the ravines and the fields there were only Forest
Guards and officials, only money-lenders and debt-bound
slaves.

Chapter 15

Each day, father and son would leave home early in the
morning and work all day long for their master—
travelling on various errands to distant villages like Kana
Pai, Kutinga or Pipalpadar, many miles away, returning
only in the evening. By then the gourd-shell flasks slung
from their shoulders would be empty. Each had his axe on
his shoulder and wore a kind of cap and a cover for the
back, made of leaves sewn together.

By the time the day's work was over and they began
their journey back home, their palms felt singed with
labour their calves seemed to be bursting in pain, their
mouths were parched. They were tired and spent, and
hardly spoke. Silently they threaded their way through the
dense and murmuring jungle. They moved largely by
guesswork, except when a clearing gave a window onto
the twinkling stars. Jackals howled. From time to time a
barking deer would sound its peculiar warning note, or a
king-deer would bugle out its cry as it ran for its life. For
the jungle was infested with tigers. And through it all, enveloped in darkness, two defenceless human beings toiled
across hills and ravines to their rest.

For a debt-bound labourer, one day was no different from another. Each day was one of hard labour. The Sahukar measured their daily output almost as if with a pair of scales. Any goti who happened to arrive a little late was not only abused in foul language but was given a specially heavy load of work.

And so a goti was hardly aware how the days passed; all his nights were dark and he never knew the bright phases of the moon.

Chapter 16

Mandia Jani was not unduly depressed because his father and his younger brother had to serve as gotis. The greater part of their crop of mandia millets had already been harvested, brought home and stored; only a patch was still left in the field. Some arum tubers which they had grown had been dug out in November and gathered in, and there was some dry maize too. The little kitchen garden in front of the house, with its fence of twig netting, bristled with pointed chillies, now ripe and red, which attracted peacocks and mynas from the jungles, so that Bili had to keep constant guard, flourishing a stick to drive them away. They also had a creeper of the kunduru gourd, which had spread luxuriantly on a flat roof of twigs and bamboos and, while Mandia Jani raised the earth round the roots, green, smooth-bodied kunduru fruits peeped at him through the leaves.

He shared his father's buoyant nature, and the days ahead were bright with promise and hope.

He would glance at their rice-land in the distance and comfort himself with the thought that in just over a month the crop would be ripe for harvesting. Their land was the choicest in the village, and would provide enough for the family's needs. He could also grow a variety of other crops on the land and reap the harvest in due course.

The village buzzed with activity, for it was the month of January. Soon, the harvest of rice, mandia, olsi, suan and red gram would be cut and gathered. Consequently, no one had any leisure and all the people of the village were on their lands as soon as daylight came. Mandia Jani was too busy to think of his troubles.

At times, while he reaped the remnants of his mandia crop on the hill slope, he could see the village girls pass by on their way to the stream. There was something majestic in their leisurely movements as they walked down, chewing on their little bits of green twig, which served as toothbrushes. And Mandia Jani glanced sideways at them as he worked in his field, marking each one as she went to the stream. Some of the girls carried bundles of clothes for washing; others carried leaves of the edible gurdi shrub, or tubers collected from the jungle, which they would wash in the stream before taking into the kitchen; others, again, merely carried earthen pitchers for filling at the pool.

Sometimes he could see his Kajodi, dressed always in her favourite sari of red and blue stripes. Her legs were bare to the thighs, like those of all Paraja women. There were bright red flowers in her shiny hair. Her face glistened in the sunlight, and she invariably giggled as she passed Mandia Jani. He could not take his eyes off her.

At times he could hear the reapers singing in chorus in the neighbouring fields. Their voices rose and fell, as the trembling notes lingered on; and his thoughts were carried away by the song. Soon, the harvest would be gathered, and Mandia Jani would sell a part'of it. Then he would go to Kajodi's father and offer him the bride-price.

And then he would bring her home.

He gazed at his rice-field across the rivulet where the ripening paddy rippled in golden waves. Beyond it were the mountains and dense jungles, stretching across the horizon in a wide arc. The landscape was a picture painted in blue, black and green. The rice-field was a legacy from his ancestors. Generations of his forefathers had laboured on that land and the touch of their hands had made the soil smooth and soft. To Mandia, it was no mere piece of land, but a record of the history of those past generations, of their bygone tales of sorrow and rejoicing and of tradition and change. And he thought of all the generations before him and of those that were yet to come; and how the ashes of those who were dead and the seeds from which future generations would spring up had been mixed together in that soil.

And then, suddenly, all his thoughts would be interrupted, and one image would fill his mind, gliding stealthily, as it were, from behind the standing paddy. It was the image of Kajodi.

His rice crop and his Kajodi, his house overflowing with rice and his heart overflowing with Kajodi, became one and inseparable in his consciousness.

Chapter 17

Sometimes, Sukru Jani and Tikra had to work so late that they were unable to return home for the night; they would sleep in the Sahukar's house and go out to work again next morning, exactly as they had done at home. On some days, the Sahukar would send them out into the jungle with his herds of cattle, to keep watch over them as they grazed. On others, they were sent to cut down trees for him.

The Sahukar rode around on his little nag, making sure that all his gotis were really working, and giving him full value for his money. But for the goti it was fruitless labour; he earned no wages, was paid no salary, but sweated his life away in trying to work off the loan—insignificant in terms of money—which his father or grandfather had been unfortunate enough to ask for. At first, it seemed deceptively easy for the goti to work off the loan. He would eagerly count up the days of labour against the expected day of deliverance. But as the days passed he found himself no nearer to the end; somehow, mysteriously, the period of unpaid labour went on prolonging itself. And then he lost all count of the days, all sense of time, all feeling of purpose. He lived only to work, and never asked himself *why* he worked. But the money-lender never forgot to calculate his compound interest on the loan that he had once advanced; and so the links in the chain that held the goti in bondage became stronger as the days went by.

Sahukar Ramachandra Bisoi rode his horse around the area, searching constantly for new lands to annex, new gotis to enslave, new kingdoms to add to his empire.

As Sukru Jani and Tikra continued to work as gotis, their nerves became dead to all sense of pain. They never complained. The sun grew hotter as the day advanced, the leaves drooped from their branches, the entire jungle fell into an exhausted sleep. But Sukru Jani and Tikra never stopped working for longer than it took to drink a little of the mandia gruel that they carried in their dried gourd-shells. At long last there came the hour when the sun grew dim, as though it were running out of fuel, sinking lower and lower until it disappeared behind the Dharam-Dooar mountains, and the labouring men became aware that another day had ended.

As father and son, bent double under the load of the day's harvest, dragged their footsteps towards their master's house, Sukru Jani would ask Tikra, as though to reassure them both:

'Isn't your brother Mandia worth more than a hundred of us in the field, Tikra?'

'Yes, father,' Tikra would reply.

Chapter 18

Back home from work in the evenings, Mandia Jani would sit on the veranda of his house, his legs dangling over the edge, wiping the sweat from his face and chest with the flowing end of his loin cloth. He had stepped into his father's shoes and the entire burden of the family lay on his shoulders. He felt himself grown in stature now, and had begun to affect many of his father's mannerisms. He would pull out his half-smoked cigar from behind his ear, put it in his mouth and light it, and then speak gravely to his sisters in a tone of authority.

'Listen, Jili, and you, Bili, how long are you going to take to heat a pot of liquor for me?' he would demand.

'Are you going to get drunk again this evening?' they would reply in an equally severe tone.

'Hold your tongue and do as I say. Put the pot on the fire at once. I want the liquor to be fresh. Do you understand?'

He liked his liquor hot and freshly distilled and as strong as possible. He had made himself a small earthen still for distilling it from sweet mahua flowers. Between swigs he would sing the same song over and over again:

> Here comes my Kajodi,
>   my Kajodi,
>   bonny Kajodi,
> Here comes . . .

Singing would be invariably followed by an order to one of his sisters to fetch his dungudunga, so that he could accompany himself as he sang, in true Paraja fashion. His sisters knew what to expect as he got more and more intoxicated. They would roll with laughter, until, in the middle of his lyrical outburst describing the scene when his bride entered his home, he would pass suddenly into a deep sleep and start snoring. His sisters would then finish their work and go to the young women's dormitory. As the evening warmed up, eager voices from the young men's dormitory would rise in passionate songs of wooing, to which the women would reply suitably, also in song, while the dungudungas twanged lustily.

'Why don't you go out, my dear?' Kajodi would whisper provocatively in Jili's ear. 'Can't you hear your young man calling to you?'

'It's you he wants, not me,' Jili would answer in the same vein.

Sometimes, at dead of night, Jili really did go out of the young women's dormitory. The still night hummed with a sound that seemed to come from nowhere in particular. Something would stir within her and she would get up, give a shake to Kajodi to see if she was really asleep, cast furtive glances around her and then leave the room noiselessly to melt into the darkness outside, her excitement overflowing painfully. She would look up at the sky; it was a void under which she felt lost. She would fidget about restlessly and then come back into the dormitory and lie down by Kajodi's side. Kajodi, after pretending to be fast asleep as she lay full-length with her face pressed against the ground, would explode with laughter and ask:

'Back so soon?'

Jili would snore.

'Why didn't you go over to the other dormitory?' Kajodi would ask. 'You must learn to be brave, my girl.'

Jili would snore again.

Kajodi would shake her and pinch her, then suddenly fling her arms around her, press her face against Jili's and whisper:

'Be careful now! If you lie in bed snoring like that I shall steal your Bagla from you one of these nights. Do you hear?'

Meanwhile, Mandia Jani lay in drunken sleep on his veranda and dreamed of Kajodi while the fat moon poked a finger at him through a chink in the thatch and laughed.

'We needn't worry about harvesting our rice, my son,'
Sukru Jani told Tikra. 'Mandia will take care of everything.'

'Yes, father.'

'He can work like twenty men, you know,' Sukru Jani
continued.

'That's true, father. No one else can do half as much.'

'Yes, he's a wonderful lad. It's time we found him a
wife. It's a pity we haven't been able to manage the bride-
price yet, but with any luck we should be able to take care
of that after this harvest.'

'That is certain, father.'

'Charming girl, Kajodi,' Sukru Jani mused to himself.
'A wonderful pair she and Mandia will make. Puri Jani is
lucky to have such a daughter.'

'Yes, father, she is a nice girl. And she is easily the best
dancer at the Spring Festival.'

'I was not talking of how she dances, my boy, but of
how she works.'

'Well, she does all the work in Puri Jani's house,' Tikra
said. 'She even looks after his herd of cattle. And she never
seems to get tired.'

'Are you on good terms with her, Tikra? Remember,
she's going to be your sister-in-law and if you don't
humour her she won't give you enough to eat,' Sukru Jani
laughed, and added: 'Take my advice and win her favour.'

'Don't worry about me, father. It's you who needs to be
careful with her.'

They shook with laughter over this.

While they worked on the money-lender's land they
would talk of the happy times that lay ahead, and this
lightened their toil.

Chapter 19

Puffed with the sense of his great responsibilities, Mandia Jani became more and more of a prig. He worked like a bull all day, brewed his liquor in the evening, drank his fill and slept like a log at night. Often he would carry liquor with him to the fields; it seemed to give him added zest for work.

Jili and Bili used to rise early in the morning, drink mandia gruel and then go out into the jungle to gather edible tubers and yams. Many other girls would join them on the way, and while they dug out tubers they would sing. The cowherd boys grazing their cattle on the neighbouring hill slopes would pick up the song as it echoed up the ravines. The jungle was alive with varieties of birds and the birds too sang.

At times, in the jungle, the girls would come across Kau Paraja, the goti of the village headman. The name Kau meant 'crow', and he was a dwarfish, loose-limbed, bow-legged scarecrow of a man, whose appearance and ill-coordinated movements readily provoked laughter. His face was too long for his body. When spoken to, he had a manner of listening to every trivial matter with an absurdly rapt and intent expression on his face. If the girls asked him what had brought him there he would say that he was searching for missing cattle or that he had come to look after cattle (though there might not be a single animal in sight), speaking always in a tone of extreme urgency as if the matter was one of life and death.

The girls enjoyed making fun of him.

'Now, brother Kau, will you please dig some yams for us,' Bili would ask. He would open his eyes wide and come running to her and say:

'Yes, yes, come with me.'

Then he would start scurrying into the jungle, pause and look back over his shoulder to see if she was coming, and then run on again; but nobody followed.

On other occasions Jili would say:

'Now, brother Kau, do sing us a song.'

'A song? All right,' and Kau would grunt out some music in a way that made them rock with laughter, while he looked at them in wonder.

Nothing seemed to throw him and no words could sting him; he took everything in good part.

Jili and Bili would return home, their heads and faces half buried under huge loads of edible leaves and yams.

Mandia Jani would often pause in the midst of work and, with his pick-axe resting on his shoulder and the sweat on his bare body shining in the sun, he would stand with his legs apart, his eyes riveted on the watering pool where he expected to see Kajodi. Then he would shake off his trance with a jerk, take a sip of liquor from his gourd-shell and resume work, like a clock that has stopped but only needs winding to make it run again.

'You are drinking too much, Mandia,' Jili warned him. 'Be careful.'

'Why are you so sore about it?' Mandia retorted. 'Do you want a drink?'

'God help me if I do. That stuff would go to my head and make me dance. And who would play on the dungu-dunga then?' she laughed. 'But I say, brother, your Kajodi dances exquisitely.'

Mandia changed the subject and assumed a serious air. 'Now listen, children,' he said in a gruff voice, 'I have something to tell you. Collect as many mahua flowers from the jungle as you can and we shall brew more liquor. I know it's an offence against the law to distil liquor. But you see, we've no money to hire labourers to reap our paddy for us, but we could get labourers if we gave them liquor instead of paying them wages in cash. I spoke to some people in the Domb street and they are willing to reap our paddy if we can give them liquor.'

'All right,' Jili said, 'we'll try to get you some mahua flowers but don't count on it.'

'Let's make a bargain. You get me mahua flowers and I'll get you combs from the market.'

'Pooh! Don't we have legs for getting to the market? Do you think we depend on you? Now listen, Mandia, those chilies in that patch belong to Bili and me, since it was we who raised them. Well, our chilies are ripe now and one of these days I'm going to take them to the market and sell them. But you shan't have any of that money unless you buy a new cloth for me and another for Bili.'

'Ah, well!' said Mandia. 'Now be a good girl and get me some mahua flowers and then you'll see what gifts I shall buy for you.'

Jili laughed. 'I know what it will be, you miser,' she said; 'just a few of those cheap sweets with rice and molasses.'

Mandia was offended. 'So you think I'm a miser, do you?' he said.

But this was only the beginning. They hung round him like cow-flies, pestering and teasing him.

'By the way, Mandia,' Jili said, 'why were you gaping at Kajodi today?' Both the sisters tittered.

'You'd better watch out, or she'll eat up everything in the house,' Bili said.

'Your Kajodi is no good,' Jili added. And there was more in this vein. Mandia snarled at his sisters but in his heart he liked them to tease him about her.

Not a day passed without his resolving to go out that night and join his friends in the young men's dormitory; but as evening fell he would get drunk and go to sleep on his veranda. He saw her only in his dreams, and some of these dreams, rising out of the fumes of liquor, were weird and feverish. He would see himself wandering through strange, dim forests, where little streams gurgled through the hills; and then he would feel himself plunging headlong over endless rocks, or trying to climb up the sides of slippery hills.

Chapter 20

Physically, Mandia Jani was all man, with a powerful body; but he was shy when facing women. Words formed themselves but never reached his lips, and he had to gulp them down again. His love for Kajodi found expression in stealthy sidelong glances, and if he happened to become aware of her presence he would feign indifference and devote all his attention to whatever work he happened to be doing. Even though he was hungry he was ashamed to speak.

It amused Kajodi to think of him and his shyness. She remembered how on some occasions he had forgotten himself in the young men's dormitory and, inflamed by the music of the dungudungas, had addressed passionate songs to her; and next day, when she passed him in the field, he had craned his neck and stood gazing at her, his nose in the air, as if he was sniffing some perfume that she left in the air as she passed. But his normal behaviour was very different. He would be humming a tune as he reaped the mandia but if she chanced to pass that way he would stop singing and pretend to be absorbed in his work.

Once, while she bathed in the stream, he had stood in his field staring at her. She had taken off her sari on the bank; she was aware that he was staring at her, but she behaved as though she did not know it. She was alone. She could not suppress her laughter; she had turned round to face him, but he had fled. And she had found that his modesty did not please her.

On other occasions, as she walked to the stream with her friends, laughing and joking, she would deliberately fall behind. She would look at him steadily, meaningfully; but all she ever got from him was a flash of white teeth, and then he would return to his work.

She would feel herself growing impatient, even though she laughed at his shyness. 'Is there no one else?' she would think.

She knew of a cave on a hillside in the forest, completely secluded among the trees; sometimes she would sit there all alone, enjoying the view of the hill slope plunging into the valley below.

And one morning, as she sat there, concealed, she saw the peacocks dance.

It began when a peacock came and stood on a flat stone in front of her and called out, and six peahens ran to meet him from under cover of the shrubbery. The peacock spread his wings, arched his neck, raised his multi-coloured tail erect like a fan, shook it and danced, and the flock of peahens circled around him in a mad whirl.

As Kajodi gazed at the dance of the peacocks she felt strange urges within her.

She knew that Mandia Jani loved her and she was willing to accept him as her mate. In the little world in which she lived, it was taken for granted that they would marry. But secretly she burned with a sense of discontent. She had wanted something from Mandia and yearned for it with a deep, unashamed longing; but he had not given it to her, and so an unrest had remained within her, an aching void which she could not account for.

There was no shame or delicacy in the jungle. The peacock felt no shame, nor did the stag; but Mandia Jani cowered in his bashfulness and did not even look up.

She had met Mandia Jani near the cave on two occasions, which she remembered vividly. The first time, she had been startled to find him standing a little distance away from the entrance to the cave. They had stood for a long moment, staring wordlessly at each other. Then she had asked him lovingly:

'Where have you been?'

'I was felling logs.'

'You look tired,' she had said. 'Come and rest.'

But he had not spoken again. He had stood in a trance while she looked at him with inviting eyes. Then, suddenly, he seemed to wake up ʳ ' moved away without a word.

On the other occasion she had found him walking towards the cave, with his axe on his shoulder. She sat alone inside the cave.

'Come, take me with you,' she had said.

'Come with me,' he had replied.

'But I can't get up. My legs are aching.'

Mandia had stood there dumbly. With an abrupt movement of annoyance she had got up and walked briskly away, leaving him to follow, but almost immediately she had trodden on a thorn and sat down again, shivering with pain. The bunch of flowers which she had tucked in her hair had fallen out. Mandia had plucked another bunch and tucked it tenderly into her hair; but then he had seemed ashamed of this little expression of feeling and had stood silently apart until Kajodi got up and moved away again.

It was not that she did not understand how deep his love for her was. She knew that well enough. And she knew that he would do anything for her. But his love left many things incomplete and unfulfilled in her; and her ripe young body felt impatient and tense, as if every particle in her being was about to burst.

The dance of the peacocks brought back several scenes to her mind. Often she had stolen out of the young women's dormitory at midnight, following Jili unobserved as she went out into the darkness. She had seen Bagla come forward, and had watched how Jili leant her face against his chest as she threw herself on him. She had felt the blood boil within her like water from the cooking-pot boiling over onto the hearth, and she had felt something pounding in her heart. On these occasions she would hide her face in her hands and slink back into the young women's dormitory.

Bagla had come but Mandia had not.

Dungudungas had been twanged by other hands than his. Their sound had died away, but he had not come. The whole world had gone tipsy with the intoxication of the moonlight, and Kajodi had gone out into the night, but still he had not come.

Chapter 21

Late in the night, Jili woke up again. Kajodi was fast asleep. Jili went out. A curved moon had just begun to peep through the fork of the tall pipal tree, its light filtering through the mist like a shower of dust particles. She was reminded of the twilight hour when herds of cattle return home. The jungle was asleep, and the light and shade and the mist wove dream-like patterns around her. She did not mind the cold. She thought she had heard someone call out softly to her, as she lay unsleeping on her bed. She had come out but found no one.

Glow-worms twinkled in the dark under the trees and she began to collect a handful of them; then she felt someone's hands cover her eyes, and she was pulled back and held in muscular arms. She turned her head, looked up and saw that it was Bagla, wrapped from head to foot in a mantle of rags sewn together. The moonlight trickling down through the leaves of the pipal tree had painted a checkered pattern on the ground. Across this checkerboard they walked till they came to a large flat stone, on which they sat.

There lay their village with the tall pipal tree standing at its centre; the doors of the houses were closed and behind them, stretched out round the dying fires, lay dogs and human beings, asleep and soundless.

They saw another figure come out of the young women's dormitory, to be joined by a shadow moving away from the young men's. The pair removed itself to a distance, and no one interfered.

Jili and Bagla sat together undisturbed.

'Why don't you come to the woods in the day time?' Bagla whispered.

'How can I?' Jili whispered back. 'I'm so busy at home, and Bili and Mandia are hanging around all the time. But what about you? I hardly ever see you now.'

The lovers had much to say to each other.

At length Jili asked petulantly: 'How long must we continue like this? Why don't we run away together?'

Bagla caressed her and said: 'Haven't I thought of it, my darling? But . . .'

'You wouldn't be afraid if you really loved me,' she said, turning her face away, 'but your promises mean nothing.' She was bitter.

Bagla continued caressing her warmly as he tried to appease her anger. 'You know I would run away with you now if I could, my darling. But tomorrow morning your father and all his kinsmen would come to our door, demanding the bride-price. How could I face them?'

'Why don't you pay the bride-price, then?' she demanded. 'Is your father, Rengu Paraja, so poor that he can't find a few rupees?'

'But it's two or even three score of rupees, my
sweetheart. Where could we find such a sum straight-
away?'

'Then stop making a show of love, Bagla. And don't
give me any more of your sweet words. But your money
wouldn't be wasted on me, I can tell you. I'm not like one
of those lazy women from the plains who do no work and
only eat and sit at home. I'd work for you in your house.
But that's enough—let me go now.' Her lips trembled as
she spoke and she burst into tears.

But she forgot her anger and her bitterness as he held her
hard in consolation, and her eyes closed with pleasure at
the touch of his body.

'When will you take me, Bagla?' she whispered to him
urgently. He warmed her heart as he embraced her again
and said: 'Very soon, my darling. I'm only waiting to harvest my paddy. As soon as I have the money I shall come
for you, and if I can't find the money any other way I shall
borrow it and become a goti.'

'No! No!' she exclaimed, wringing her hands. 'I'll never
allow you to bind yourself as a goti.'

'Don't worry, my love,' he said. 'What must happen
will happen. But I shall take you home on the first possible
day, when the season of marriages comes.' And Bagla and
Jili went back to their respective dormitories.

There are only four months in the year when people of
the Paraja tribe may marry: February, March, April and
May; and Chaitra (March—April) is the month of the
Spring Festival, when they spend their days and nights
dancing, hunting and feasting.

This spring, Jili thought, she would dance with her
Bagla—but as his wife. She and Bagla would have their

own home. She would go out into the jungle for firewood, and leaves and tubers to eat, while he went to the fields to work; and then she would carry warm mandia gruel for him in a gourd-shell flask. She would fish with him in the brook and catch chenga fish, the ones with big heads and smooth, scaleless bodies; and she would prepare a tasty dish for him with the fish, leaves from the forest, mandia flour, and a little salt, which he would love to eat.

And she would have her house—hers and Bagla's.

Bagla too was lost in thought. He must find the money for the bride-price somehow. Should he go to the Sahukar? The idea was frightening. Besides, did he really want to tie himself down to married life, and give up the freedom of the dormitory? He wasn't sure.

But then again, the image of Jili's face with her quivering lips and tearful eyes rose in his mind. He felt guilty. But as he slept the faces of several other girls flashed through his mind as if competing for his favour.

Chapter 22

There had been no rain in December, and Ramachandra Bisoi, the money-lender, was having a new barn built to store the freshly cut crops from his fields. Several of his gotis were working on it, together with some hired day-labourers, among whom were a number of girls. Sukru Jani was helping to build a mud wall, while Tikra was working at one of several pits from which clay had been dug out. The clay had been moistened and puddled, and the sticky paste had been stacked in heaps ready for use. Tikra was in charge of one such stack. Five labour-girls were engaged in carrying clay from the stack to the work-site. They would come to Tikra with empty baskets which he had to fill with the oozing mud and lift on to their heads.

Tikra was now in his twentieth year and beginning to grow conscious of his manhood. As he filled the baskets and lifted them onto the heads of the girls, he felt buoyant and gay. At times, while he worked, he would stare at them, his gaze lingering on their faces or breasts before returning to the mud stack.

There was lynx-eyed Manguli, who, while she bent her head to take her load from his hands, looked up into his face with pouting lips and gurgled with suppressed laughter, until Tikra gasped and broke into a smile.

'What a strong young fellow you are!' she teased him. 'Why, you're panting for breath after lifting up a single basketful of mud!' Tikra bit his lip and smiled. Manguli went. Next came Reni for her basketful. She came running up on light feet, her face rippling with laughter, and while he lifted the load to her head she whispered: 'Look, my flowers have fallen off. Will you put them back in my hair?'

'Yes, yes,' he said. 'Now off you go with this load and I shall set it right when you come back.'

Next was a girl named Olsi. Her movements were languorous and she seemed barely able to stand; as he raised her basket to her head she would appear to collapse against him, and look at him with deep, languid eyes as though to

size him up. Then she would walk away with slow steps.
And so it went on.

'Now let me have my bunch of flowers,' Reni said when
she returned with her basket ready for filling. Tikra had
picked up the bunch of flowers that had fallen off her head
and now he held it behind his back and refused to let her
have it. She managed to snatch it, almost falling on him in
the process, tucked it in her hair, smoothed it back, and
stood adjusting the folds of her sari, which had come un-
done in the struggle. Somehow, she seemed to be finding
it difficult to tie the sari around herself; she made a number
of attempts, but did it wrong each time and had to start
again. And all the while she looked at him with reproach-
ful eyes. 'Now look!' she exclaimed, 'see what you have
done to my sari!' Then she burst out laughing.

Tikra was pleased with himself. He felt as if he was the
master there on that clay-heap, lording it over all those
girls, dispensing his favours as he pleased, filling Reni's
basket with a lighter load of clay and putting a heavier load
into Olsi's.

While the girls worked, they sang in chorus, and Tikra
puddled the clay with his hands and feet and listened.

He had grown up. Now when he looked at women he
felt a strange stirring in his blood. It was frightening at
times.

Manguli stood before him scratching her body with
both hands.

'Now tell me, young man,' she jeered at him, 'are you
really as strong as you look?' The others laughed. He felt
his face shrink and grow hot, but he mustered his courage
and said challengingly: 'Why don't you find out for yourself?' This only made the girls laugh all the louder. Tikra

stood silently with his arms crossed over his chest, trying to hide his confusion.

Reni came running again, placed both her hands on his shoulders, shook him and said:

'Hurry up and fill my basket, will you? The people over there are waiting for more clay.'

He tried to concentrate on his work, but he felt his blood grow hotter and race in his veins like wild deer in flight, then collect inside his heart and roar like a hillstream in spate. He heard a drumming in his ears and his head spun; for a moment he could see nothing but black and white spots before his eyes.

At times he felt a longing to run away.

Sukru Jani was a neat worker, but his work failed to absorb him. As he went on raising the mud wall, adding one lump of clay to another, he remembered how he had once planned to build houses for his sons. He had nursed visions of himself and his children labouring together. As the walls rose higher and higher, the wooden frame for the roof was laid, and the thatch plaited out of long strands of piri grass, gathered from the jungle. As he slaved for the money-lender he could see it all as it would have happened.

Only, it had not.

In the fields below the hills, the olsi plants were in flower. The landscape had been washed in delicate shades—the light yellow of the olsi flowers, and the grass a light green. The jungle was black in the background, while the hills and deep valleys beyond it merged into patches of ochre and brown and blue; the cattle grazing on the hills and the men in their fields were tiny specks of grey.

Sukru Jani looked at the scene with eyes that registered

nothing but emptiness. His hands continued to work, mechanically smoothing one layer of mud over another. And the Sahukar's house rose higher and higher.

Sahukar Ramachandra Bisoi sat basking in the sun, watching his new barn rise out of the mud, the latest symbol of his wealth and power. He stroked his bushy moustache and scrutinized the girls who were working for him, appraising their firm, taut bodies as they walked to and fro with their baskets. If his glance met some girl's she would shudder, smile to hide her confusion, and move away with downcast eyes. But the Sahukar never smiled.

Just then, Sukru Jani walked up to him; on his face was the expression of meekness which a tribal finds convenient to assume when dealing with a man from the plains, particularly if the latter is rich or powerful or both.

'Lord, may I have two days' leave to go home?' he said to the Sahukar in a low voice.

'What for?' the Sahukar growled.

'I want to harvest my rice, sir,' Sukru Jani said humbly; 'this is the season for harvesting.'

'Get back to work, you fool!' cried the Sahukar, 'you certainly can't have leave!' Sukru Jani went back to his work, and the Sahukar, who had been annoyed at the disturbance, returned to his pleasant occupation of examining the bare bodies of the working women.

Olsi stumbled and fell against Tikra, as he was lifting a basket of mud to her head. He lost his own balance and slipped in the mud, and Manguli clapped her hands and cried out: 'Bravo! What a strong man!'

Everyone laughed.

Tikra's face fell but he managed a sheepish smile.

Chapter 23

On Wednesdays, people from all the neighbouring villages within twenty miles travelled to Podagod—about twelve miles from Sarsupadar—for the weekly market or *haat*. All over rural India, these periodic village-markets are important events in the lives of the countryfolk; but they are especially significant for the tribals. Men and women think nothing of trekking many miles through dense forests or over steep hills to buy a copper's worth of salt or oil, or to sell a few red chilies from the garden. In the uneventful lives of these people, the weekly market becomes more of a festival or a social event than an outlet for commerce. The women dress up in their brightest clothes and their gaudiest beads; their chattering becomes higher-pitched than usual, their songs are louder and their smiles broader. The market is the place for meeting friends, new and old, and exchanging gossip.

And the market is also, often, the place where lovers meet.

It was market day at Podagod and the market was at its busiest.

There among the crowds was Lili Paraja. He had walked twelve miles for two coppers' worth of sweet condiments, made of rice and molasses, for his little son. There too was the wife of the headman of his village; she had come to purchase a copper's worth of kerosene which would light her hut for a whole week.

Here, among the forbidding hills, as in the great commercial centres of the world, business thrived by appealing to the instincts of women. The most popular stalls of all, where the crowd was thickest, were those where ornaments of copper and brass were displayed, and beads, combs and mirrors in which the mountain beauties could admire themselves. All these fineries cost only a few coppers.

Whenever Bagla remembered his betrothed, Jili, the thought of her companion Kajodi somehow came to his mind and he felt that if he were to buy presents it should be for both of them and not for one alone.

Jili was pacing up and down in front of the stall where clothes were being sold, looking for her brother, Mandia. He had promised to buy a sari for her. But he was nowhere in sight. She felt bitter and impatient and suspected that he had gone into hiding to avoid her.

She scanned the crowds that were pouring in. There were tall Dombs from the villages in the interior; they were Christian converts who arrived in groups, shook each other by the hand and then moved away. There were people of the Kondh and Paraja tribes. There were girls of the Gadaba tribe, with their striped garments, and huge ear-rings of copper which hung down to their shoulders. It was a medley of new faces and fashions and quaint dresses and ornaments, of colour and noise and constant movement. Jili felt lonely.

Suddenly she saw Bagla. She rushed after him, her face wreathed in smiles; then she felt someone tugging at the end of her sari, turned round and saw that it was Kajodi. The two laughed.

'I'm looking for my brother but I can't find him,' Jili said.

'He is here,' Kajodi murmured shyly. 'I saw him.'

'Of course,' said Jili with a smile. 'How could your eyes miss him?' Kajodi laughed and moved away.

Then Jili caught up with Bagla. 'So, here you are?' she exclaimed. 'But I can't find Mandia!'

'Can't you, indeed!' Bagla said, laughing. 'Look, there he is, behind that big tree.' He pointed into the distance. 'And if you ask me what he's doing I'll tell you: he's selling kerosene.'

'Kerosene!' Jili exclaimed.

Bagla laughed. 'Yes, yes,' he said. 'Why don't you go and see?'

As Jili went towards the tree she wondered why Bagla had joked about her brother Mandia selling kerosene. Then she saw him. He had a huge turban tied round his head, and he sat on the ground at his ease, smoking a cigar made of a rolled leaf. Arranged in a neat row before him were a container of the kind used for selling kerosene, and some bottles. The place was not crowded.

'Well!' Jili exclaimed.

As soon as Mandia saw her he began fuming at her. 'What are you doing here?' he shouted. Didn't I tell you to stay at home?'

'Keep your questions to yourself,' Jili retorted angrily. 'You think you're very clever, don't you? You promise to buy me a sari and then you disappear!'

Customers arrived. 'A bottle for me,' said one. 'And one for me too,' said another. Each customer placed two annas before him and he poured out liquor in bottles which they gulped down.

'So *that's* the kerosene you're selling,' Jili said, laughing, when the customers had gone. 'You must have made a pile of money. Now you can come and buy me a good sari.'

'Be reasonable, Jili,' Mandia pleaded. 'We need the money to hire labourers for the harvest. We've still got to pay the rents. The sari will have to wait.'

'Very well,' she said, making a wry face. 'Save all the money you can so that you can pay the bride-price for your Kajodi. I don't want anything from you.'

This started a quarrel. Finally Mandia said: 'Don't let's quarrel. Have patience. If I can sell this tin of the stuff we shall see.'

Jili was hurt. She no longer cared whether he bought a new sari for her or not. But she waited as the market swelled.

Chapter 24

December is bitterly cold among these hills, and in every home a small charcoal brazier is lit in an attempt to keep out the cold; at night the villagers huddle round a communal fire on one of the verandas, and gossip.

In December, the tribes observe one of their major festivals, to mark the gathering of the harvest; this is followed, fifteen days later, by the ritual eating of the new grain. Tribal life is punctuated with many festivals, but chief among them is the Festival of Spring—a fortnight of revelry, hunting and feasting. Work is forgotten and the drums throb incessantly, day and night, to the rhythm of the dance; the old year is drummed away and the cycle of back-breaking labour begins again.

At the time of the harvest festival, the men all return to their own villages – even those who have been serving as gotis. Budra Jani had come back from his labours, and so had Kakna Paraja and Tendaw, Gora and Cheetum – old cronies of Sukru Jani who now shared the same fate as he. At last, only one day before the festival, the Sahukar told Sukru that Tikra and he could go home, but that they must return to work directly the festival was over.

As they walked through the hills, they saw groups of other people, also homeward bound. All were wrapped in makeshift rugs pieced together from the remnants of discarded clothes. The men carried their axes on their shoulders. The hills were no longer golden with the flowers of the olsi, but grey. The fields were brown and the crops had been cut, with only an occasional patch of ripe paddy or mandia still remaining, and here and there a straw hut, put up to shelter the harvesters in the field. Everything looked sad and desolate.

Night fell while they were still some miles from the village, and the hills turned black, as though plastered over by an invisible hand. Some of the travellers lit faggots, and little fires sprang up all around them like fireflies where the last of the harvesters watched over their crops, shouting and blowing their horns to scare wild beasts away. Women were returning from the streams with earthen pots full of water, and Sukru and Tikra overtook the stragglers, walked with one group for some distance and then hurried on to join another group ahead.

At last the lights of Sarsupadar appeared, peeping through the hills. Sukru and Tikra lengthened their strides up the steep ascent, and the twang of dungudungas floated up from the young men's dormitory. It was the night before the harvest festival, and preparations for the dance had begun.

Homecoming had brought no happiness to Sukru Jani. He had not been allowed to return in time to harvest his own fields, and he had grave misgivings about Mandia's ability to manage on his own. The occasion was merely another reminder of his misfortune; he had brooded so long and so often that the gift of joy had dried up with his bones, and he felt he could never be whole again.

Tikra was glad that he was returning home, but felt something of a stranger; his thoughts were more on the girls with whom he had worked in the Sahukar's home. He missed them.

Chapter 25

It was the morning of the festival. People rose early and were soon out in the streets, teeth chattering from the cold. The sunlight filtered through thick shrouds of mist which hung over the village, blurring the outlines of the huts. But even on that cold, misty morning, spirits were high with expectation. The menfolk hurried through their morning meals of mandia gruel and dashed off into the jungle to collect wood for the bonfire which was to burn all night.

The young women rushed from their beds to fetch coloured earths for painting the floors and walls of their huts. They did not stop even to wash their faces. The walls were

daubed over in white and red; the verandas were plastered
black and yellow, and gay designs were painted on the
walls and verandas in powdered rice mixed with water.
Finally, the floors inside the huts were smeared over in
different colours, and the wooden frames of the doors and
windows were painted with powdered charcoal mixed in
oil. The little huts glittered like new brides.

Other women were busy laundering clothes, boiling
them up with wood ash to make them white, and pounding them vigorously over the rocks in the bathing-pool to
remove all traces of dirt. Then it was the turn of the
women to wash themselves and dress their hair. The final
touch was the scrubbing of the heavy brass bangles which
they wore round their wrists; these had to be rubbed and
polished until they shone, and it was usually midday before the women were satisfied that their bangles were
bright enough.

Then they would put on their most colourful saris,
draped in tight folds round the waist and reaching no lower than the knee, and disappear into the jungle in groups to
look for fresh flowers to tuck into their hair; for there
could be no dancing without flowers.

Jili, Bili and Kajodi linked arms and walked down the
narrow, winding path into the jungle, moving as graceful-
ly as pea-fowl, with that fluid effortless walk which comes
so naturally to tribal girls, and to nobody else. Their
movements were sure and firm, whether they were stepping lightly from stone to stone, or jumping the narrow
gullies which the streams had gouged out of the hills.
When the streams were too wide to jump, they waded
through the clear, icy water, splashing each other merrily
as they went. Other girls were out in the jungle, alone or in

groups; the forest echoed to the sounds of their shouting and laughter. Sometimes they would break into a chorus, and the notes would linger in the still, cold air. The last drooping ears of ripe paddy, nodding imperceptibly in the wind, leaned over to catch the melody and then lay down again to sleep.

Some distance away, a hill rose almost vertically from the bottom of a deep ravine. Tikra stood near the edge of the precipice, leaning on a forked stick and peering into the darkness below, where a stream came crashing down in a series of foaming cataracts. The roar of the water was reassuring as he stood there alone under the cobalt sky, surrounded by hills rearing and plunging violently between dark valleys, thick with vegetation. Tikra had grown up. The soft, dimpled body was now hard and erect; the arms and shoulders bulged with muscle, and when he turned his neck sinewy cords stood out prominently on either side. And he had grown aware of strange new desires - those of a healthy young animal in the forests.

Everywhere in the village there was a fever of activity; the preparations for the night's orgy seemed to be endless. As daylight faded, the first batches of men and women returned from the forest, carrying armfuls of faggots for the ceremonial bonfire. There was a gleam in every eye – the result of something more than sheer high spirits. Already, the cups were brimming over; Mandia Jani and his associates were hard at work at their stills in the forest, making sure that no throats were dry, so that the voices round the bonfire that night would be loud and clear. Some of the men were carrying lengths of the slender siali creeper, with its leaves and fruits intact; these would be hung from the entrances to their huts, for the tribesmen believed that this plant had magical powers and could ward off all evil and protect them from misfortune. The faggots were arranged in a pile on high ground in the centre of the village; it was here that the fire would be lit.

Sukru Jani had gathered his share of firewood, but his heart was not in the festivities. As a goti, he felt he had no home, no family to rejoice over; the merrymaking and singing only mocked him. All day, he sat on the flat stone in front of his hut where, in the old days, he used to rest his limbs after a hard day's work. He realized that no one could share his feelings: his children were young, and knew nothing of sorrow. They were like young seedlings, growing ever upwards, though the husks of the seeds out of which they had sprouted still clung to them. Jili dreamed of her Bagla. Bili did not yet have a young man, but, no doubt, all her fantasies were woven from processions of brawny young men in loincloths, chanting her name to the plaintive accompaniment of the dungudunga. Tikra was a mere child, even though the first signs of manhood were appearing. As for Mandia, well, he was too young to be entrusted with the cares of a household, but one could not help feeling that he had been negligent. Sukru Jani had left the house in perfect order when he went away to serve the Sahukar; now everything was a shambles. There lay the fish-trap which he had started to weave out of fine slivers of bamboo—still incomplete—exactly as he had left it. The old wooden bedstead had not been repaired. Usually, at this time of the year, his kitchen garden was overgrown with the thick stalks of runner beans. This year, the creepers were half withered. Worse still, the rice crop was still not fully harvested, though December was nearly over. The mandia had been harvested, but the grain had not been properly stored; the earthen containers had been left open and the rats had undoubtedly got at the millets. Yes, Mandia had been something of a disappointment. What was there to celebrate?

As dusk fell, there were sudden loud cries of 'Thief! Thief!' This was the signal for the festivities to begin. By tradition, the fun started with some of the young men breaking into their neighbours' houses and 'stealing' anything that they could lay their hands on: a metal water-pot, or a basketful of vegetables from the garden. It was all a game, of course, and next day the stolen articles would be restored to their owners, for a nominal 'price'.

The evening meal had been cooked and eaten, and now everyone was hurrying to the spot where the fire would be lit. Already, the inmates of the young men's dormitory were there with their dungudungas, and the first voices rose in a tentative chorus. The young girls, now fully dressed for the dance with their flowers and bangles, stood in a semi-circle, arms linked to form a chain, with the tallest girls at one end. Their faces had been lightly smeared with oil. The taut bodies swayed rhythmically backward and forward as the tempo of the dance quickened. Small fires were lit in a wide circle round the groups of performers so as to light up the scene.

And then the dance of the Jhodia tribe began.

Traditionally, it was the privilege of the young men to call for a particular dance, which the girls would have to perform. The request was always made in song: the young men now asked for the dance known as 'The Clashing of the Bangles'. This was the song they sang:

> Let the bangles on your wrists ring together,
> Let them clash, O my beloved!

Let us all join in the dance of the Clashing of the
   Bangles,
As it was danced by our fathers long ago.
Let this ancient village ring again with the sound of
   your bangles –
This Village of the Mango Fruit or Village of the
   Blackberry,
Whatever we choose to name it. So dance, and make
   merry, and laugh,
Till the belly begins to ache.

Then the girls brought their heavy brass bangles
clashing together like cymbals and danced to the music of
the dungudungas. The ageless soul of the forest awoke, intoxicated with the dance. The earth throbbed, and the
dance of the Jhodias and Parajas, repeated by countless
generations, rang out again. And the past lived once more:

When there was no poison in the fresh air,
But only faith;
And no mosquitoes drank our blood,
And there were no snakes to bite at our heels;
When there were no paths in the jungle for the out-
   sider,
Jhodia shoulders carried no burdens except their own.
And when it was time to die,
They laid themselves down on land which they,
And not the outsider, possessed.
And in this land of hills and valleys,
The earth belonged to the Jhodia,
And to nobody else.

The dance had already begun when the Jani, or tribal
priest, arrived. The prescribed ritual had to be gone

through: a black rooster was killed in front of the pile of logs, and the fresh blood was allowed to ooze into the soil. Then some liquor, freshly distilled from mahua flowers, was poured on the same spot and mingled with the blood. This was the libation to the Earth Goddess, sealed with an offering of flowers. Next, the rooster, still dripping blood, was held over the pile of wood; a few flowers were placed ceremonially on the logs, some more liquor poured on, and the flame was lit. A great shout went up as the logs crackled and blazed; the drums beat frenziedly, the dungu-dungas became more and more insistent, and the long chain of girls snaked round the fire in writhing, twisting coils. The red firelight was reflected in their mahogany faces, gleaming with oil and perspiration; the flickering, dancing shadows wove strange designs on the ground. The dance quickened as the music built up into a climax; the girls were singing with the young men in chorus. Sud-denly, as if by a pre-arranged signal, the singing stopped. The drums took on a new, orgiastic rhythm, and a new chorus was taken up, the burden of which was:

Dhangdi! Dhangda!
Girls and boys!
Come together!

'Dhangdi! Dhangda! Dhangdi! Dhangda!' the drums panted, faster and faster; the girls ululated, the dungudun-gas twanged in their nasal monotone, and the Parajas danced on in the intoxication of the night.

At midnight, Sukru Jani sat on the flat stone in front of his house, looking around him. The fire had almost burnt out, and only the glowing embers lay winking among the ashes. Everywhere, people were lying in huddled groups

on the ground – dead drunk. For the moment, the festival
had reached a quietus, but the fires would burn again, in a
different village in another part of the hills. The festival
would continue, relay fashion, for an entire month; but for
Sukru it was already over, since after one more day he
would have to return to his master.

Next morning, it was the children of the village who
took charge of the festivities. They organized themselves
into groups and moved from door to door, collecting doles
of food-grains for a feast. Each child had one cheek painted
white and the other black; their clothes, hands and feet were
dyed a variety of colours and they carried little sticks. As
they came to each door they would clatter their sticks on
the grounds, dance and sing:

> Chher Chhera, Chher Chhera,
> Give us money and bundle up your straw.

The owner of the house, or his wife, would come to the
door, laugh, and return with a handful of rice or mandia.
This would be poured into the alms-bowl, and the group
would move on to another house.

In the street of the Dombs, who were the professional
music-makers, the drums were still beating; from time to
time a group of young girls would suddenly swing into a
dance. The mahua flowed freely; men gossiped, the
women sang or giggled, and the girls danced. At evening,
the sound of drumming was heard from neighbouring villages, and the people of Sarsupadar prepared for another
night of revelry. There was no more work to be done in
the fields, and life was one endless round of merrymaking.

Chapter 26

Long before the festival began, Mandia Jani had foreseen the demand for his liquor which it would create. He had set up his distillery in a ravine, some distance away from the village, Here, he felt, he would be safe from prying eyes; for it was illegal for anyone to distil liquor in the hills without a licence from the revenue authorities, though it was well known that all the tribes distilled their own liquor.

Mandia Jani loved the place where he had set up his still. The ravine ran like a tunnel between two high hills, with a thin stream trickling through it. Varieties of fern grew densely on each bank. In places, the matted roots of great trees stretched across the water like nets, obstructing the flow and forcing the water to skip over them. Here, Mandia felt as safe as a king, protected by the hills, the jungle and the ravine.

The process of distillation was simple. Mandia collected the sickly-sweet flowers of the mahua tree, which grew profusely in the forest, and soaked them in water in a large earthen pot with a lid until they were rotten and fermented. The pot was then boiled over a large open furnace, which he kept well stoked. A clay pipe connected the pot to a second earthen vessel at a much lower level. Mandia had set up his still right next to the stream, and he very ingeniously used the stream itself to cool the vessel which served as the receiver. He had rigged up a piece of bamboo, split in half along its length, with one end dipping in the stream and the other just touching the receiver. As the

fermented mahua boiled in the pot over the furnace, the
fumes collected in the receiver and were condensed into liquor by the running water of the stream.

While the other men from the village had been in the
forest fetching firewood, Mandia had been busy making liquor. He had worked feverishly for days, scarcely bother-
ing even to come home, and now he had several drums of
liquor hidden away in the ravine, which he would sell on
the day of the festival. It was so ridiculously easy to make
liquor and sell it on any market-day; liquor was such an
important part of life here that a tribesman would rather
forgo a meal than a bottle of pungent mahua wine. There
could be no festivities without liquor; no ritual was complete without it. The tribesman needed liquor not only to
propitiate his gods but also to drown his hunger and his
misery. With mahua wine in his veins, he was king of the
forest again; sober, he was only a weak, miserable, snivell-
ing creature, easy prey to the ruthless official and the wily
money-lender.

Mandia Jani had hit upon a goldmine. His clay pots and
piece of bamboo would soon bring him the sixty rupees
which he needed for the bride-price, to bring his Kajodi
home. As he worked, stoking up the fire in the hearth, or
putting more mahua flowers into the pot, he saw only the
dark eyes of Kajodi. Yes, he was doing it all for her, and as
soon as he had saved enough, he would go straight to her
father and claim his bride. Mandia's mind, like that of all
tribals, could entertain but one concept at a time; for the
moment, Kajodi filled his consciousness to the exclusion of
everything else. He was scarcely interested in the festival.

Sixty rupees is a lot of money in the jungle, and Mandia
found the target receding further and further away as he

worked himself to a standstill. Exhausted, he stood beside
his still, looking despondently at his pots, which seemed to
be failing him now. His eyes were smarting from the
smoke that rose from the hearth. Would he ever have the
money? He *could* have saved a little more, but he had to
buy saris for those wretches Jili and Bili, and they would
give him no peace until he had kept his promise to them. If
only he could coax a few more pots of liquor out of his still
each day! If he could brew enough liquor to fill the ravine!
The little stream might turn into mahua wine. But now it
all seemed so slow and tedious. And other young men had
followed his example and set themselves up in competi-
tion; there were at least three stills in other parts of the
jungle.

Sixty rupees. How much had he now? Ten? Fifteen?
Surely it must be more. He had sold gallons of liquor on
the day of the festival. And he had worked all night, while
the two boys who were helping him had come running
back to him for more and more. The liquor had sold so
quickly. Another such festival, and Mandia would be
home and dry! No need for him to go to the money-
lender; to become a goti; like his father, and Tikra, and all
others that he had known: oh no! But how else? Come on,
let's get back to work, boys.

Mandia never even saw the group of ten or eleven men
who walked into his ravine at dusk, on the day following
the festival. He had his back to them, and he was busy
stoking the hearth with brushwood. Then he saw the
terror-stricken faces of the two boys standing in front of
him, and turned round. It was the Sub-Inspector of Excise,
with four Excise guards and three or four other men
whom Mandia had never seen before. With them was

Chamru Domb, of Mandia's own village.

There was no escape; he had been caught red-handed. It was no use cringing or begging for mercy. He had broken the law, and he must suffer for it.

Mandia was ordered to carry the pots and drums of manufactured liquor on his shoulders and follow the Excise officials into the village. The dancing has started again. Several of the women were dancing in a kind of trance: they were 'possessed' by one or other of the goddesses in the tribal pantheon, and they howled and contorted themselves while the others watched reverently. But as soon as the Excise officials entered the village, the goddesses left them, and dancers and drummers fled helter-skelter into their huts. Within minutes, the entire area had been cleared. It was a visit from the dreaded 'Saltu' – the Salt and Excise Department.

There followed a thorough search of all the huts and surrounding patches of jungle for contraband liquor. Were there other stills in the village? The officials entered every hut and probed the walls and searched under the thatches and turned over the kitchen gardens while the villagers cowered and trembled, but never said a word. More stills were discovered, some no longer in use, others still hot. There were empty containers, old kerosene canisters and broken bottles in which the smell of liquor still lingered. All these articles were seized and a detailed inventory prepared by the officials. There were witnesses at hand to testify to everything, should this be required. The officials made them sniff the pots and even the ashes gathered from disused hearths, so that later they could swear in court that everything the officials said was true.

Now the officials were busy recording statements by the

offenders: they did not so much record as dictate, and the accused were given long confessions of their guilt to 'sign', which they did by placing the inked impressions of their thumbs on the paper. They were required to declare that everything recorded had been read out and explained to them; but few had any real idea of what was happening. They put their thumb-marks where they were asked to, and that was that. The 'Saltu' officials were pleased with their haul: authority had been asserted and vindicated.

That night, there was mourning in the village. The unknown informants who had brought about the visitation were cursed in helpless anger. Several people were suspected, and there were hot words and blows exchanged.

The harvest festival was over.

Chapter 27

Mandia Jani was tried, along with the others, in the magistrate's court.

'Accused in the dock, Mandia Jani,' the magistrate droned, 'it has been alleged against you that on such and such date, at such and such place, you illicitly distilled liquor and were found in possession of articles used in illicit distillation, namely. . . . Do you know of any cause why you should not be convicted of the offence under such and such section of such and such Act?'

Mandia stared at the magistrate with the dumb eyes of a

bullock. He knew the reply which was expected of him: his people had the words by heart.

'Great lord,' he said mechanically, 'I am guilty.'

The ritual went on. The magistrate read out his sentence.

'I accept your plea of guilt and convict you of the offence under Section such and such of such and such Act as alleged, and sentence you to pay a fine of fifty rupees, in default to undergo rigorous imprisonment for fifteen days. Next case.'

A police constable led Mandia Jani away, and another offender took his place. The trials continued: it was nearly time for the court to rise and the magistrate was in a hurry. Who would listen to Mandia if he told them that he had no money to pay the fine? He sat on the veranda outside the courtroom with his head bowed. It was getting dark and lanterns were brought in. Beyond the court compound, Mandia could see the bare fields, lifeless after the harvest. They were not his fields, but they made him feel sad. The first stars appeared, as though they had strayed there by mistake. People came and went; no one even looked at him.

Mandia Jani petitioned the court for time in which to pay the fine. He had to execute a bail bond and offer a surety, and then he was allowed to go home. He set out for his village along the dark and narrow mountain path, with that old, effortless stride of his, like a panther's. Outwardly, it was the same Mandia; the head was still carried high and the powerful chest was thrown out. He was like a sal tree seared by lightning: the sap had dried up inside, though there were no visible signs of damage—unless you looked in his eyes. The future had been blotted out entirely; Kajodi was no longer even a memory. From the moment of his arrest, he had lain in a trauma. There was no sorrow, no pain - no time to reflect on the experience that had overtaken him. And now, as he retreated to his hut, he imagined he was a young barking-deer, pursued by hunters at the Spring Festival, running for its life. And still the sounds pursued him: 'Kill! Kill! Don't let him get away! Fifty rupees, or you go to jail! Shoot! Kill!'

In a panic, Mandia started running.

Chapter 28

It seemed to Mandia as though everyone in the village was unusually considerate to him. Nothing was said at all about the raid, or the trial. The elders of the village came to Sukru Jani, and there were long and earnest conversations which Mandia, naturally, did not join. When the others did speak to Mandia, it was only to talk of other things. Mandia spoke very little now. He wanted to avoid everybody, and he hardly ever came out of his hut. In point of fact, he had no reason to feel ashamed, for nearly everyone in the village was involved in the affair in some way or other. Many others had been convicted like himself, and they too would have to pay fines or go to jail. The whole village had been brought together in misfortune. No one laughed now, and all voices were low. Occasionally, the womenfolk would stop to converse as they went to the pool for water, speaking in whispers of the calamity that had overtaken their sons and husbands.

It was time for Sukru Jani and Tikra to go back to the Sahukar's house, but Sukru Jani could not possibly desert his eldest child now. Tikra returned alone, and Sukru stayed on. He had borne this new grief in silence; there was not a sign of dismay on that granite face.

Once more, there were protracted conferences with the Naika, the Barik and the Chalan. The money would have to be found; there was no question of Mandia's not paying the fine and going to prison. For the ignorant tribesman, there is no terror greater than the terror of the prison: it is altogether beyond his comprehension, for it belongs to a system in which he has no part, though he lives on its fringes. Labour he understands, even unpaid labour under a tyrannical money-lender, for this he is born into; but anyone who goes to jail is forever stamped a criminal, and ostracized. It cripples him socially and economically; the law never relents once it has you in its toils. It is far better to become a goti and raise a loan from the money-lender.

And so Mandia Jani accompanied the Naika, the Barik, the Chalan and his father to the Sahukar's door. It was a long march, and to Mandia it seemed to have no end. Even in December, the sun was hot at midday. They stopped to rest beside a stream, and ate the mandia gruel which they carried in their gourd-skin flasks. They chatted nonchalantly of this and that, and even Sukru Jani joined in the conversation, though Mandia was silent. Doves cooed in the forest, and a few dry leaves fell from the trees. Mandia's mind could register nothing. At last, they reached the Sahukar's home. There was no need to explain their errand; it was only too obvious.

It was nearly four o'clock in the afternoon or, as the Parajas like to describe it, when the sun was only the length of a walking-stick from the horizon, before the papers were drawn up. Mandia Jani smeared his left thumb with lamp-black mixed with oil, and the Sahukar told him where to press it down on the document. Money changed hands, and Mandia Jani became a goti like his father and his brother.

Chapter 29

It was the month of Phagoona—that is, February—and spring had arrived. The fields, still bare after the harvest, gaped at the sky, which was unrelieved by even a single cloud. The hilltops were almost bald; a few vivid red leaves were beginning to sprout on the slender trees.

It was time to hoe the fields for the next crop. The rocky soil was hard and dry, as though unwilling to yield itself up to the human beings who were trying to woo it, softening it with their sweat, coaxing the fields to smile again. Each day, Sukru Jani and his sons rose at dawn and remained bent over their hoes till the sky grew crimson in the west. They stopped work only for a few minutes at about midday, when they ate the gruel from their flasks. There was no pleasure in this work, for the fields which they hoed belonged to the Sahukar. Being on the hillside they could not be ploughed with bullocks; human muscles had to be used, but the Sahukar had gotis in abundance. The yield from these hillside fields was always the best, and the Sahukar's granaries overflowed with the fruit of his gotis' labours.

As Mandia Jani put down his pickaxe and stopped to wipe away the sweat from his forehead and chest, he was silhouetted against the setting sun like a massive granite boulder. The sweat glistened on his firm body. Mandia had adjusted himself to the life of a goti far more easily than the others; perhaps it was because of his greater resilience. He rarely brooded like his father. The shock had worn off and he had grown buoyant again. He never bothered to count his tomorrows, for he was sure that his time would come. Optimism comes naturally to the tribesman; he is never quite cured of it. Or maybe, when one has lived long enough among the mountains, one is no longer aware of the peaks and troughs of existence, and everything appears to be level ground. After centuries of trial, the Paraja has learned to be like the earth, patient and enduring.

Mandia Jani sat under a tree, mopping the sweat from his face. The brisk spring breeze whipped up clouds of dust among the hills, and the rich fragrance of champak flowers was wafted down to him. Woodpigeons were cooing softly in a nearby jhodi tree. Further on, some cowherd boys were fluting a Kondh tune; every bar ended in a kind of wail. Mandia leaned back against the tree and allowed his mind to wander away into the distance, across the hills. Familiar images floated up: the little stream, broadening out into a placid pool, where the girls bathed and filled their earthen pots; the fields of ripening mandia and olsi, sloping down to the water's edge, where on other days, he had rested after work, savouring the fragrance of the breeze. And then he saw Kajodi. There were red flowers in her hair, and her sari was red like the dhatiki flower. Her lips were like the vermilion berry, and the aroma from her body was more maddening than that of mahua. Her eyes twinkled as she smiled and beckoned to him, pouting and teasing.

For a long moment Mandia sat under the tree on that bare hillside, thighs pressed together, knees drawn up under his chin and arms clasped round them. He was as motionless as the upright stones commemorating the dead in the centre of his village. Time stood still. And then the bubble burst. The hills were black against the sun. Mandia rose silently, shouldered his pickaxe and spade, and trudged back to the Sahukar's house.

Each night, the Sahukar would call his gotis together and give them their orders for the next day. He loved to shout and nag, and the more they argued with him the happier he was.

'Listen to me, you idiot,' he would shout at Sukru Jani. 'For heaven's sake, can't you do anything right?'

'But I've done everything you told me, Sahukar,' Sukru Jani grumbled.

'Well, how much longer are you going to be over that barn you're building?'

'Is it my fault if you keep on moving me from one job to another? You never give me time to finish anything. One day it's 'Sukru Jani, clear the weeds from the paddy fields'; the next day it's 'Sukru Jani, go and bring firewood from the jungle' or 'Go and plough the fields'. I have to attend to everything; and on top of that, I must build the new barn. How do you expect me to finish so soon?'

'No arguing, you lazy old ox,' the Sahukar shouted back. 'The barn must be completed this month. And Tikra, you go and work there too.'

Sukru Jani did not retort.

'And didn't I ask you to repair my rope-bed, Sukru? But you just can't remember a thing. And you should have put up the thorn fencing round the plot of land where I'm going to plant sugar-cane this year. What am I to do with such a useless old man? All he can do is sit and chew the cud like a bullock and growl like a dog!'

By this time the men were too tired to argue; they rested their heads on their palms and listened while he ranted and screamed obscenities.

Chapter 30

Spring came to another village too—the village of Sukru Jani and Mandia. It dyed the leaves scarlet and tickled the flowers into laughter. The girls wore mango blossoms in their dark hair, and the white, wild niali flowers; honeybees, drawn by the fragrance, lost their way and hummed round their ears. The hills grew festive once more, their splendour undiminished.

Kajodi bathed alone in the pool, splashing absent-mindedly. Her red sari hung from the nearby mango tree, merging with the new leaves. As she dipped her head, the wild flowers floating down the stream got entangled in her hair. She shook them loose, and they went drifting on in the current. The gulmohur tree, weighted down with long-tasselled flowers, drooped over the stream and drew golden patterns in the flowing water. As she sat in the water, listening to the warbling of the stream, Kajodi's eyes grew heavy with sleep; but at once the wind began to play with the strands of wet hair over her ears, sending a shiver through her.

As usual, Kajodi found herself brooding. Her thoughts would never leave her, however hard she tried to shake them off in the evening dance, or in the day's activities. Jili never came out with her now; they no longer walked in the forest together, or dreamed away the afternoons in the secret cave in the hills, where the peacocks danced. They did not bathe together in the pool, scrubbing each other's backs. For Jili was now the head of the family, the breadwinner. She had to go out into the jungle each day and collect edible roots; there was no time for play.

When Jili was with her, Kajodi seldom thought of Mandia. She never had time to think of him, for Bagla occupied most of their time, joking with them and teasing. Often, when she and Jili were together, they would talk about Bagla; and as soon as Bagla's name was mentioned, he would appear before them, as though he had been hiding somewhere, waiting for his name to be uttered. Why did he follow them everywhere? Kajodi felt sure it was not for Jili alone. He would turn his face towards Jili, and she would giggle happily; but once or twice Kajodi had been startled to find Bagla's eyes searching for her own, even though he appeared to be looking at Jili. And her eyes had been caught in his, and they had burned through her like a flame. She had teased Jili about Bagla's love for her; it had made her happy to think that he belonged to Jili. And then, her thoughts would grow confused and turbulent and, to her bewilderment, she found herself drawn towards Bagla.

When she had joked with Jili about Bagla, some of her jokes had been definitely barbed, and Jili had been stung to retort about Mandia and herself. Everything would be said as if in jest, but Kajodi would feel uncomfortable and guilty. A wave of tenderness for Mandia would surge through her then; but later, when she weighed up her feelings dispassionately, she saw that the man she loved had the form of Mandia Jani, but the spirit and personality of Bagla. There was no peace for Kajodi after that, though she prayed to all her gods to give her peace of mind. She felt herself being dragged, like driftwood, over a roaring cataract, and she could not see what lay below.

Where was her Mandia now?

There was no one to fling bouquets of wild flowers at her, unseen, as she walked through the forest; no axe, thudding on the trees, echoed the beat of her woman's heart; there were no probing eyes to search for the treasures of her body.

Her world was forlorn.

Kajodi felt a langour creep over her limbs; she needed someone to lean on. She closed her eyes and drifted away on a tide of fantasy.

For a woman's heart can never lie empty.

And Kajodi thought: how often had Bagla come to her and asked, 'Where is Jili?' Once or twice, she had teased him in reply, but inwardly she had flared up: 'Does the fool think I am Jili's bodyguard?' And sometimes she had answered him roughly, though with a smile. Bagla had grinned back sheepishly and walked away; but her woman's instinct told her that she had hurt him, and she was glad.

As she sat there alone, Kajodi could remember exactly how she had behaved with Bagla on each occasion. But Bagla belonged entirely to Jili – he was nothing to her. And yet the thoughts of this non-person sent a pang through her heart and she thought: what has he done to deserve this? Why do I hurt him; what glory do I gain by doing so?

And only the gurgling stream and the silent trees that fringed it knew of her repentance.

Poor Bagla! How cheerful he was, in spite of all her rebuffs – as eager as ever to begin a conversation! Her heart warmed to him more and more. She might not belong to Bagla, but he was hers entirely. Ah, how could she have hurt him? And gradually the non-person came to fill her entire consciousness.

Memories flowed through her mind. As one image arose, stepping down to the water – it seemed to her – from the high bank opposite, the other receded into the jungle on the other side and grew faint, like the footsteps of a forester as he vanishes among the trees.

Kajodi rose from the water, dried herself, dressed, and climbed the path that led to the village. A little way along, while she had been bathing, somebody had offered a sacrifice to the Earth goddess; right in the middle of the path there lay a little shrine, about two feet high, thatched like the doll's houses children build at play. Varieties of coloured powders were sprinkled on the ground in front of it, and a broken eggshell lay on top.

In the village, a number of men and women were walking busily along the narrow lane between the two rows of huts. Manglu Jani sat basking in the sun on his veranda, while his wife, newly married, searched for lice in his hair. In the centre of the village was the open square where the people usually congregated. Only Milku Muduli was there now, with his betrothed – the daughter of Sania Paraja. They laughed and flirted and tugged at each other. Milku, having no money for the bride-price, had become a goti in the house of his prospective father-in-law; when he had worked long enough for the bride-price to be realized, he would claim her and take her away. He was perfectly happy with the arrangement.

In front of Kudumi's hut, his young bride was pounding suan millets into flour in a wooden mortar, her bangles and bracelets jingling merrily. Yes, Kajodi thought, each woman had her home and her man, and the whole world was tied together in pairs; those who were still unattached were like driftwood, aimlessly floating on the surface.

In the past, Kajodi had often felt disgusted with the noise and disorder of life in the village – the little urchins, who had no sense of hygiene, and the chickens and the pigs. And the endless chatter-chatter; and the smoke that hung over the huts every morning and every evening. The sheer drudgery of having to worry about others all the time, having to carry gruel into the fields for somebody, boil somebody's clothes for the wash. And a husband who was drunk every night, foul-mouthed, abusive and violent. A household full of want and difficulty. She had thought then that the only happiness lay in the freedom of the dormitory, when a girl received nothing but endearments and kindness and had no drunken husband or father-in-law to please.

But the time comes when every sparrow begins to build

its nest, when the butterfly grows tired of its flight, and human shoulders ache for the yoke. Now Kajodi felt that life had passed her by and forgotten her, as other women marched proudly past, their foreheads ablaze with the vermilion marks that proclaim marriage, their noses and ears bristling with rings, their bunches of house-keys dangling from the knots at the ends of their saris. How triumphantly they carried their filthy brats in their arms! Her heart cried out. She longed for the touch of a husband who would come to her after the day's work, damp with sweat; and the muddy child that she could hug in her arms, streaming nose and all. She only wanted a little corner for herself in the great hall of society – a cheap ticket, which would entitle her to squat inconspicuously on the floor.

Kajodi walked past the house of Sukru Jani. Jili stood on the veranda; the cooking was not yet done. Kajodi felt very uncomfortable every time she looked at that house. Of late, she had begun to avoid it, choosing another route to return home through the fields.

A string of memories came back to her. That house had long lain desolate, without a master. No one waved to her when she passed. There was no Mandia to stare at her with big eyes, in which she could read the language of the heart. Tikra was not there to crack his jokes. She no longer saw Sukru Jani walking to his fields with his spade in his hand, stopping to nod to her, his eyes full of a father's blessing.

She had heard that Sukru Jani and his sons still came home sometimes, but a goti has little time to spare for meeting friends, and nobody in the village ever knew of their coming. They were never discussed now in the village assemblies. No one said: 'This piece of work must wait till Sukru Jani comes back.' The memory of man lasts no longer than the lines one may draw on the surface of water. And the world plays its game with only those players who are present; those who are absent are forgotten – they do not exist.

A time had been, Kajodi remembered, when Mandia's name was linked with hers on every tongue. And in Chaitra they were to have been married; their friends had counted the days to the event, happy that it was coming. Expectation had made her days beautiful, and her happiness had been reflected in her looks, her talk, her manner of walking.

But now the stream had run dry. Only the puddles remained.

Chapter 31

The February nights were heavy with dew, and the cold pierced to the marrow. But the moon rose clear behind the hills, as cheering as a bonfire. The jungle lit up with a smile. The mountains and valleys were a dream of floating shadows. On a night like this, one could forget the disappointing mirage that life really is. For one deceitful moment, life was good.

Jili sat on a low mound in front of her hut, gazing into the night sky, forgetful of her existence. Bili crept up softly behind her and put a hand on her shoulder.

'Come to bed, sister,' she said softly. And Jili got up and

followed her into the hut, while the sounds of the night still called to her.

Several months had passed since their father and brothers had left home. At first, life had been easy; the mandia had already been harvested, and there was enough food. When the meal had been cooked, there was time enough to wander off into the forest and join the dance in the evening. There was no cause for anxiety.

But then the stores of mandia and paddy, kept in the attic above the ceiling, ran low. This was a development which no one had foreseen. The Paraja lives only in the present. When Sukru Jani had left home, he had said: 'There is food in the attic.' He had never stopped to calculate how long the food would last; nor had Mandia. As for Tikra, he had resented the fact that he would not be allowed to sit lazily at home and enjoy the harvest; instead, he would have to labour and sweat, while other young men danced and sang.

And even if Sukru and Mandia had known that the food would not last forever, there was nothing that they could have done about it. It was quite common for people like them—poor labourers scratching for an existence—to leave their homes suddenly whenever there was a call for their services. The call would have to be obeyed at once, and everything else must wait; there was no time to think of what *might* happen while they were away. They were sustained by a simple faith that nothing could go wrong, no one would die of hunger at home.

But Jili did not share this simple, rugged faith; she did not have the courage of the men. Hers had been a carefree life, even if, like all girls in the hills, she had to work hard: digging in the fields, cooking and taking care of the home,

walking enormous distances to the weekly market with a
basket of home-grown vegetables on her head, in the hope
of selling them so that she could buy a little salt for the
home, or a bundle of cigars for the men. But until now she
had worked only under her father's direction: she had carried the basket on her head, but no responsibility on her
shoulders. And so she had always had time to dress her
hair with flowers and drape her sari in such a way that it ac-
centuated the roll of her hips when she walked, and laugh
at the young men as they ogled. When she had travelled
through the mountains to the weekly market, it had been a
festival and not a drudgery: she would chew sticks of
sugar-cane as she walked, stop to pluck flowers in the
jungle and arrange them in her hair, and sing her loudest.

But now the magic was gone. The vines were still
loaded with blossoms, but the props had been taken away
and they were left trailing in the dust.

The truth had dawned on Jili.

She had woken up one ecstatic morning and rushed out,
in her imagination, into the forest, past the fields of olsi,
past the little rivulet that sparkled at the foot of the hill, the
thicket where peacocks grouped together for their dance
and the stag with tall antlers looked up to sniff the breeze.
For she had seen Bagla as he walked to his work, and he
had looked at her and laughed; and the day had been transformed for her. She had been adrift before and had suddenly touched land.

How quickly she had gone through the day's work! And
she had asked Bili to run and fetch coloured earths, so that
they could paint the floors and the walls. When Bagla returned after the day's work, bathed in sweat, she was
going to invite him to the house. They would sit together

in the dusk, and he would tell her meaningless little stories. And later she would ask him to take Bili and herself for a walk in the moonlight, to the other side of the hill.

When Bili had gone out for the earth, Jili had lit the fire, filled the pot with water and set it to boil. And she had climbed the rickety ladder and poked her head into the dark attic under the ceiling, where rice and mandia were kept in two bamboo containers. Whenever Jili had need, she would push her arm into one of the containers, take out a handful of grain and replace the lid; she never looked inside to see how much was left.

But that day she had suddenly realized that there was only a small amount of grain left, at the bottom. It would soon be gone.

What would she do then?

She stood transfixed like a statue, with one foot on the top rung of the ladder and the other on the floor of the attic. Her head reeled.

What was she to do?

Her father and brothers were away.

The fields were lying fallow.

Where could she find food? Tomorrow, it would be gone. What would Bili eat?

Whom should she ask for help?

No one ever came to see them now, not even a kitten. None of her father's old friends ever came to ask them if they needed anything. They were never asked for subscriptions for village festivities, though in the old days the Naika himself came to wheedle her father into giving money. Ever since Sukru Jani and her brothers had gone, the village looked on them with disdain, as though they were destitute widows living in misery. No eager young men lounged before their door now with songs of invitation. When Jili did go to the communal dance, she seemed to be commiserated with, rather than welcomed.

Here, as elsewhere, the attitudes of the community to the individual depend entirely on the known extent of his possessions. Only, in this primitive world, the individual's wealth is measured in terms of the quantity of grain in his attic. On the surface, there is little evidence of class snobbery or prejudice, but sooner or later its existence becomes inescapably obvious.

As Jili stared at her empty stores of grain, a hundred forgotten incidents came back to her—little insults and humiliations from those who had been her friends, and neglect and indifference.

She was filled with a sense of shame. For the first time in her life, she understood poverty. She wanted to hide herself and her misery, melt away into some dark corner, away from the pitiless glare of a hundred inquisitive eyes which pried into the privacy of her hut, turning up pots and pans, raking up her rags, looking into the attic where the grain had once been, searching among the few sticks they possessed. And those eyes pierced through the mud walls and the straw thatch, exposing all her disgrace; they scorched her dry, leaving her stark and leafless, like the bare trees on the hillside in summer.

Jili climbed slowly down from the attic and slumped on the floor. Soon, Bili came home with the coloured earth, but Jili did not get up.

'Come, sister,' said Bili, shaking her, 'let's paint the floor.'

But Jili only said: 'No, not today.'

Chapter 32

Many tracks converged near the house of Ramachandra Bisoi. There were always a few bullock-carts parked in front of his house; some were waiting to be loaded or unloaded, while others were being repaired. Crowds of fascinated children hovered around them. The money-lender's mangy horses nibbled at the few blades of grass, hopping about, their forelegs hobbled together. Bullocks dozed in the shade, flicking their tails to drive away the flies from their sores. The money-lender had many bullocks, all large and robust.

To enter the money-lender's house, one had first to pass through his warehouses, stuffed to overflowing with paddy, rice, mandia and other grains, stored in jute bags or containers made of bamboo matting. After a series of these warehouses, one came to the big inner courtyard where paddy, chilies, oil-seeds and other crops were drying in the sun. After crossing the courtyard, one came to the rooms which he himself occupied with his family. The plan of the house was typical of homes of rich money-lenders in the South. The veranda also was stacked with bags of grain; in a corner stood a huge pair of scales used for weighing grain, among a pile of old chairs, broken bedsteads and other accumulated junk. The entrance was guarded by massive wooden doors, studded with huge knobs of iron to reinforce them.

The whole house stank of musty grainbags, manure and sweat from the Sahukar's cattle and servants; to the Sahukar, however, it had the fragrance of money. And that miasma filled the air for miles around, proclaiming the Sahukar's magnificence. He owned everything that the eye could see—the houses and granaries, the wide fields stretching out into the distance and the orange orchards.

On either side of the Sahukar's empire lay two small, miserable villages where the tribesmen lived, or rather existed. The ragged, mud-walled huts drooped as if they were too tired to stay up; the thatches had grown bald from the wind and the rain; tattered rags hung from the rafters, and men, women, children, chickens, dogs and swine grovelled in the same dust.

The only sound to be heard in these villages all day was the wailing of hungry children; their parents slunk out of the huts at sunrise and did not come back until dark. Their lives, between the hours of sunrise and sunset, belonged to the Sahukar. They were his gotis.

The two miserable colonies of gotis on either side served as a foil to the Sahukar's splendour.

Yet these huts could have told their own tale too. The wretches who huddled in them had once been hard-working peasants, living lives of dignity. Their ancestors had owned all the land. Then, the first distillery had sprung up near the villages. The tribesmen could never resist a pot of liquor after the day's work, and the money-lender was so eager, so willing to oblige. When they had no money to pay, which was often, he would insist on their drinking; payment could wait. And many days later he would stop one of the men in the fields and tell him: 'Look here, you owe me three score of rupees for the liquor. Are you going to pay up or give me your land?' Afterwards, the Government took away the money-lender's liquor shop; but the money-lender had taken all their lands. It was the old story.

And these huts had witnessed much else besides. They had watched the money-lender's power grow and new houses rise up on the land which was now his. And the huts had stared mutely at these strange events, until they had grown bleary-eyed and haggard, and their mouths had gaped open in astonishment. They had sagged with age, while the money-lender had laid new roads and planted orchards. He had thrived; but the huts were now over-grown with wild grass and littered with dirt and rubbish. The occupants of these huts lived in perpetual terror of the Sahukar, of his being annoyed with them and setting the police on them. For the Sahukar had many friends in offi-cialdom; all the 'great lords' and 'masters' camped in his house when they went on tour. The police had innumer-able ways of harassing the tribesmen; if no other charge came to hand, they could always be hauled up for fouling the public thoroughfare.

After the liquor shop was closed, the money-lender had started a general merchandise shop. He began lending grain to the tribesmen, and collecting it back, with in-terest, after the harvest. All his dealings had been shady, and legends had grown up around him.

A tribesman comes to the Sahukar for a loan of mandia, and the Sahukar agrees to let him have it. The deal is closed and, as the man is about to go, the Sahukar asks him: 'Have you taken your grain?'

'Yes, Sahukar,' the man says.

'How much are you taking?'

'One putti.'

'All right. Now go and tell my clerk that you are taking a putti of mandia. He will write it down in his books.'

The loan is entered in the clerk's ledger.

'Have you informed my clerk?' the Sahukar asks again.

'Yes, Sahukar.' The man prepares to leave.

'Wait,' the Sahukar says. 'You haven't informed my wife. She is inside the house. Go and tell her. And tell my servant also.'

The poor Kondh or Paraja has to inform three other persons, besides the Sahukar himself, that he is borrowing a putti of mandia, at fifty per cent interest. And each time an entry is made.

Next year, the borrower returns with a putti and half of mandia, which should clear him of the debt.

'Is that all?' the Sahukar asks, looking at the pile of grain.

'Why, yes, Sahukar. I took one putti from you, and the interest is half a putti.'

'One putti! Are you mad? You took one putti from me, one putti from my clerk, one putti from my wife, and one putti from my servant. How many puttis is that? There, count: one and one and one and one makes four. And the interest on four puttis? Two puttis. So you should have brought six puttis in all; instead of which you have brought only one and a half. Why, even the interest is more than that! Do you understand?'

'No, Sahukar,' the bewildered tribesman says. 'But you must be right.'

And the poor man is hooked. A goti is born.

All this the huts had witnessed. And every stage in their decay had been marked by a new chapter in the Sahukar's prosperity.

The tribesman has a natural horror of the law; he is afraid of doing anything which might be unlawful. To this is added his awe of the mighty Sahukar. He is caught between two fires. The poor goti has no idea of the terms of contract between the Sahukar and himself. He has his own rough-and-ready system of accounting—a length of rope in which he ties a knot for every year of goti-hood completed by him. By counting the knots, he is able to tell how many years have passed, and how many years still remain before he can regain his freedom. But the Sahukar does not recognize these crude accounts. He has his own ledgers, filled with strange scribblings in red and blue ink, the mysteries of which the bewildered goti can never unravel. And the magic figures in the ledgers grow and grow, and the goti's debts increase from year to year, and his bondage never ends.

From every hill the red tracks came down and converged at the Sahukar's house like the threads in a spider's web, and along these tracks came many a tribesman from the remotest hills. Some brought their wives' ornaments to the Sahukar, wrapped in bits of rag. Others brought the produce from their fields. Others again had nothing to pledge but their own bodies. And the Sahukar's house swallowed everything up, and nothing that entered ever came out again; and the house grew and bulged.

Sometimes the tribesmen whom the Sahukar had in his clutches grew restive, driven by hunger to acts of defiance. But the Sahukar knew how to put them in their place. That year, the Sahukar's wrath had fallen on Sania Paraja.

There was a patch of land from which the Sahukar had dispossessed one of the tribesmen, on the fraudulent grounds that it had been mortgaged to him. He had put up a fence around it and posted a watchman; the maize crop had been excellent. Sania Paraja had nothing to eat for two whole days, and he was going down to the river for the second time that night to fill up his empty stomach with water. The ears of maize were too tempting: he thrust his hand through the fence and plucked a couple. A neighbour saw him eating one of the ears, while the other was still in his hand. Sania confessed that he had plucked them from the Sahukar's field. Inevitably, the Sahukar heard of the theft. Sania was caught, tied to a tree and mercilessly beaten.

And that was not all. The Sahukar lodged a complaint with the police; an Assistant Inspector arrived with some constables, and an inquiry was started. Many witnesses deposed on behalf of the Sahukar. One said that he had been squatting down to ease himself near the scene of occurrence and had seen everything; another man had been searching for his bullock. A big pile of maize, freshly plucked, descended on the police party as though it had rained down from the sky; someone else produced a big basket and a sack—the instruments of the crime. It was alleged that Sania Paraja had broken into the Sahukar's field at night and filled the sack with ears of maize; he had been filling up the basket when the sound of snapping maize-stalks alerted the watchman, who caught the thief red-handed. Further, Sania Paraja had pulled down a part of the fence to make his entry. The evidence of the two witnesses, he who had been easing himself and he of the missing bullock, clinched the case. Sania Paraja was charged, tried, convicted and sentenced to four months' rigorous imprisonment. And the villagers learned their lesson.

The Sahukar was not content with suppressing possible mutinies; like all successful tyrants he knew the importance of sustained terror. Whenever a touring official came to the village, the Sahukar would meet him with a long list of grievances. His crops were being plundered, his orchards robbed and his servants assaulted; it was becoming impossible for an honest man to live in peace with these thieving rascals, and he had no option but to seek the protection of the law. And the officers, who loved nothing better than to parade their authority, called the people from the offending villages and warned them of dire consequences unless they mended their ways. And the Sahukar puffed himself up like a bullfrog.

The Sahukar hired every variety of labour for a hundred odd jobs: some of the men were promised food in payment of their wages; others were paid in cash. But he would never advance money to anyone, for he was afraid they might run off to the tea-plantations in Assam.

These men also had to perform all kinds of duties for the officials when they came on tour: carrying their baggage to the next camping-place, chopping firewood, setting up camp and so on. Sometimes they were paid a few coppers by some generous official; but this was not expected. They were the Sahukar's men, acting under his orders; it was the Sahukar who was praised for his hospitality.

When the Sahukar was bored and could find no other diversion, he would ask his servants to fetch a few tribal girls from one of the two villages 'to dance for him'. Who had a better claim to their services than he?

On hot summer afternoons, some goti of the Sahukar's might walk into one of the huts of the Bisras or Parajas for a drink of water, or for a burning ember from the fire to light his cheroot. And the good housewife would ask, in a voice full of sympathy, 'Have you been working too hard, brother? Look, you are sweating all over! Do come inside and rest.' The goti would sit down and relax in that hovel, among the filthy children who reminded him of his own, and share the food and even help himself to the home-brew in the flask. A stricken man easily accepts another who is like himself.

In the evenings, the men from the two villages and the other gotis would club together round a roaring fire under the big banyan tree, light up their cheroots, and compare notes. Each man would try to condense all his grievances against the Sahukar into a single puff of smoke and so lighten his chest.

'He'll work us all to death,' Buda Paraja complained one evening.

'You could work yourself sick and still not get a day's rest.'

'Oh, don't talk of him,' Aita Paraja said. 'There isn't a meaner man in the whole district!'

'Why should he worry about what happens to us?' said Mandhu Muduli. 'All he cares about is gold.'

'And women, don't forget!' Angra Paraja added quickly. 'Anything will do for him – the lecher: Domb, or Christian, or Paraja. A young girl makes his mouth water.'

'Ah, well – that's only natural,' Durja Paraja said sagaciously. 'Gold does make a man randy. The trouble is, this old goat won't spend a penny on a girl; he's capable of snatching a girl away from her home, keeping her for a couple of days and then kicking her out. And it wouldn't worry him if she went back to her people in disgrace or drowned herself in the river.'

'Oh, he's a rogue,' said Sida Paraja bitterly. 'I should never have come to work for him, but I had no choice. I didn't have the money to get married and the girl just wouldn't wait; she said her father might sell her out to anyone if we didn't hurry up – and he would have done it too, that leech of a Bandhu Paraja! I *had* to give him his twenty-five rupees, and so here I am – the Sahukar's goti. The only way I can be rid of him is to run away with my wife.'

Sukru Jani and his sons sat there, smoking and listening to everything that was said.

And it was unanimously resolved that the Sahukar's ancestry was uncertain. There *must* be some low Domb blood in him.

The great ones of the earth are unconcerned about the opinions that such insignificant folk hold about them. Their eyes see only the ashes remaining from the holocaust that they themselves have caused, but not the fire that smoulders underneath. And the fire feeds on itself and waits.

Chapter 33

March is the month of the Spring Festival. During the two weeks of the festival no tribesman does any work at all, and even the goti must be released from his labours. To compensate, the Sahukar would work his gotis extra hard in the preceding weeks. Sukru Jani, as well as ploughing the Sahukar's land, had to complete the barn he was building; Tikra had to help him, as well as make four bedsteads for the Sahukar and the rope netting which was slung from them. There was no rest. There were mountains of grain and dried chilies to be packed in jute bags and taken to market; Mandia had to load them on the backs of pack-oxen and drive them through the jungle. As he walked along behind the bullocks, he thought that perhaps he would see Kajodi in the market-place. But these hopes were never realized.

Tikra's normal duties were at the plough, but sometimes he was sent out into the jungle to graze the Sahukar's cattle. This was a job he enjoyed; he would leave the cattle to graze at will and loll under some tree, or play with other cowherd boys. Often, he would see a group of girls plucking leaves or gathering twigs in the forest; then he would play on his flute, or sing a Paraja courtship song, and the girls would sing back in answer. And Tikra would be happy.

Chapter 34

The March sun is hot, because the sky is absolutely clear. The new leaves·dance in the wind, for March is the season of dancing.

The jungle is aflame with the blood-red flowers of simili, dhatiki and palasa. Butterflies emerge from their cocoons and flit on the March winds - specks of vivid colour.

The new flowers and leaves, as well as the new birds, all seem to favour a single colour − red.

And the blood goes mad with so much redness; the little mouse-deer prods the big spotted doe with its tiny horns, and young men begin to look at young women with new eyes. Everyone is drunk with the spring.

But there is another side to March; for spring does not stay long in these hills. And soon – too soon – the ground is strewn with dead leaves, which the wind sends wheeling round and round in clouds of dust. And the dead trees sob in the wind for the passing of spring.

The tribesmen start preparing for the festival at least a month in advance, storing up all their provisions, husking paddy, pounding rice and millet into flour, and getting as much of the ploughing done as possible. For during the festival there must be nothing but dancing and singing, drinking, hunting and feasting: there is no place then for sorrow or care.

Spring is crowded out by the scorching months of April, May and June; then, suddenly, the first rain comes. The monsoon follows: days of unceasing storm and rain, when the sky frowns darkly and the ravines and valleys turn into mighty rivers in flood. The paddy seedlings are in danger of being swept away now, unless they have grown sufficiently strong, before the rains come, to cling to the soil with their roots. This means that the rice-fields must be made ready for sowing very early, long before the rains: and in the days before the Spring Festival the tribesmen are busy ploughing, manuring, puddling and so on.

And these days before the festival are also the time when the sites are selected for new clearings in the jungle. This must be done with great care – the hillside must not be too steep, nor the jungle too thick, and the soil must be deep enough for cultivation. Selection is followed by the usual

ceremony of propitiating the gods, after which the peri-
meter of the intended clearing is marked out by burning
down some of the trees on its edge. The Spring Festival is
no sooner over than the entire village gets busy with axes,
and when the Forest Guard comes round again on his visit,
he is faced with a fresh pile of glowing charcoals; the trees
are gone, and he cannot even calculate their value in order
to penalize the offenders.

So the days before the festival are days of frenzied activity for everyone. The young children are busy collecting
firewood in the jungle; the men are busy in the field, and
the women are busiest of all.

Even Sukru and his sons, as they slaved for the Sahukar,
felt the excitement all around them. And Sukru Jani remembered that his fields were going to lie fallow that year,
for there was no one to plough them. He was helpless.

And while everyone else in the village worked, Jili and
Bili merely looked on. There was nothing for them to do
this year; they had no share in the excitement of preparing
for the festival. How different it had been the year before,
when they had worked breathlessly, helping their father
and brothers! What pleasure there had been in that work,
in which their hopes, their future, were mingled! Mandia
and Tikra would order them around and even Sukru Jani
would be annoyed if they did not carry out his instruc-
tions; and they had been happy to feel that the men needed
their help. But now they were unwanted, unnecessary.

Last year their father had presented new saris to each of
them, and they had browbeaten Mandia into buying
bracelets for them, and yellow bead necklaces, and little
bells that tinkled on their ankles. But this year there was no

money even for a little molasses to put into their rice-cakes.

Everyone else in the village had bought their new clothes for the festival. The Domb girls proudly wore their new blouses when they went down to the pool for water, and the Paraja and Kondh women were trying on their new clothes to make sure that they would look their best at the dance. Jili and Bili would say polite, admiring things about the clothes; but when they returned home they would look at each other in silent understanding.

In the days before the festival, strings of hawkers visited these hills, with bale upon bale of cloth, piles of metal bracelets, coloured beads, and other finery. The boys and girls swarmed round them like flies, and their baskets were emptied in no time. In the evenings, the girls would cavort like butterflies in their new clothes, as though the bright dyes had coloured their spirits as well as their dresses. Jili never went out to look at the pedlars' wares, even though she could see all her friends crowding round their stalls. But Bili was unable to contain her excitement; she would hover round the hawker's basket, shouting, gesticulating, offering comments, snatching away things from her friends in order to examine them and running back to Jili with some little trinket held in her eager hands, crying, 'Look, sister! How lovely this will look on you!' But there was nothing they could do except admire, and crave.

At last Jili decided to ask the Naika for a loan: only one rupee, not more, which she would return to him as soon as her father came back.

And the Naika laughed, scarcely believing his ears. 'Are you mad, my daughter? Where should I find a rupee?'

The Chalan was equally unhelpful, and so were the other elders in the village.

Should she ask Bagla?

No, that was out of the question. And she warned Bili: 'If you ask Bagla for the money I shall never speak to you again.'

Jili no longer danced with the other girls at night, but Bili danced for all she was worth. She wanted to wipe away the disgrace of poverty in the triumph of her dancing.

There was only one person in the village who showed the slightest interest in their welfare now, and that was Kau Paraja. He would call out to them in the street: 'When are your father and brothers coming home, my girl?' Or he would say: 'It's time they were home to look after you.' And he would pucker up his ugly face and frown, as though he alone were responsible for their safety.

No one in the village had a more hideous face. His features were distinctly simian; the nose was like a mass of dough, and the low, sloping forehead vanished into a receding hair-line. He had one large tuft of hair, like coarse coconut-huskfibres, into which he was fond of tucking little flowers. His limbs were thin and knotted, the arms of unusual length; his body was stunted and misshapen, and the face grave and unsmiling.

But he was a man of many talents, useful in his own way. He had a wonderful memory for details; if he was asked to carry a message for somebody, he would remember every word. His own speech was blunt and often offensive, but there was no malice. If people were annoyed by his speech, he never stopped to argue, for he knew that they despised him.

And Kau Paraja had been keeping constant watch on Jili and Bili ever since their father and brothers had gone.

He tried not to think of the beating that Sukru Jani had given him, for he was used to such treatment. But now that Sukru Jani and his sons were gotis like himself, he had realized that they were no better than he, no higher in the social scale. Suddenly, he began to think of Jili and Bili as eligible brides for himself. After all, it would be cheaper to marry a girl of his own village; the bride-price would be less. The problem was: which one to choose. He could not decide. The idea of marrying one of these girls was certainly pleasant, and Kau Paraja enjoyed many a train of pleasurable day-dreams. At the same time, he knew how absurd it was for someone like himself, a human pariah, to harbour any such dreams. His desires became detached, disembodied: a vague, uncertain, twilight yearning.

And now Kau Paraja was frequently to be seen in places where Jili and Bili were likely to be. He walked home from the fields several times each day - to eat, he would tell the others; and each time his path lay across the bathing- pool. He would suddenly remember that his master, the Naika, needed firewood, and walk off into the jungle at the strangest of hours; but it seemed that the best firewood in the entire forest was the tiny bushes which grew near the spot where Jili and Bili dug for edible roots. Nobody ever bothered to ask why he followed the girls or stared at them; his ugliness seemed to have given him that privilege.

Bili, the livelier of the two, often teased Kau Paraja and made fun of him; and he soon decided that she would not be a suitable match for him. She was far too young and childish; moreover, she did not seem robust enough to make a proper housewife.

Yes, there was no doubt about it: Jili was better in every way. She was beautiful and healthy; she would bear sturdy children. And she was understanding too - she never hurt his feelings. Indeed, it was surprising that she was not already beseiged by rival suitors. The field lay open for him.

He followed Jili everywhere — a hideous shadow, like a black cloud floating behind the moon. The shadow kept its distance, but it was a shadow nevertheless.

One shimmering afternoon, he walked up to Jili as she sat in her garden, looking at the bean creeper which was beginning to turn grey. Her thoughts were elsewhere, and she never even looked up as he approached.

Kau Paraja silently put a new sari on the ground, in front of her, and stood there wiping the sweat from his face.

'Here, it's for you,' he said, trying to sound as casual as he could.

'Why have you brought it?' Jili asked tonelessly, eyes still on the ground.

'I want you to wear it,' he said.

'Well, take it away. I don't want it.'

And Kau Paraja picked up the sari and walked away. Jili remained as still as a statue: a stone goddess that could not be moved by the votary's offering.

But when Kau Paraja had gone, Jili wept for shame. It was the first time she had wept in many months.

Chapter 35

A huge bonfire blazed under the jhodi tree which stood in the centre of the village, painting its leaves red against the darkness. A dance was on; the fire cast enormous shadows of the dancers on the banana trees in an adjoining garden. From her veranda Jili heard the singing and the laughter—but her mind registered nothing. However, when Bili asked her a few minutes later if she might go to the dance, she herself walked out into the square, quite unthinkingly.

The girls danced in a ring around the young men, arms interlaced behind their backs. The men wore red turbans, and coloured shawls draped round their shoulders like sashes.

The next moment Jili herself was in the ring, wheeling round and round while the gigantic shadows flickered faster and faster; her feet moved instinctively and the old, familiar rhythm surged through her. The trees in the jungle craned their heads forward to watch. The night was suddenly full of magic.

In his dark, rich voice, Bagla was singing the Paraja song of the coming of rain—though the rains would not arrive till June or July. For on a night like this the tribesmen relive their entire lives: their songs and dances enact the cycle of the seasons, the total sum of human existence.

And this is what Bagla sang:

> O my darling jayi flower!
> My sweet malli bud!
> Come with star-white flowers in your dark hair;
> I wait.

I know that you will come, beloved;
For you are as unfailing
As death is.

There are only two things I know to be true –
Your love, and the fear of death.

I play each day with death
And so I know that you will come –
Mingling your black hair with the dark clouds;
For the rains have come.

The sky grows dark,
My eyes are blinded by the lightning.
The moon's fire is extinguished, the stars are put out.
The earth gropes in the dark.

The raindrops patter on the thatch-eaves;
The river sings and the mountains join the chorus,
And the frogs make music.
And the kadamba tree listens in ecstasy –
Its flowers bristle, like hairs standing on end.
And your coming to me in the rain
Is the bride's home-coming.
For the new bride washes the feet of her elders
In the custom of our tribe.

You are the rain, the new bride.
The raindrops fill my heart with joy.

The coming of the rains was also the motif of the dance.
The chain of girls whirled round dizzily, then fanned out
suddenly and sinuously like a streak of lightning. The dan-

cers would break away in little groups, like floating
clouds, only to mass together again and advance in an undulating line, to suggest the marching clouds. Rhythmically
they leapt and swayed; their hands and feet and bodies
were convulsed with the madness of the monsoon rain,
they bent backward from the waist, touched the ground
with their heads and then straightened out again, as the
young paddy seedlings do in the fields. And the thunder
rolled out from the drums, the rivers broke their banks,
the parched forest lapped up the life-giving rain. And the
new bride came to her husband's home and religiously
washed the feet of her father-in-law and all the elders, to
signify the beginning of her new life.

As Jili danced, she felt the warmth of Bagla's breath on
her face; and she saw the bridegroom coming to her in procession, amid the lights and the fireworks. The dance became slower: the heavy downpour had turned into a light
patter, and soon it would stop altogether.

The girls were bathed in sweat. Their breasts heaved,
their dark faces were flushed. The flowers had fallen from
their hair and been trampled in the dance.

Jili came back to her senses. The girls were resting
between dances, talking in excited gasps. But Bagla was
not by her side now; he was in the centre of a group of
admiring dancers, and in the group were Kajodi, Sajodi,
Sambali, Saniadan and others.

She slipped away quietly, not even calling to Bili. No
one noticed her; the chain re-formed and the dance was resumed. The gay sounds seemed to mock her, and she fled.

Suddenly, at the bend in the road, she saw Kau Paraja.

'Where are you going, Jili?' he asked her. 'It's very late,
you know.'

Jili stopped running and slowed down to a walk, but said nothing.

'Shall I see you home, Jili?'

He followed her home, though he kept his distance. She never said a word nor looked back; but she could hear his stick thudding on the ground as he walked behind her.

She reached her hut, climbed the steps onto the veranda, unlatched the door and walked in.

'So now you are home,' Kau Paraja said. 'Well, I must be off. I can't stay, I'm afraid; it's very late.' And the stick thudded back down the road.

Jili lay silent inside the dark hut.

Chapter 36

The Spring Festival coincides always with the dark phase of the moon, and it begins on the night of the new moon.

The day arrived at last, and Sukru Jani and his sons picked up their axes and started the long walk home. It was a little after dawn; the sky was still dark, and the mountain air was cold. Their feet grew wet with the dew.

The sun rose higher as they came to the foot of the Girlighati pass. As they climbed through thick jungle, it grew hotter; the clouds round the hilltops rolled away, and the valleys far below sparkled in the sun. In the distance, the fields were brown.

Little telltale wisps of smoke rose from the jungle: these were the villages, still hidden among the trees. There was a sudden clamour of voices as they pointed out what all of them knew. 'There's Dandabad, on the right, and there's Kondhbeda Padar; and that's Pedisil, and the other one is Sargiguda!'

They were almost running now as they went down the hillside—as excited as children. They traversed the Karaghati pass; Dandabad was left behind and Sargiguda was fast approaching. The jungle was full of the heavy perfume of kurayi flowers.

They sat down to rest on a flat rock beside a stream, under the shade of twin jhodi trees. It was a favourite spot with people who travelled among these hills.

Mandia Jani picked up a dry twig of kureyi, peeled off the bark with his knife and carved a small hollow in the side. Then he took another twig, trimmed one end into a sharp point, and held it vertically over the hollow he had made in the first twig. He gripped the twig between his palms and began to twirl it vigorously round and round like a milk-churn. After a minute or so, a little smoke rose from the twig, and soon it was burning. Mandia lit his cheroot, then passed the piece of wood to his father.

They sat and smoked, and Sukru Jani wiped away the sweat that trickled into his eyes. The same thought arose in each of them: the festival was due to begin that night, and they had no time to make any preparations. The Sahukar had not agreed to release them a single day earlier. There would not even be firewood at home.

They got up silently and began walking again. By the time they reached the Malingjodi pass, the last on the way to their village, the sun was already low in the sky.

The hillsides were already swarming with crowds of young men and women. The girls had their saris dyed yellow with turmeric, in the traditional colour of spring.

'Father,' Mandia Jani said suddenly, 'we might run into Kajodi's father tonight, at the village. What shall I say to him?'

'Oh, don't worry, brother,' Tikra laughed, 'no one is going to steal your Kajodi away.'

But Sukru Jani nodded gravely.

'Yes, my son,' he said at last. 'I must speak to Puri Jani.'

After an hour they came to their village. The sound of drums was everywhere: it must have begun at sunrise that morning, and it would continue all night, without a stop. The girls were moving in groups, dancing rather than walking, their faces and bodies smeared with turmeric paste. Men sat chatting together, boisterous with liquor.

As they walked past the other Paraja homes and reached their own hut, Jili and Bili rushed out to meet them.

Sukru Jani stroked them with slow hands. 'How thin you have become, my children,' he said, tenderly. But he was happy.

Mandia was making a frantic inquiry about Kajodi to a laughing Jili, while Tikra wanted to know how things were with her Bagla.

Tikra shouted loudly to Bili: 'Well, we're here now. Hurry up and bring some food – I'm hungry.'

Chapter 37

Kajodi sat on the veranda outside her hut, rubbing turmeric paste vigorously into her face with both hands; but it would not cling to the skin, and kept falling off. Annoyed, she started once again. She was in a hurry to finish.

'Kajodi!' someone called suddenly.

Mandia Jani's cherubic face smiled at her through a gap in the fence. The eyes were bright against the dark skin.

Kajodi picked up her pot of turmeric and fled indoors, leaving Mandia to stare foolishly after her. The dead leaves from the jhodi tree scraped dully on the ground; pigs scampered away with their noses rooted to the earth. Everything else was still.

In a little while, Kajodi returned, with her sari rearranged. Mandia still stood as before.

'You are back, Mandia?' she asked feebly, after a very long silence.

'Yes, I came back today.'

'It has been so long."

'Yes.'

She looked down at the ground. He came a little closer, but remained a few yards away from where she stood. He gazed fondly at the top of her head.

And Kajodi stood there, waiting. But he never touched her.

'Will you dance with me, Kajodi?' he said at last.

She laughed – a harsh, grating sound, very different from the bubbling laughter one usually associates with a tribal girl.

'Oh yes,' she said, 'I shall dance with you indeed! But tell me, who danced with you when you were away? And now you have remembered Kajodi at last, when spring is here!'

Again she went inside the house. Mandia sat down on the veranda, feeling rather more confident now.

She returned and they chatted easily of this and that. He wanted to know all about the arrangements for the dance and the hunt that would follow. She laughed at the eagerness of his questioning.

Presently he said he had to go. Then, abruptly he asked, 'Where is your father?'

'Why?' Kajodi said warily, feeling herself grow tense. 'He has gone to the village.'

'Oh, nothing,' Mandia said. 'I wanted to ask you to . . .'

'To dance with you?' she interrupted drily. 'Yes, I know. But there will be time enough for that. You had better go.'

And Mandia walked away like a chastened schoolboy.

Kajodi shook her long hair loose and absent-mindedly began to rub castor-oil into it. Then she examined herself in a hand-mirror. In spite of the turmeric paste, she thought she looked pale.

She sat thinking for a few minutes. Then her lips seemed to twist into a smile and she hummed softly to herself as she applied a final coat of turmeric to her face.

Chapter 38

In the hills, all events planned by human beings require the sanction of the divine.

The Kondh and Paraja tribes each have their own systems of communion with the supernatural. The Kondhs have their astrologers, who can read the stars and know the most suitable times for the performing of marriages, or even of agricultural operations. They can forecast rain or drought, and warn the tribes of evil days which may bring disaster. But among the Parajas the Disari, or diviner, finds the clues to all future happenings from the almanacs which the wise men of the past have handed down through the generations, recorded on palm-leaves. To the Paraja tribesmen, the Disari is all-knowing: he can tell them, with equal confidence, the prospects for agriculture in a particular year, or the most auspicious time for setting off on a journey. He can communicate with the spirits of ancestors, and learn their wishes, which must then be fulfilled. When a child is born, the Disari can tell which particular soul has been reborn. To help him in his divination, the Disari uses a medium, known as a Beju (or a Bejuni, if it is a woman), who is possessed by some ancestral spirit or tribal god or goddess, and temporarily acquires supernatural powers of prophecy. Every village has its Beju, through whose lips the gods or the spirits of ancestors speak, and only the Disari can interpret what they say.

The beginning of the Spring Festival had to be carefully calculated by the soothsayers of all the tribes. The Kondh astrologer had made his own calculations from the stars, the Paraja Disari had consulted his almanacs, and they had arrived independently at almost the same results. There was only a slight difference in the times declared by each as propitious for the commencement of the festival. The god of Spring had to be invoked: the Kondh wanted the rites to be performed at the exact moment when two stars appeared over Elephant Hill, while the Paraja said that the appropriate moment would be signalled by the call of three barking-deer in the forest. Finally, the Jani, or village priest, hit upon a compromise: the chicken would be sacrificed at the altar when the barking-deer called, while the pigeon would be sacrificed on the appearance of the two stars. During the interval between the two sacrifices, the headman must lie prostrate before the god's altar, with his face to the ground, a bit of straw held between his teeth and a halter round his neck, as a mark of humility. Thus the god would find no cause for annoyance, no matter when he chose to make his appearance, unseen by human eyes.

After the invocation, the festival would begin. All the villagers must walk in procession to the god's shrine and beg him to grace their festival, singing:

> O god of joy, god of dance and song,
> God of the hunt,
> Come, make us gay.
> Be our guest;
> Drink the liquor we have brewed for you,
> Accept the fowl and chicken that we offer.
> Then, when the few days of the feast are spent,
> You may return to your home.
> Only come, come, come.

The god lives deep in the jungle, breathing air that no human breath has contaminated, walking on soil untrodden by the feet of men. He lives among his divine neighbours: Basumati, the Earth goddess; Jhakar, the god for all seasons, and Bagh-Debta, the tiger god who rules the tigers that devour men and cattle. These gods have their shrine in a deep valley hemmed in by hills and overgrown with thick forest. Gigantic trees and thick creepers have interlaced their branches and tendrils to form a leafy net, through which the moonlight filters down. The tendrils hang from the trees, forming a swing for the gods. The long, trembling shadows of the sal trees sloping down into the valley dances for the gods every morning and every evening; tiny rivulets, born nobody knows where, come running to join hands together and dance; masses of wild flowers dance in the breeze and peacocks dance in all the wealth of their finery.

The sun had set, the preliminary ceremonies were over; the villagers gathered together in a procession and walked off into the jungle to invite the god of Spring. They walked up steep hills, through thick jungles of sandalwood, sal and bija trees. Far below them, a rivulet leapt dizzily through a gorge in the forest, dashing for cover into the undergrowth, like a wild animal, as suddenly as it had appeared. A range of high hills stood forbiddingly on the other side of the gorge.

The villagers walked in a double column, the men in one file and the women in the other. As they went, they beat their drums and danced.

As they reached the top of the ascent, the sky, previously a brazen yellow, turned pale and then dark, blotting out everything from view. The jungle lay peaceful and quiet. They began the descent into the valley by another path. They could hear the sounds of animals scampering away into the forest, roused by the beating of drums. They lit torches, and came at last to the shrine of the god.

The shrine itself was an ancient and enormous mango tree. It stood on the bank of a stream, like a pot-bellied old man with outspread arms. The trunk was covered with knots, and mango blossoms had appeared on it, even where there were no branches. Crowned with a ring of tender red leaves and festooned with orchids, the mango tree looked positively dandified; the two thick branches that grew sideways like arms wore bands of the guluchi creeper, and a thick siali creeper was ·draped across its shoulders, and down to the waist, like the sacred thread worn by a Brahmin. The upper branches were covered with massed garlands of wild flowers: the white malli, with its fragrant blooms, and niali, and red-and-yellow tiger's claw. The big, coral-coloured fruits of the mahakala creeper hung round its neck like a garland of beads. The mango tree was everything that divine body should be— huge, beautiful, powerful, wild and free; the very sight of it inspired awe and devotion.

They smeared the tree-trunk with the sacred vermilion paste which they had brought with them. The pigeon and fowl were sacrificed, and offerings of liquor poured into the soil, which was then decorated with patterns drawn in coloured powders. The drummers beat furiously on their drums, and everyone shouted and danced, so that the god would awake from sleep. Suddenly, all noise ceased; in the hush, the priest climbed on top of a huge boulder facing the tree, raised his torch to the sky, and began the incantation to the god:

O mighty god of Spring,
Awake!
Shake off your sleep.
See, the trees are heavy with flowers;
The Chaitra moon is in the sky.
We are all dressed up for the dance

In your honour.
And the young men and girls are waiting.
Wake up, and come!

It is you that the young man remembers
As he stands with his sweetheart
Under the liquor-palm tree,
Arms linked together.
You inspire their songs;
You are the light in lovers' eyes.
You bring the new-born babies to our land,
Like a welcome shower of young mango fruits,
So that we may never lack strong arms
To plough our barren and rocky lands.

Wake up, god of the hunt!
For the trees are beginning to shed their leaves,
And there are fires in the forest;
And the wild beasts are driven out of hiding.
The wild boar swarm in the sandy river-beds;
The spotted deer,
And the king-deer with big, branching horns,
Roam everywhere in the glens.
Of the wild hare also no count can be made.
Come, lead us in the hunting,
And we shall feast together.
Those who were old are dead,
But we shall not mourn them.
For such is life,
And each must go in his turn.

But every year, when Spring comes,

Every year, in this month of Chaitra,
Your rites will be celebrated
In this sacred valley where you live,
And through your grace
The mango shall blossom again,
The crops shall grow in our fields,
And our cattle grow fat,
And men shall prosper
In this land of forests and hills.
This is our sacred pledge,
O god of Spring!

The spring wind blew in gusts; the tree shook, and several blossoms and tender mango fruits were shaken to the ground. By these signs the god indicated his acceptance of the sacrifice and manifested himself.

The torches flamed in the darkness. The drums beat in unison, the big drum boomed louder and louder, and the men and women danced in the madness of spring, the Spring whose god had set their blood on fire. A thin sliver of moon appeared over the mountain on one side of the valley.

The valley itself lay in darkness as the mountains grew luminous in the faint moonlight. The ghostly shadows on the mountains trembled, and zigzagging lines of deep black arose from the bowl of darkness and climbed up the slopes, into the patches where light and shadow mingled to form delicate traceries. Every stone and bush came to life.

Then the ceremony ended. The dancers, forming ranks again, climbed slowly up the hillside in columns, torches held aloft, like some huge incandescent centipede crawling along the slope.

Chapter 39

Later that night, in the open square in the village, the dance was about to begin. The bonfire had been lit, and the stones placed in honour of the ancestors lay in rings encircling the fire – erect stones representing the men, and the flat ones the women. It was as though the ancestors were spectators at the dance, watching the tradition continue in an unbroken line. Many springs had come and gone, and one group of dancers was replaced by another, but the stones remained to watch. The dead and the living came together to worship the joy of spring.

But in Sukru Jani's hut that night there was a discordant note, for Jili was loud in her accusations of her father and brothers.

'No, I'm not going to the dance,' she shouted. 'Just look at my clothes—how can I wear these rags at the dance? But did any of you ever think of us? Did you ever care to find out how things were with us? No! We might have starved here, for all the difference it would have made to you!'

Bili had also declined to go to the dance. Nevertheless, the two sisters had washed their old saris clean, and braided flowers in their hair.

'Don't be impatient, Jili,' Mandia Jani teased her, 'you will have plenty of good clothes and food before long. How much longer do you think Bagla is going to delay?'

She sprang at him with an arm upraised.

'Go on, tease me,' she shrieked, 'that's all you're good for! You never give me a present, but you're always ready to torment me. You bear me witness, father.'

Sukru Jani was relieved to find the attack shifting from himself to Mandia. Now he became the arbitrator and said: 'Oh, do leave her alone, Mandia. Never mind him, Jili—go and join the dance.'

And then he spoke to his children in the stern tones of the patriarch: 'Go, go! Go out and dance, and be merry. It is not proper to quarrel during the Spring Festival.'

Hand in hand, Jili and Bili went skipping off to the dance. Mandia Jani shook with laughter and said: 'She hasn't changed a bit, father. She is angry because she has no new clothes or ornaments. Always thinking of herself! She just can't understand the state we're in now.'

'She's only a girl,' Sukru Jani said. 'Can you name a girl who doesn't like new clothes? She has a right to expect new clothes from us. Is it her fault if we weren't able to buy things for her? You wouldn't have dared speak to her like that if her mother were alive today.'

The words went home to Mandia, and he suddenly grew angry with his lot. He flung up his arms violently, as though shaking off chains, and said: 'If only those rascally Dombs hadn't reported me when I was distilling liquor, there would have been no problem. Jili and Bili would have had their new clothes.'

Sukru Jani said nothing. At last, with a deep sigh of weariness he said: 'Well, what's past is past; let's not think about it. On this day there should be nothing but rejoicing.'

The three of them sat smoking on the front veranda, chatting in low tones. The sounds of the dance grew louder, but none of them was interested.

Tikra yawned, stretched his limbs and said: 'Everyone is worried about Jili and Bili, but what about me? Do I get new clothes too, father?'

Sukru Jani caressed his back and said: 'All right, son. I shall remember. It will be made up for you next year.'

Mandia laughed and said: 'Just wear your old clothes, Tikra, and if anyone asks tell him they're new. That will make everything new!'

Sukru Jani continued to stroke Tikra's back slowly with his hand. There is magic in the touch of a father's hand or a mother's lap, no matter how withered and bony it becomes; it makes the offspring forget all his troubles. Somehow that physical touch brings the seed and the fruit together again, though each has been growing independently of the other: the dried-up streams begin to flow once more, and there is the harmony of deathless music.

They sat quietly for a while. Mandia continued to suck vigorously at his cheroot. Suddenly Tikra mumbled, as though talking in his sleep: 'I'm going to the dance, father.'

'Go, my son. But don't be too late.' And Tikra went out.

A little later, Mandia said: 'Father!'

'Yes?'

'It's about my marriage, father.'

'Yes?'

'What have you decided?'

'Eh?'

'I'm asking about my marriage.'

Now the old man was attentive. He put away his cheroot, stamping it out with his heel.

'What can I do?' he said. 'Why don't you think of something?'

Mandia understood his father. Yes, it all hinged on the problem of finding the money. No father would consider giving him his daughter unless he could pay the bride-price. But how was he to raise the money? He couldn't mortgage his body a second time.

'I don't know how much Puri Jani will demand for his daughter,' Sukru Jani continued. 'All we have left is the two small plots of land. I *might* sell or mortgage them, but then there will be nothing left to feed the new bride when she does come to my house. And what about the two girls?'

Sukru Jani felt annoyed because Mandia could only brood and brood, and weigh up all the consequences without ever acting—just like an old man. That was not the way of youth! Youth must be impetuous, and rush head-long through trackless jungle: the paths would appear by themselves, magically. Why, when he was that age, Mandia had already been conceived!

Mandia should go out and grab some girl for himself, and bring her home by force. The marriage could be regularized afterwards: the bride's relatives would come, strike Mandia the few blows required by custom, and demand a bride-price, which they might consider paying at their own sweet will. Such marriages were common in their tribe.

Yes, that was what Mandia should do, and that was what he himself would have done if he had been young. Did Mandia expect him to shed his years and demonstrate how it should be done?

At the same time he felt sorry for his docile, good na-tured son. So he said encouragingly to Mandia: 'Now lis-ten, my boy. It's Chaitra now—the season when young men court their sweethearts. Don't ask me—*do* something. I shall be only too happy if you bring a bride to my house. And I know that nothing would have pleased your mother more. So you may be sure we shall approve of anything you do.'

Mandia took the hint, and his heart went out to his father.

'I'm going to the dance, father,' he said gruffly. 'I have some good tobacco here, tucked in my waist-cloth. You can have it.'

And Sukru Jani stretched out his hand for the tobacco. His son's face was hidden in the darkness.

The old man was now alone in the house. The cool breeze fanned him. The sounds from the dance seemed to wish to enter his mind and drag something out into the open. He tried to rest his thoughts by focusing on a clump of trees in front of the hut, but the trees were studded with thousands of fireflies, which alternately glowed and faded, and while this continued his mind remained restless too.

The intoxication of the spring dance was spreading through his blood. He grew conscious of his body again: of his limbs, of the weight and proportion of every part, of the life that was there. He rose to his feet, picked up his stick and walked in the direction of the dance.

The dance was on. The married men and women, young or old, were supposed to have no share in it; they could only sit and watch. The ring of unmarried girls, like a garland of half-opened buds strung together, arms laced behind their backs, moved round and round the young men who formed the pivot of the wheel. The dance had grown almost uncontrolled in its frenzy. The bonfire blazed and the liquor flowed abundantly. The girls spun round and round in quickening circles; their bodies were glazed with perspiration, their breasts rose and fell and they swayed rhythmically from the waist. As the hours went by, many of the spectators, now completely drunk, leapt into the dance; young and old danced together, all restraints forgotten.

Bagla Paraja was among the young men in the centre of the ring, playing on his dungudunga. Each time, as Jili circled past him, she would look into his eyes. Sometimes they would collide and smile at each other; at other times, she would catch him laughing with one of the other girls, and her own eyes would grow bloodshot. Then she would feel the blood drumming in her ears and her vision would blur for a moment. The rhythm of the dance would change, unnoticed by her, as the chorus took up a new tune, and she would occasionally find herself dancing alone, out of step with everyone else. She would change step hastily, looking around to see if she had been observed, and slip back into the group.

She wanted only a word with Bagla, to get a clear answer from him, so that everything could be settled for good, one way or the other. But the shouting and the clapping and the sound of the drums never gave her a chance. Her head swam as she went round and round, but her mind was stagnant with unresolved thoughts.

Mandia Jani was there too, with his dungudunga. The company of the other young men had made him bold, and he was being specially attentive to Kajodi. He would advance a few paces towards her and strum his dungudunga loudly in her ears and smile. She would smile back with a sidelong glance and move on with the other girls, swept away in the dance. Several of the other young men would advance on her: Bagla would throw flowers at her, and so would Milu Paraja and Ratan Paraja. But she brushed them all aside and danced on.

And Kau Paraja danced too, wordlessly, as awkward as
a banana tree being tossed from side to side by the wind.
He was draped in a loose-fitting shroud. His eyes searched
only for Jili.

The spectators laughed and exchanged jokes. The open
space echoed to their shouts, and amid all that laughter
hearts were being won and marriages made, scarcely
noticed by the others.

The young men would break into a chorus, addressed to
all the girls at once; but this could carry an individual message too, and the singer would stress a particular phrase,
and the person for whom it was meant would understand.
And while lovers communicated thus in code, others, still
unattached, poured out their emotions in loud song, hoping to raise an echo in some responsive breast. The girls
roared back their answer to the song of the young men:

Oh, oh, oh!
Boys and girls, come together!

The dance turned into a riot. The night stretched on.
Here and there someone would flop down, drunk. Mandia
Jani had filled himself with drink, and now lay snoring on
Lelli Paraja's porch. Sukru Jani, incoherent with liquor,
muttered to himself as he stumbled home, supported by
Bili. Tikra walked off into the darkness, following a group
of young girls. Clothes were disarranged after the dance
and the drinking. But on this night, as on the other nights
of the festival, all excesses were pardoned. Boys and girls
paired off, and went where they chose. The crowds at the
dance grew thin, but still the music did not stop; those
who had no particular company to keep seemed reluctant
to go home.

Kajodi, Jili and Bagla were among those who continued
to dance when the others had gone. Kajodi's feet were tireless, and the smile never left her face as she danced on,
triumphant and ecstatic. The garlands of flowers round her
neck had snapped, but she was unconcerned. The plaintive
song of some forlorn lover would rise and tremble in the
air, the words lost, but the meaning clearly perceived in the
haunting tune. Kajodi and Jili floated away in the dream-
like movements of the dance. The madness, the seduction
of that song, urging the beloved to abandon herself to love!
It was the intoxication of moonlit nights drenched in the
perfume of white chameli flowers: lips remained fixed in a
pout, as though carved out of stone; eyes, half shut, were
as sharp-edged as daggers; limbs and muscles rippled with
life. The girls swayed like snakes dancing to the charmer's
pipe; the singing voices were vibrant with pathos, with the
agony of the unfulfilled moment. Yes, one could see it all:
the supreme moment had arrived, and it would slip by,
leaving everything silent and empty:

> Say 'Today', and 'Today', my darling!
> Say 'Now', and 'Now'; say 'Yes!'
> Come, dance and play with me.

And the young men would prostrate themselves, offering their breasts to be trodden upon by the dainty feet of
their loved ones, who disdainfully accepted what was
theirs by right.

Finally, the roseate mists swirled away, and flesh clung
to flesh in hunger, and grew still.

Chapter 40

The moon had grown pale and the bonfire had burnt itself out. The night was full of a strange humming. The dance had come to a halt and the crowds had melted away, until only Jili, Kajodi and Bagla remained. Then, before Jili's very eyes, Bagla lifted Kajodi in his arms and rushed away into the jungle like a tiger carrying off its prey.

A few drums still boomed into the darkness. Jili tottered to the edge of the open square and slumped down on one of the stones commemorating the dead. The sound of the drums gradually faded away, and the last glimmering lights went out. Darkness lay heavy and frozen under the big trees. Presently a bright star rose in a corner of the sky. It was the planet Venus, come out in the dark with a torch, to look for a tiny, lost soul.

Jili lay on the stone with her face down, pouring out her tears on the ground as the dew came down on her in large drops.

Jackals began to howl in a clump of trees behind the village, and were then quiet; a spotted snake hissed in his lair in the hollow of a tree. Startled, Jili rose and walked slowly homewards.

In the dying hours of the night, that strange humming sound still floated down from the jungle, carried on the soft breeze. There was in it neither the delirium of joy nor the bitterness of grief: only that steady, monotonous ringing, which was strangely comforting.

Chapter 41

The sun was already high when the booming of the drums awoke Mandia Jani. He stretched his limbs and looked around. The square was deserted. The events of the night were dim in his memory, but he saw the withered flowers on the ground, the remains of the pots which had held liquor, and the ashes from the bonfire. The air was heavy with the delicious smell of liquor, and, as he inhaled, confused recollections came back and merged into daydreams: he saw himself bearing Kajodi off into the jungle, along the mossy bed of a narrow, dried-up stream. And as he walked he kept asking her: 'Whom do you belong to, Kajodi?'; and with one arm twined round his waist and her lips pressed to his ears she whispered: 'I am yours, yours.' The journey and the catechism had no end, and still their feelings were not fully expressed. Then they came to a deep gorge, with high jungle-topped hills on either side; the moist sand was stamped with the imprint of deer hoofs. He sat down on a rock with Kajodi in his lap, stretched out his hand to pluck wild flowers growing on the bank and tucked them in her hair. Suddenly, a herd of deer stood facing them. The great stag who led the herd lifted up his proud head, crowned with long, branching antlers, sniffed the air with distended nostrils and prodded at the doe nearest to him; then he leapt to the other bank, as graceful as a bird in flight, and the herd followed him into the trees. And still Kajodi and he sat there.

But these were only dreams.

The drums continued to boom. The great hunt was about to begin. The men would go out into the jungle, prepared to face the taunts of their women if they should return empty-handed. The women would tie their clothes together and hang them up on a rope, and anyone who failed to kill something would be made to crawl under the garments; he would be pelted with dung-balls and other filth, and the women would shout at him: 'Look at the mighty hunter! Aren't you ashamed of yourself? Go back into the jungle.' Such was the custom; but success was greeted with garlands and dancing and rejoicing.

Mandia Jani got up and went home. His beautiful dream had left him unsatisfied. Yes, it was true that Kajodi loved him, but what had she ever given him? Then the bitterness faded; the vision returned, and his confused senses were unable to separate dream from reality. He was again certain that he had everything he wanted, for Kajodi was his very own.

He laughed happily. He felt sure that the hunt would go well for him. He had seen the deer, and he knew where to find them. He would wander away from the other hunters and wait in the gorge where the deer had appeared – maybe he could get Kajodi to join him there. And then he would shoot them down.

All the men of the tribe had breakfasted much earlier than usual and marched off into the jungle, armed with guns, bows and arrows, hatchets, knives, sticks and anything else they could lay their hands on. The women escorted them as far as the end of the village, singing and dancing, and all the dogs in the village followed them into the jungle. Drums were beating, and trumpets brayed;

everyone was flushed, excited.

When they reached the flat-topped hill they stopped to confer together. Plans were carefully laid and each man was assigned a specific post. After much debate, the hunters split into three parties, each of which was to approach the jungle from a different direction. The women looked on.

Mandia Jani walked off, as he had decided, into the ravine; there were five other men with him. The jungle was thick here; the leaves were gone from the trees, but the dry branches were matted together in an impenetrable net. From the higher slopes they could see a number of villages in the distance, and several large streams; lower down, the jungle enveloped them completely. Along the banks of the rivulet which they were following the trees grew particularly thick; there were many varieties of trees and creepers whose names they did not know. The tiger creeper was in bloom – so called because the flowers have the heavy odour which the tiger carries with him in the jungle. Tiny red flowers grew like pinpoints of fire. Nothing had disturbed the primordial sway of the leaves and the flowers; it was their kingdom. A tiger had killed a peacock not long ago, and dragged it up the slope; its tail feathers still lay scattered among the trees, and the bright feathers from its neck had left a vivid trail along the tops of the half-dried bushes, like a string of banners. The Paraja boys picked up the long plumes and stuck them in their hair. The pugmarks of the tiger were still visible, and dried pellets of its dung, the colour of chalk and mud ground together, lay along the narrow track. When the pellets were broken up, they were found to contain fragments of bone and hair.

Under a jhodi tree a small pile of stones lay heaped

together; two wooden staves, about three feet high, had been planted in the ground, and bunches of mango leaves, long since dried up, hung from them in festoons. On one side lay the remains of a palm-leaf umbrella. This was the spot where a man-eating tiger had killed a cowherd boy the year before, and these were the relics commemorating the event.

The hunters picked their way carefully through the pits and boulders, down the slope into the ravine. They crept through dense patches of wild banana, and other creepers whose wild fruit hung in clusters—some of them five feet long. Ferns grew twice as tall as a full-grown man, waving their fronds like elephants' trunks.

The hill sloped abruptly into a deep gorge, through which a river flowed, as though gashed out of the mountains with a sharp knife. The stream was almost dry now, and bright-coloured pebbles glittered in the sand of the bed. They walked across the sand, into the centre of the gorge. They could hear shouting from the upper slopes, where the others were beating the forest. Looking up from the gorge, they could see only a narrow strip of sky overhead, framed by the steep cliffs on either side, winding away like a snake. On the highest ridges the dense jungle petered out and the tops of the cliffs were quite bald. It was as if the hills had stretched themselves out in complete repose; huge rocks leaned into the gorge, dotted with trees growing at various angles. In the cleft of one such rock grew a gnarled banyan tree, and a python lay coiled around the trunk; now, startled by the sound of the drums, it was retreating into a hollow in the rock. For a while its huge tail hung dangling over the edge, then it gradually disappeared. Further on, a troop of monkeys chattered angrily at them through the leaves of an overhanging tree. Here the sand had been trampled by herds of deer as they stood waist-deep in the water, drinking, or bathing, or merely frolicking after a feast; the hoof-marks were too numerous to count, and the hunters were overjoyed. The rivulet wound on through the ravine, joined by other streams which had cut their way through the hills, and the sound of falling water echoed through the gorge like the ceaseless patter of rain.

The hunters selected suitable spots overlooking the ravine and posted themselves in readiness. Mandia Jani had taken the post furthest ahead, and sat with his ancient matchlock loaded and ready. A smaller stream had joined the main stream here, forming a circular pool; the falling water had bored several small pits into the polished rock, and as the water flowed over them it formed eddies which looked like gaping mouths. Moss and ferns grew luxuriantly here, and other small plants with yellow flowers had sprung up in the damp soil, forming a little jungle of their own. Mandia Jani made a screen for himself out of some twigs and leaves, behind which he crouched and kept a sharp look-out.

The voices of the other hunters were faint now, and the jungle was quiet, almost sinister in its silence. From time to time Mandia Jani was startled by what sounded like snapping twigs, but he could see nothing; most of the time the only sounds were the bubbling of the stream, the whistling of the wind through clumps of prickly bamboo and the drone of honey-bees in their hives in the trees. The scene was one of peace and beauty, and yet Mandia expected a tiger to charge out of the thicket at any moment. Once he had seen one scampering effortlessly, almost gaily, up a sheer hillside, with a nearly full-grown buffalo gripped in its jaws. There were bears in the forest too; they liked to feed on termites, and he had seen several ant-hills, or what remained of them, scarred with the claw-marks of bears. But the killing of bears was taboo. Tigers were another matter, however; besides, his own mother had been killed by a tiger, and revenge would be sweet. But what if the tiger should kill him? He saw himself stretched out on a bier of yellow flowers, with Kajodi grief-stricken at his side, tugging disconsolately at one of his dead arms. And the other arm was being pulled by the Sahukar. Mandia laughed when he saw the look of utter frustration on the Sahukar's face: the thick lips pulled back from the teeth, the corners of the mouth dribbling with saliva, the eyeballs rolling. So much money gone to waste!

And Mandia thought: how much of his life was really his own? How much remained to him, when Kajodi and the Sahukar had each claimed their share?

Presently he heard a rustling in the trees, and looked up to see a jackal standing not a dozen yards off. Their eyes met, and the jackal slunk away. But why had it come? There was sure to be some game around; he hadn't seen a hare so far, and that was a good sign. But the jackal? There had been a familiar twinkle in its eye, as though it were trying to say something to him. Where had he seen that look before? Then he remembered: long ago, when he had gone stealing ears of maize from the Sahukar's garden, and there had been sounds of the watchman approaching, someone had given him just that wordless look of warning. It had been his mother, Sombari.

Mandia Jani shivered. He tried to see which way the jackal had gone, but it had disappeared. At that moment a huge stag leapt straight out of the clump of trees on the water's edge and stood poised on a slab of rock, surveying the scene majestically. Quickly Mandia Jani picked up a handful of burning straw which he had kept in readiness, and held it against the fuse of his ancient matchlock. Then he took aim and waited.

But the action of the quaint old weapon was painfully slow. The gunpowder sizzled and crackled while Mandia turned it round this way and that, aiming in the direction of the stag. At last the gun went off with an almighty crack that thundered through the gorge. But by then the stag with the branching antlers had gone.

Mandia Jani reloaded the gun with powder and shot. It was no use waiting in that spot any more, so he and his friends moved to another part of the gorge, further downstream. The hoof-prints of deer were everywhere. Though Mandia had missed once, they were all certain that the incident of the stag was a sign of better things to come. As long as no one saw a hare their luck would be good.

The hours passed. The shadows on the hills sagged into the ravine, as though by sheer weight. The stillness grew, a stillness endowed with millions of sharp eyes, like needle points. The hunters waited, pricking their ears at every sound. For a long time, a big vulture could be seen wheeling around in the sky; perhaps it was searching for the tiger's kill. By now the hot sun blazing down on them all day had dried up the hunters' spirits; they resigned themselves to failure, and crept wearily out of the jungle, nodding silently to each other, as though to say: 'It was not fated to fall by our hands today.' The darkness in the ravine was now the colour of ink. The guns were heavy on their shoulders, and they trudged on, heads bent low. As they

began the ascent, the sound of a horn rang through the
jungle; the notes melted into the darkness and dripped
down from the leaves, saying: 'Come back, brothers,
wherever you may be; we are returning home.' And
though the sound was sad it was full of the love which the
community felt for every individual within its fold, and
the five hunters followed that call.

On the outskirts of the village, the disappointed hunters
stopped to argue away their failure. The guns held the beaters responsible, and the beaters blamed the guns. 'There
we were, waiting,' said the guns, 'and you worthless fellows couldn't find us a single animal.' 'Oh, yes?' said the
beaters, 'perhaps you waited too long. It's too bad we
couldn't tie the animals up for you to shoot.' And the wiser
ones among them said that Fate was to blame, if anything
was. 'I saw my bullets hit the deer,' said one, 'but it just
walked away.' Another said, 'Oh, I had two deer in my
sights, but someone came between them and me, and I
didn't fire because I was afraid of hitting him.' The argument was heated and unending; everyone was dejected.

They crept into the village as silently as they could after
it had grown dark, but the women were there, ready with
their taunts and insults and missiles. Both Kajodi and Jili
searched out Mandia Jani, but he shrugged off their abuse
quite gaily. Kajodi must still regard him as her man – else
why should she bother even to taunt him?

Chapter 42

Jili lay in a corner of the hut, nursing her shame and bitterness. Love had first come to her like the song of the blackbird in the stillness of the morning; it had caressed her like the dew and slowly unfolded her being to a world grown suddenly bright. Only half awake, she had become oblivious of her own self.

First love is like a blackbird's song, or like a slender creeper which twines itself round an object, glorying in its own weakness. It is like a narrow stream, filled with the sound of its own gurgling. And, like the stream, it loses itself in the jungle of conflicting emotions. Other objects begin to attract; values are readjusted to a scale of profit and loss, and the blackbird's song is left behind.

And then the drab, brown paths stretch endlessly under foot. Suddenly, night descends, blotting everything out.

The dark night comes for different people at different times; but when it comes nothing matters any more. What remains is mechanical and lifeless—like boulders ceaselessly falling down a hillside.

The night had come now to Jili. Somewhere within her a door had banged shut. The tender creeper had become gnarled and tough. The magic of early love was past.

Jili buried the tenderness that had lain in her, but not without effort. She was determined that from now onwards Bagla should mean nothing to her—but all around her was the revelry of spring, and it seemed only to mock her.

She groped in the dark for the little presents that Bagla

had given her: the cheap necklace of beads, the little red comb with its broken teeth, the tiny mirror in which she had admired herself, and the cake of soap. Deliberately, she ground these objects into powder with a heavy millstone and threw them into the fire.

Then she sat down to prepare supper for the family. But the tears came, uninvited; the fire died out and the hearth grew cold, with the meal still not cooked. She remained motionless. She heard herself sobbing; she did not know what she was doing.

Sukru Jani came, put a hand lightly on her shoulder and said softly: 'You are crying, my daughter!'

She leaned against her father and sobbed. The night screened the grieving father and his daughter.

Outside, the Kondh flutes were calling: 'Come out, beloved! Come!'

The dance was like a raging fever, but Jili was not there.

Chapter 43

When Mandia Jani woke up, he had a premonition that something important was going to happen that day.

The morning was bright with promise. Most people were still asleep, the doors of their houses shut. The ground was littered with leaves, rolled into cups for drinking. Every home had in front of it a pile of mango kernels, thrown away after the fruit had been eaten. Turmeric paste, which had been rubbed off human bodies, lay everywhere. Mandia found the piled-up rubbish and the stale odours in the wind deeply comforting: these were the sights and smells of home.

He had gone to sleep thinking of Kajodi and now he had arrived at a decision. He would not waste any more time: Kajodi must come to his home at once. Already one day of his leave was gone and only five days remained. Time was running out.

One of two things must be done immediately. Either Kajodi must be carried away by force, or her father must consent to their marriage and pay off the debt which bound Mandia to the Sahukar. Later, Mandia would become *his* goti, and work for him until all debts, including the bride-price, were paid.

Mandia hummed to himself as he went down to the stream to wash. Already he was thinking of the priest and the drummer that he would hire for his wedding. There would have to be a feast as well; Mandia's thrifty soul shrank back, but only for a moment. He sang:

> Kajodi, my Kajodi,
> I sing of the walls of the lovely Saria's house
> And of the porch of the Sundhi's house.
> Come, my lass—
> Let me see how strong you are in your youth.

As he was climbing up the bank he saw Kajodi going down to the water, carrying her pitcher. On seeing him she stopped.

'Kajodi!' he called.

'Yes, Mandia?'

'Will you come hunting with me?'

'What, me?' She laughed, wriggled and looked mischievously at him out of the corners of her eyes.

'Yes,' Mandia replied, advancing towards her.

She scampered quickly down the bank, as though trying to escape. He started to follow her, whistling to himself, then paused and looked around. There was nobody else in sight. Mandia was confused. He climbed back to the top of the bank, and watched Kajodi as now she walked sinuously down to the stream. It was still quite dark down there by the water, though the forests around him were beginning to catch the sunlight.

Then his feet began to move of themselves: he was rushing down the slope, and the trickling of the water was like a roaring in his ears. In a flash he had pounced on Kajodi, and his arms closed around her. His breath hissed in her ear.

Kajodi felt her cheeks grow hot and her body tingle with a feeling of shame. She struggled fiercely as he continued to hold her.

'Let me go, Mandia,' she gasped.

Mandia released her and stepped back a pace, panting; but he continued to hold out his arms to her, his face distorted with passion.

'I can't bear it any more, Kajodi,' he said huskily. 'Come with me; we'll run away and get married.'

But with a defiant toss of her head she flung back the tresses of hair which the brief struggle had sent cascading over her face. Her answer was plain. And Mandia's moment of passion was over.

He turned away quietly and walked back towards the village. And Kajodi followed him with eyes that suddenly filled with tears.

Mandia had been the first man to come into her life; she

was still betrothed to him. But nothing was the same since she had grown aware of her feelings for Bagla. It seemed so easy to choose between them: Bagla was free, while Mandia was a debt-bound slave; Bagla was lively and gay, and knew how to flatter a woman's heart, but she had rarely seen a spark in Mandia's eyes.

Still, it was not easy to tear away old memories: the pain lingered, though she willed it away. Mandia continued to occupy a corner of her mind.

Kajodi filled her pitcher and returned home.

Chapter 44

Mandia was hurt by the rebuff. But when the drums boomed out again that afternoon, calling everyone to the hunt, he felt his manhood renewed by their challenge, and the pain of rejection was dulled.

The men had failed so utterly on the first day that now the women were coming out to show them how to hunt! As the drums sounded they rushed out of doors, gay in their flowers and turmeric paint, chattering and laughing excitedly.

At the edge of the forest they stopped and broke up into groups before going any further. Deeper in the jungle, the groups scattered and shrank as various young couples wandered off in different directions. It was March and the trees were almost bare; the thin scrub provided little cover for wild animals. The hunters moved easily and fearlessly through the trees and were soon lost in the privacy of the jungle.

The forest was alive with the sounds of drums, whistling and shouting. They were all reckless with drink: the men had drunk mahua wine and the women pendom—strong mandia beer—or landha, which is only slightly less potent. They covered each other with wild flowers, and the young men carried off the women of their choice, slung over their backs or shoulders or hanging from their necks, giggling, deeper into the trees, and rolled them into the beds of fallen leaves. There were no restraints. Life renewed itself in the total abandonment of spring; old ties were revived and new bonds forged in the shade of those trees; the disapproving eyes of prudish society were a million miles away.

Tikra had crept into a narrow ravine with two of the girls; they had hidden themselves among the trees, soundlessly, and allowed the others in their group to go on ahead. But now Tikra found himself embarrassed in his riches; how was he to rid himself of one or other of his two admiring females? He climbed up into a mesh of intertwining vines, pretending to look for birds' nests. It worked. Soon he had lost one of the girls; whereupon he and the other slipped away into a clump of amla trees. Here, perched on a drooping branch, they fed each other with the sour plums. After a while, they jumped down and started their little housekeeping by the bank of a little stream that trickled into a ravine. For them, that marked the end of the hunt.

The older men saw the numbers dwindle and asked each other: 'Where is everyone? There were scores more when we started – where have they all gone?' And someone

laughed and said: 'How can a man keep his mind on hunting when he comes to the jungle with a woman tied to the
ends of his clothing?' But none of them went to search for
the stragglers; they only smiled at the sounds of laughter
from behind each bush, and took up their positions for the
beating of the jungle.

Kajodi found herself in a group with several other girls
and boys. But after a while, some of them got separated
from the rest and only Bagla and Mandia were left to
escort Kajodi, Fulmati and Sariaful. They were moving
downhill now and a stream lay in front of them. Fulmati
leapt nimbly from stone to stone and crossed to the other
side, while Kajodi stood lazily on the bank, watching her.
Then Mandia picked her up in his arms and carried her
across. She wanted to snuggle close to him as she lay in his
arms, with the water splashing and gurgling around her.
Bagla was almost halfway across when Sariaful called him
back: she wanted to be carried too. By the time they
reached the other side the girls were giggling happily but
the men were quiet.

Mandia said: 'Bagla, walk on ahead and see if you can
find any wild boar tracks.'

'Whatever for?' Bagla retorted. 'Do you think they're
going to wait beside their tracks until I'm ready to walk up
and take a shot?'

A little later they came to a hillock with a stream flowing
on either side, and Bagla said, 'Mandia, why don't you
climb to the top while I keep a lookout below?' But now it
was Mandia's turn to find this an unreasonable suggestion.

By now the scrub had given way to continuous jungle
which rose thick and dark up the sides of steep, forbidding
hills. Immediately in front of them was a high peak already

swarming with men. The beating of the forest had begun. Shouting themselves hoarse, the hunters almost flung themselves down the slopes in their excitement. Mandia and the others would be directly in the path of any animal that broke cover and ran. There was no time to lose. They ran towards a narrow ridge, densely covered with sal trees, which streaked the mountainside like a vein.

Mandia said: 'Bagla, Fulmati and you can wait here. I'll go ahead with Kajodi and Sariaful and see if I can find a better spot.'

But Bagla said: 'No, we should all stick together. There may be tigers, and the girls will start screaming.'

The girls, for all their bravado, were indeed scared. They crept closer to Mandia and Bagla as though to support what Bagla had said.

So Mandia's stratagem came to nothing.

They huddled together, waiting, crouched high above the valley which could be seen only through the gaps in the trees and the undergrowth. The hillside plunged into a deep ravine directly below them, where the hiss of a stream could be heard. In the distance lay the villages of Tunupar, Kanapadi and Diansil, easily identified by the rounded tops of the mango trees that ringed them. On either side, the mountains rose abruptly in an almost unbroken wall—thatched with dense jungle; between the two ranges the ground sheered away into a deep gorge stretching into the distance, melting into the swamps where paddy grew, beyond the village of Champi. This was the fearful Cat's Ravine, at one end of the knot of hills that formed the Dharam-Dooar range.

Kajodi looked at the hill which rose, turret-like, on her left. 'What hill is that?' she asked. 'It looks like the back of a tortoise.'

'That's Pandarmali,' Bagla said, but at once Mandia contradicted him. 'No, no. That's the Barigaon hill near Dasmantapur.' They began to argue excitedly, to the great amusement of the girls. Mandia grew angry because Bagla seemed to be getting the better of him, turning him into an object of ridicule.

Now they were both silent, but it was a silence charged with thunder – a thunder which Kajodi could easily detonate. The shadows lengthened.

Suddenly, they became aware that the drums had fallen silent. The jungle was still; only faint voices muttered tonelessly in the distance, like ghosts conversing. Bagla and Mandia looked anxiously at each other.

Some fifty yards away stood a stunted jhodi tree, whose short trunk ramified into two projecting limbs. With one accord they moved towards it. Bagla helped Kajodi into one of the branches, but before anyone else could make a move Mandia had leapt on to the other branch, leaving no room for the others.

'Why don't you climb into that other tree?' Mandia shouted, pointing at another jhodi a little further on. 'Hurry, there's no time to lose.'

He sounded insistent. Bagla nodded gravely, and Sariaful and Fulmati, really frightened now, clung to him fiercely and almost dragged him to the other tree. Bagla looked Kajodi full in the face and laughed, before allowing himself to be led away.

Kajodi and Mandia sat in the jhodi tree, hidden by the leaves.

'How quiet it is,' Kajodi whispered.

Mandia moved closer to her until his body pressed lightly against hers.

'Don't be afraid,' he said. 'I'm here.'

'Who's afraid?' she laughed.

He grew bolder and put an arm around her. She leaned on him.

The long creepers hung from the trees like swings, weighted with massed flowers. The mountainside, ribbed and creased, looked like the fruit of the karmanga tree. On the stump of an old mango tree on the slope below, peacocks sat perched.

'Shall I try a shot?' Mandia asked. 'They're too far away, but perhaps I could crawl nearer.'

'Oh, no!' Kajodi said. 'Such pretty birds!'

The silence of the jungle drew them close. Together they shared the blue-black of the sky, the hill slopes ablaze in the setting sun, and the inky darkness of the ravine – as though it all belonged to them alone, the last two human beings left alive.

Suddenly, on a ledge of rock above the ravine, a dark shape appeared, moving very fast. It looked like a man holding an umbrella. Kajodi shivered.

'A wild boar!' Mandia exclaimed, preparing to climb down. But Kajodi held him tightly. 'Don't leave me alone,' she said. 'I'm scared.'

Mandia did not go. He held her close to him and said, 'I won't leave you Kajodi; don't be afraid.' His voice was husky with feeling. And he told her, in whispers, what he had felt on that morning when she had spurned him, and during the days and nights that had gone before. He wanted to tell her all that was locked up inside him and, though he was often incoherent, the memories they shared told her all that he intended. She lay in his lap and smiled at him, afloat on the tide of shoreless, fathomless dreams which come only to the young.

Then, suddenly, from the jungle there came a series of noises which told of an immensely heavy body padding cautiously over the dry leaves. They were accompanied by a peculiar, nauseating smell like the burning of putrefied flesh and – something most unusual at that hour – a loud cry from a barking-deer. Mandia's trained senses were immediately alert; his face assumed the hardness of the true hunter. The crackling noises came nearer; he could see the bushes in the undergrowth quivering and rippling as they parted to let that heavy yet lithe body through. Kajodi was trembling. Mandia pressed his hand to her lips to prevent her from crying out. Then the sound grew fainter. Kajodi breathed again.

'The tiger's gone,' Mandia said. 'He must have passed under this very tree.'

Kajodi said nothing.

'What would have happened if he'd seen us?' he teased her.

She slid closer to him and gripped his arm. He laughed; he felt as though he had just passed a trial by ordeal and won Kajodi for a prize.

'Now, this fellow Bagla,' he continued mockingly, 'I believe he has his eye on you. But isn't he betrothed to Jili?' He had intended this speech to be loaded with meaning, but somehow the words, or the intonation, were not quite right.

The sound of a gun echoed across the hill and a bugle sang out, signalling: 'Come at once! An animal has been killed.' They scrambled out of the tree and were at once caught in a scurrying, jostling crowd which surged towards the hill. Mandia pushed his way through and ran, stumbled and fell, picked himself up again, and finally, breaking through the dense circle of people that had formed near the top of the hill, he saw a huge buck with long, branching antlers, lying in a pool of blood. They swarmed round it like ants, yelling, gesticulating, admiring; the story of the killing was being told and retold in immense detail. A little to one side sat the veteran hunter Agadhu Baidya, short and stocky, cleaning his gun with a rag, quite unaffected by the praise and excitement and the staring eyes. 'Oh, it's nothing,' he said, smiling through the acrid smoke of his cigar, 'pity the tiger got away.'

A bundle of bamboos appeared from somewhere; these were made into a litter on which the carcass was tenderly laid. The girls had woven garlands of flowers, which they now used to cover the deer. Willing shoulders carried the prize, the drums began to throb and the frenzied procession started down the hill, singing, dancing, rejoicing, celebrating, growing wilder with each step.

That night the carcass of the deer lay in the centre of the square, and all night long the mad dance went on around it, long after the bonfire had died and grown cold; the drums never stopped beating, though their rhythm was often uncertain. Afterwards, no one could recall the doings of that wild night; no one dared recall them.

Mandia Jani remained in his senses until about midnight. Reeking of liquor, he held a burning faggot in his hand as he searched frantically for Kajodi. He could not see her anywhere. Vaguely, he realized that Bagla was not to be seen either, and a disturbing thought lay coiled inside him, sending spasms of pain through him like hammer blows on his chest.

He was just beginning to grow desperate, when soft limbs twined around him in the dark, in impersonal but urgent invitation. The maddening beat of the drums set his blood roaring, and he let himself drift away on the night.

And the night was tasteless – neither sweet nor sour; it was indifferent alike to good and bad.

It was just a night.

Chapter 45

A sudden burst of crimson splashed the mountains, and the limp branch of the old salap palm caught fire. The sun rose, scattering red dust on the carpet of green. Ornamented dancing feet continued to tinkle around the dead buck, in tune with the music, though eyes were sunken and faces haggard and drawn. The outlines of the ancestral stones grew clearer through the haze. Dust had settled on the broken pots of liquor and the torn garlands of flowers. With the morning came the pigs, the chickens, the bawling, squalling children; smoke from the hearths coiled upwards, and familiar smells were carried on the wind. Wild pigeons cooed softly in the groves, and greenpigeons perched in the jhodi trees, breakfasting on the berries. The long-necked hornbills in the kochila trees let out shrill, piercing cries, and peacocks called loudly as they began to climb up the hill.

The murmur of voices grew louder and groups of people gathered by the wayside. A girl would veil her face modestly behind the end of her sari and stand with downcast eyes; another would laugh loudly.

The old routine began to make itself felt.

Except that Kajodi and Bagla were missing, and nobody could tell Mandia Jani where to find them.

The morning came also to the Kondh settlement of Kania Jhola—the Bride's Ravine. It was a tiny settlement of only twelve houses, huddled close together as if in a basket, its surrounding circle round the village coming down sharply on the patch of farmland hemmed in by the Podh Gad river and the steep, forest-clad mountains.

That morning, when – as the Kondhs say – the sun was as high above the horizon as the length of a walking-stick, Bagla and Kajodi emerged from one of the low-roofed huts, which belonged to Bagla's uncle, in the village. They stood there, facing each other in silence on that first morning; the only sound was the rustling of leaves.

At last Bagla said: 'Let's go to the river.'

They met the girls who were returning with their pitchers full, splashing as they walked. There were boisterous greetings; Bagla drew back as Kajodi was surrounded by the laughing girls, but he too was basking in the warmth of their greetings.

A Paraja marriage requires a minimum of formality. As soon as a boy and girl agree to live together as man and wife, the marriage is recognized by tribal custom. Only the conventional ritual remains: the Disari, or soothsayer, selects an auspicious day for the rites; a tiny roof, woven from twigs, is propped up on supporting sticks three feet above the ground, and pigeons and fowl are sacrificed to the sound of drums and bugles. Then comes the wedding feast. But these ceremonies merely set the seal on the marriage.

Bagla had exercised the ancient Paraja right of marriage by capture. All that remained was for him to pay the brideprice to Kajodi's father. He would have to send a special messenger, a barik, to his own village. His father as well as Kajodi's father would be informed, and then the elders of the two families would meet to negotiate the price. When everything was settled, they would bring him and his bride back to the village, in honour and glory.

It had not been Bagla's intention to carry her off, but what else could he have done after Mandia's sudden display of daring? When everyone had rushed to see the carcass, Bagla had gripped Kajodi's hand and led her away into the jungle, half dragging her. She had looked into his face but made no protest. They had rushed headlong over hills and valleys and through deep ravines, with the wind in their faces, soaking up the drops of sweat. Gradually Kajodi's trembling palm had sought that of Bagla, and she had surrendered herself to those unknown jungle paths, closing the door on the past.

When she awoke that morning, she was calm after the fever of the night, at peace with herself and the world, but conscious of new responsibilities. Her bright eyes were moist with tenderness as she looked at this man to whom she had given herself. And she asked him: 'Bagla, will you promise never to ill-treat me, or make me work like a slave?' Laughter and tears mingled as she spoke, and Bagla took her in his arms and reassured her. She rested her head on his shoulder and grew calm again. The hills, slowly waking into life, seemed to bear witness to their pact.

Chapter 46

Chaitra was gone, and all that remained of the spring was an occasional drum in some hillside village, nostalgically beating out the rhythm of the dance. The jungle looked dry and withered. Now the sound of drums would be replaced by the thud of pickaxes ringing out on stone-hard soil.

It was time for the goti to return to his master. Had the holiday really ended? So much remained to be done: the plastering of mud had begun to peel off the walls of the hut, and the thatch was gaping. The land was still unploughed and no arrangement for its ploughing had been made. The excitement of spring meant little to him, for the cycle of days brought no change. Each day he watched the sun rise, and the shadows grow smaller and smaller under the plantain trees and lengthen again into night. Nothing new entered his life.

That evening Sukru Jani sat with his children on the flat stone in front of their house. From neighbouring houses came the smell of cooking, and in the young men's dormitory the dungudungas had begun to twang. Children were shouting at play, and from nearby villages across the hills could be heard the flutes of the Kondhs.

It was the hour when the village came most vividly to life.

Sukru and his family sat quietly in the darkness, their heads bowed, as though torrents of weariness were raining down upon them out of the dark sky. Bats flitted around them like black shadows. Occasionally one of them would raise his voice and mutter something indistinctly. Sukru Jani said: 'I hear Bagla had to pay three score of rupees as the bride-price.'

After a pause he added: 'Anyway, we could not have paid such an amount.'

They were silent. Mandia and Jili sat with their faces turned to the ground, apprehensive of what the old man would say next.

'Those two are evil spirits reborn,' the old man continued. 'They were meant for each other and not for us. But don't worry, we shall find a bride for Mandia and a groom for Jili. After that, it will be Tikra's turn, and then Bili's. Maybe this summer . . .'

He went on muttering to himself: 'Who could have expected it! It's an insult! Ah, well, each one to his choice! Though I'm sure Bagla and Kajodi won't stay long together – he'll run away to the tea gardens in Assam and then she'll start looking for another husband. Then they'll come back to us begging for help. But I shall have nothing to do with them.'

His children were grateful for his words of comfort. Old as he was, he was still a prop on which one could lean. He spoke again: 'Go, my children, and enjoy yourselves. Things are bound to improve. We shall find a share-cropper to plough our land. If nothing else turns up, Jili and Bili can work as day-labourers. Or we can go to some other money-lender and borrow more money and get Tikra released from the Sahukar. Leave everything to me.'

A voice called out to Bili from the darkness, the voice of some admirer. 'Fine Rice!' he called. She rose and walked away. The sound of bells tinkling on the dancing feet of young girls drew Tikra away and he too was lost in the darkness. The old man sat alone on the stone and smoked.

Mandia got up, went into the house, poured himself some liquor from the earthen pot in a corner of the room, and then handed the almost empty pot to Jili. 'Drink,' he said. 'It will do you good.'

They would make a night of it, for next morning the gotis had to take to the road again.

Chapter 47

Sukru Jani and his sons would have to reach the Sahukar's home while the sun was still less than a walking-stick's height above the horizon; he was sure to abuse them if they were late. They hurried over the unending mountain paths, walking barefoot over the stones, always in single file, tribal fashion, with Sukru leading and Tikra in the rear. Already the April day had grown unbearably hot, and the heat shimmered elusively before them.

They walked in sullen silence, their thoughts resisting the onward movement. Sometimes they would meet a stray traveller, his bundle slung across his shoulder at the end of a stick, or a herdsman driving his goats. For a moment their loneliness would disappear, before they relapsed into that moody silence in which even the pain of their bodies failed to register. Only the sun, as it bit into their backs, would sting them momentarily out of their numbness.

They came to a flat ledge of rock, surrounded by a

clump of jhodi trees, in the centre of which was a tiny depression, shaped like the hoof-print of a deer. The place took its name from the sign on the rock: it was called the 'King-Deer's Footprint'. Water oozed constantly from the hollow in the rock, which stood on an eminence between two ravines. It was a favourite camping-place with travellers, and the relays of runners who carried the mail would rest there; the shade under the jhodi trees was strewn with the ashes of many a fire on which travellers had cooked their meals.

Sukru Jani, Mandia and Tikra sat under the trees, drank mandia gruel out of their gourd shells, and smoked in silence. They were tired after the long walk, but they could not afford the rest, for the Sahukar would be waiting.

Sukru said: 'There is much work still to be done at home. We must ask the Sahukar for a few more days of leave.'

Neither Mandia nor Tikra felt inclined to speak; Mandia was wrapped in his own thoughts and only grunted. Some other travellers who had also stopped there to rest were getting ready to move on, and Mandia suddenly woke up and said: 'Let's go!' They picked up their sticks with their belongings slung at the ends and resumed their journey.

Near Kanapari they saw the Christian preacher of Kelar village, travelling to Lulla to preach. He looked solemn in his black coat, but from his shoulder hung a live chicken.

The route to Lulla lay through Sursupadar.

'Are you going back to the Sahukar?' he shouted to them.

'Yes,' they shouted back.

'Is the Spring Festival over, then?'

'Yes.'

The preacher walked away, but when he had gone a little way Sukru Jani thought of something and shouted after
him: 'Listen, Preacher, please tell my daughter Jili that she
mustn't lose heart. I shall come back very soon. I am going
to ask the money-lender for leave.'

The preacher shouted back a reply, which they could not
hear, and turned away.

Mandia Jani said 'Do you think that rogue of a money-
lender will let you go again?'

Sukru Jani did not reply.

The money-lender's house drew near.

Chapter 48

Rengu Paraja, Bagla's father, was building a new house for
Bagla, who was expected to return soon with his bride.
Once married, no Paraja may live with his parents. Rengu
Paraja had hired several young men and girls to build the
house as quickly as possible. The foundation had been laid
and the mud walls were rising fast. A frame for the thatch
was being made out of bamboo and logs tied together with
strands of siali creeper. The house was being built beside
the path leading to the pool, where the labourers would go
to wash the mud off their hands, or fetch water to moisten
the clay for the mud walls and floors.

Jili had gone to bathe in the pool and she stopped to look
at the young men and girls working on the new house,
singing as they worked. They were singing an old ballad,

of which the chorus ran:

> Here today and gone tomorrow,
> And money cannot buy it.

It was a song about young love. It continued:

> No one can find it,
> Though many die searching.
> One moment you may see it
> By the winding jungle trail;
> But it quickly hides again.
> Money can buy everything,
> But love it cannot buy.

And then the chorus again:

> Here today and gone tomorrow,
> And money cannot buy it.

As Jili walked by the group of labourers with her pitcher under her arm one of the young men shouted: 'Hello, sweetheart! Come and see the new house we're building.'

'What for?' Jili asked.

'Well, come and see if you like it. After all, it's for you we're building it.'

The other labourers stopped singing and burst into coarse laughter. Jili turned her back on them, burning with shame and anger, and walked down to the pool.

Another girl was bathing in the stream—Kambla, a younger friend of Jili's. The two of them sat waist-deep in water rubbing the grime off each other's backs and chattering.

'How did it happen?' Kambla asked. 'It was such a surprise to all of us. How could Kajodi do such a thing to you?'

She clucked sympathetically as she rubbed Jili's back, and Jili felt as though Kambla's palms were peeling the flesh off her body, but she said nothing. The labourers were singing:

Here today and gone tomorrow,
And money cannot buy it.

She got out of the water and began to dry herself. Shiba Paraja came to the pool to wash.

'I say, Jili,' he shouted.

'Yes?' she said, growing tense.

'Why don't you come and live with me now, since Bagla has left you?'

She let fly at him, but the words slid off his back. He swung his arms wide and ran after her in mock pursuit through the water, shouting, 'Come to me! Come to me!'

Jili was shivering as she returned home. There was no food in the house, but Bili had cooked some tamarind seeds and tubers gathered in the jungle.

Bili had grown mature beyond her years. She looked at Jili's flushed face and asked, 'Has anyone hurt you, Jili?'

Jili burst into tears. Then, between sobs, she told the whole story. They held each other close and stood on the veranda outside the house hurling abuse at anyone who might hear them. Their voices rang out in the night:

'How dare anyone insult us just because our father and brothers are away! May the gods turn anyone who insults us blind in both eyes, and may the evil planet Saturn fall upon him and destroy all his children and all his cattle, and may he himself be burnt to ashes! The evil tongue that insults helpless women should be torn out by the roots!'

They felt much better when the long string of curses had been launched into the air. The song of love still floated up from the other end of the street:

Here today and gone tomorrow,
And money cannot buy it.

Chapter 49

The tribal priest had fixed the auspicious day. Four big simul trees had been cut down, and the trunks stripped of their bark and soaked in water until they grew slimy. Then they were planted upright near the entrance to the new house; a scaffolding made of twigs was laid across the four posts and a large melon hung from it. The professional drummers kept up an unceasing tattoo in front of the house.

The shadow of the salap palm grew shorter as it crawled to the foot of the tree; when it was exactly one and a half times the span of a man's palm, the auspicious moment would arrive. Rengu Paraja, with a curved knife tucked into his waist, started climbing up one of the posts of simul. The priest stood nearby muttering a chant to the gods. Rengu Paraja climbed a little way up, then slipped down the slimy post, climbed up again, and again slipped down until, sweating and tired, he managed to reach the top. He drew his knife and sliced the melon neatly in four. A shout arose from the watching crowd, for this was the ritual which inaugurated the wedding.

The wedding procession left the house—the elders of the tribe escorting the bride and the bridegroom to the bank of the stream, where the ceremony would take place. Turmeric paste had been smeared on their bodies and their heads shone with a thick plastering of castor-oil. They marched along the bank until they came to a spot where another stream joined the main one. Here, at the meeting of the waters, Kajodi and Bagla waited on the bank while the elders took a smear of turmeric from Bagla's body and a smear of castor-oil from his hair and rubbed these on Kajodi; then they repeated the ritual with turmeric paste and oil taken from Kajodi, which they smeared on Bagla. Thus bride and groom were symbolically united. Then Bagla pressed Kajodi's left foot with his right foot and spat three times in her face, and Kajodi did the same. Their necklaces and rings were exchanged; the ends of their clothes were knotted together, and each took a ritual dip in the stream. The priest offered some eggs in sacrifice to the planet Rahu.

From the stream they went to the square of the ancestral stones, offering sacrifices to the other gods along the route. And now the spirits of the ancestors were propitiated with eggs and rice placed reverently in front of the stones, and with mahua wine poured on the ground. The bride and her groom bowed low in obeisance to the dead.

Finally they came to the new house. The priest chanted mantras which nobody else could understand; and as he did so, he scattered rice and turmeric paste on the heads of the couple. A big black rooster was made to peck the grains of rice off their heads, before being sacrificed. The priest then linked their hands together and in everybody's presence Rengu Paraja hung a pair of gold ear-rings from Kajodi's ears and a gold ring from her nose and put three silver necklaces round her neck. The marriage rites were over. Rengu Paraja invited all his kinsmen to the wedding feast. The liquor flowed freely and amidst dancing and singing the bride and bridegroom entered their home.

The Jhodia Parajas, who were kinsmen to both Bagla and Kajodi, had come from villages nearby to join in the feast, which grew noisier than ten Spring Festival dances. Two brewers had set up shop in the village, and spirits were high indeed. The dancing went on all night. Jili never stirred from her hut; but several times that night Bili came out to see what was happening and report to her sister.

'What a mess!' Bili said. 'Half the guests have gone away hungry – no one remembered to serve them. And the meat! They'd cooked the two oldest goats in the village, and the guests had to chew and chew! And Rami told me the liquor they served to the guests was mixed with water from the stream.'

Jili heard, and smiled faintly. Bili kept up her commentary: 'The priest is so hoarse with a cold that you can't hear a word he speaks. . . . And what dreadful music! The drum must be cracked. . . . A fine pair Bagla and Kajodi make! She looks at least eighty and he has a face like a horse.'

They tried to draw comfort out of bitterness. The feasting went on and Jili and Bili groped in the dark for each other's hands. Their sobs mingled with the shrieks of the trumpets.

Chapter 50

Sukru Jani lay on the floor of the shed where the Sahukar's gotis slept, muttering softly.

'I can't stand it any more, Mandia,' he said. 'We must do something.'

'Yes, but what?' Mandia answered.

'Oh, I don't know. But I was thinking . . .'

'There is nothing to think of, father,' Mandia said. 'We have no money to pay the Sahukar – everything is gone. Only the two rice-fields are left.'

To Sukru Jani those two rice-fields were like the ribs in his chest. Four pieces of barren land were all that his father had left him, but by sheer hard work he had carved out two more pieces of land for himself from the bank of the Gadbajholla stream. He had had to dam the stream and wait for several years while the silt from the stream spread and settled. It was deep and fertile. Those two pieces of 'wet' land were his family's pride; on it they grew the finest of fragrant rice, which was known as 'the food of the gods'; and if the rains failed they could still grow coarser varieties of rice, together with olsi and castor-seed. Usually a farmer was not expected to pay rent for these 'wet' lands, for nobody knew when they would be washed back into the stream out of which they had grown. But the tax-collector had come and fixed an annual rent which Sukru Jani must pay. This only made the lands more precious to him, and though he had faced starvation he had never once thought of mortgaging the lands to the money-lender.

But now Sukru said: 'Yes, I am thinking of raising a loan

on those lands. I am tired of being a goti.'

'But father, don't you remember how angry you used to become when anyone suggested this to you? If you had done this earlier, we need never have become gotis at all.'

'Yes, Mandia, I know,' Sukru Jani said softly. 'But you must understand that things are different now. Jili and Bili are alone at home, and we haven't left them anything to eat. Think how they must be suffering.'

Mandia was silent. Tikra had begun to snore in his sleep, but his hand moved automatically in the dark, fanning away the mosquitoes that swarmed all over his bare body.

Sukru Jani said: 'The night is nearly over. Jili and Bili must be asleep now with the outer door bolted. The poor darlings! I wonder if they were able to get a good meal last night; they couldn't possibly sleep on an empty stomach.'

He was so lost in his thoughts he did not hear Mandia snoring. 'Are you asleep, Mandia?' he asked. 'Don't you think we should pledge those lands and get ourselves freed?'

He saw his village, his hut, his land, and then there remained only his two daughters, Jili and Bili. And his wife Sombari was with him too. His mind had travelled far beyond the Sahukar's home, where there were no bonds of any kind.

Chapter 51

A new day began, but not for the old man. His lands could not be mortgaged. He mentioned them to the Sahukar but the latter showed no particular interest. 'We shall see,' was all he said. By noon, when Sukru Jani and Mandia met again, Sukru Jani appeared to have changed his mind.

'I've been thinking, Mandia.' he said. 'Money we could find, perhaps, but land such as ours could never be found again. To pledge land to the money-lender is to lose it for ever. And it's all we have.'

Mandia showed his displeasure by saying: 'Well, do what you think best. Maybe we are fated to remain gotis all our lives.' And he returned to his work.

Sukru Jani sat alone, staring vacantly into the distance. 'How can Mandia understand these things?' he thought. 'He's too young – he can only think of his own comfort.' For Sukru Jani it was different: the land to him was not merely a patch of earth – it was part of his body. He knew every contour and depression in the land; every thorn, every ant-hill had a history. He had watered the land with his sweat and nursed the seedlings with the warmth of his own body. His four children had grown up on the soil and his wife Sombari had worked alongside him, bringing him his afternoon meal in the transplanting and weeding season, when he had been too busy to leave the fields. His children had helped him clear the land of rocks and he had told them: 'Remember, the earth is your mother. Sombari and I are nothing: we are here today and gone tomorrow, but the land will remain.' And he had sacrificed pigeons and fowl to the Earth goddess before each harvest, and she had received his offerings and smiled on him, and his harvests had been plentiful.

How could he barter away all those memories?

Chapter 52

March went by, April followed, and half of May was
gone. The sky grew heavy and swollen, ashy-pale, until
white and grey clouds burst out of the suppuration. It was
a time for despairing memories and heartache, but it was
also the busiest time of the year. In the nests that the birds
had built, the little chicks were tapping at their egg-shells,
impatient for their first view of the world; and they could
have seen human beings busy everywhere – sweating over
their ploughs or their hoes and pickaxes as they prepared
the land to receive the seed. This was also the time when
the greedy made new plans to grab their neighbours' lands,
and all kinds of disputes arose.

The Sahukar had ordered his gotis to sow paddy on the
lands of some Kondhs which lay close to his own fields.
Many years before, when he had owned the liquor shop, the
Kondhs had sold him their lands to pay for the liquor they
had drunk. But the land had since been taken away from
him, and restored to the Kondhs. An interfering government official had come to the village and looked at all the
records, and he had ruled that the sale of the land to the
Sahukar was invalid, since the law forbade anyone who
was not himself a tribal to buy tribal land. The Sahukar
fumed and raged, and declared that the official was an im-
becile; but the law was against him. The Kondhs danced
for joy, an ox was slaughtered, there was feasting and
drinking, and amid the beating of tomtoms and the
braying of pipes the Kondhs had marched together and
taken possession of the land which the Sahukar had earlier

tricked them into selling. Much the same story had been repeated in other villages. The money-lenders bided their time, and Ramachandra Bisoi, in particular, burned with the desire for revenge.

The Sahukar's mentor was Garaja Sundara, the Ribini or Revenue Inspector—a powerful man, who inspired awe and admiration. Ramachandra Bisoi had modelled himself into an imitation of the great man: Garaja Sundara wore heavy gold rings in his ears, and so did Ramachandra Bisoi; both had long vermilion marks painted on their foreheads to proclaim that they stood in the odour of sanctity. Each day, after taking his bath, the Ribini would sit cross-legged on a tiger-skin, chanting mantras to the accompaniment of mysterious gestures; this too the Sahukar had copied faithfully. Both of them smoked hemp and drank home-brewed liquor, and both were known to have a weakness for women. Both were in their fifties. They sported similar moustaches, bushy and bristling like the hairs of a wild boar. Above all, Ramachandra Bisoi imitated the Ribini in his dealings with the Kondhs and Parajas, threatening, abusing and beating them at the slightest provocation. Each was a terror among these hills. Often they were to be seen riding out together on miserable-looking. ponies, which had to be whipped constantly to persuade them to move. Each wore a garland of red hibiscus flowers round his neck, and the hill folk would look at them wide-eyed as they went on their errands of exploitation. The tribesmen believed that Garaja Sundara (the name means 'he-whose-roaring-is-beautiful-to-hear') possessed occult powers, some of which he passed on to Ramachandra Bisoi. Sometimes, when fires broke out in the jungle, the tribesmen would watch the mountains

glowing in the night and whisper to each other: 'It is Garaja Sundara who has set the forest on fire with his magic.'
No one dared question the actions of the Ribini, however
oppressive they might be.

And the Sahukar followed in the Ribini's wake as the
jackal follows in the tiger's. Some of the Ribini's awesome
reputation among the tribesmen had rubbed off on the
Sahukar. Moreover, his cordial relations with officialdom
paid him dividends. He played host to every touring official. Most of them were fond of hunting, and Ramachandra Bisoi always came to know of their visits in advance
and was able to anticipate their every wish. His servants
were sent far afield to fetch bananas and oranges, cigarettes
and foreign liquor – which the tribesmen called 'red water'. The visitors were offered cabbages from the Sahukar's
garden, bags of the finest fragrant rice, and large canisters
of butter-oil. And if they suffered from loneliness, the
Sahukar would provide them with companions for the
night.

Garaja Sundara had outlined for the Sahukar a foolproof
plan for repossessing the lands which he had lost to the
Kondhs. First, he had to win over the Amin or tax-
collector, who was superior in rank to the Ribini. The
Sahukar played his cards well, and the Amin sent a long report to the higher officials in the district containing numerous allegations against the headman of the Kondh village.
Whereupon the headman was replaced by another Kondh,
who was much more tractable. The simple tribesmen believed that all their lands were a gift from the headman,
who was the real owner. There were no records of ownership, and the headman could transfer any land from one
tenant to another without question. Now, when the head-

man was removed, the poor Kondhs were confused. They did not know to whom the land belonged.

Three years before the final phase of the plan was launched, the Sahukar applied to the revenue authorities for a reassessment of the rents which he was expected to pay. Strangely enough, he wanted the rents to be increased. It seemed as though he actually owned more land than shown in the records. At the same time, the rent paid by the Kondhs on their land had been correspondingly reduced. The revenue records were doctored to show that the lands in question really belonged to the Sahukar and not to the Kondhs, since it was he who paid the rents.

When the new headman was appointed, the Ribini obtained his thumb-print on a legal-looking document which stated that the Kondhs were being obliged to pay rents on lands which did not belong to them at all but to Ramachandra Bisoi, and that the Government should look into the matter and exempt them from further payments of rent.

The Ribini then entered Ramachandra Bisoi's name in the records as the rightful owner of the lands who had been paying the rents regularly. No court of law could have questioned his ownership now.

And so the Sahukar had ordered his gotis to march on the disputed lands with their ploughs and oxen and take formal possession. Some of the lands had already been ploughed by the Kondhs and paddy sown on them, but the Sahukar's men ploughed them over again. The Kondhs stood looking on and cursing the Sahukar and his gotis; but the latter were armed with sticks and axes, and there was nothing the Kondhs could do. The gotis felt elated at their own bravery, even though it benefited only the Sahukar. Their degradation was complete.

The Kondhs asked for a panchayat—an assembly of elders who would arbitrate and decide the ownership of the land. They claimed that the Sahukar had occupied their lands forcibly. The Sahukar, on the other hand, claimed that he had only recovered land which had always belonged to his family—and there were the rent-receipts to prove it. The arguments on either side went on; the crowds grew and no one could be heard above the shouting. The Kondhs, as was their custom, swore an oath and said: 'The Earth goddess is our witness, and the sacred Kodingamali mountain is our witness. May our hands wither away and all our cattle and children die if we speak a falsehood: the land is ours.'

It was an impressive oath, but useless against the sharp logic of the Sahukar, supported by every legal document. The victory was his.

The Kondhs shouted and cried until they were tired and then went home, and the panchayat came to an end.

The Sahukar's flag had been planted on the land, and all the courts of law and all the authorities would stand by him. 'Thank God there is still some justice in this land,' the Sahukar said, 'or else these rascally Kondhs would have walked away with my lands.'

And the Sahukar threw a single rupee to his gotis and told them to celebrate the victory.

Chapter 53

A freak wind wheeled round and round like a miniature
hurricane over the ploughed fields, raising a pillar of dust,
and then passed by. The men were resting from their
labours in the fields. It was their mealtime, and they were
drinking mandia gruel from little cups rolled out of leaves.
Their children surrounded them. The wind flung eddies of
dust into their cups, but they only laughed, waited for the
gust to pass, and resumed their meal. It was wonderful to
be working on one's own land. The shimmer of the heat-
waves seemed to turn into the dance of lush green crops,
and then into the golden festival of ripening grain. They
could see an endless procession of harvests stretching into
the dim past, when their ancestors had coaxed life out of
the reluctant soil. Each harvest came as the climax of an
unending cycle, and bound them harmoniously to the
land. The life in the soil lay dormant until they watered it
with their sweat and warmed it with their breath; then it
awakened, borne up on tender stalks. The miracle of the
harvest had become to them as common as breathing; for
the land never failed them. Out of the profusion of the soil
the crows and sparrows and ants and grasshoppers were
fed, and there still remained enough to nurse their joys and
sorrows in the months to come, until the next harvest.

The tiller of the soil counts his years in the harvests he
has reaped, waiting for the day when he himself will ripen
and fall like his crops, and others take his place. He knows
nothing of what lies beyond his fields; he is indifferent to
the rise and fall of kings. But he knows that someone is

sure to be lying in wait for him by hedgerows, with hands
outstretched to snatch away a share of his harvest. That is
the only reality.

Chapter 54

Sukru Jani's fields lay fallow that year. None of his neighbours were prepared to share-crop his land. As the headman said, 'Why should anyone waste his labour on that
land? Sooner or later Sukru Jani will have to give it up to
one of us anyway.' Jili stayed at home, watching her
neighbours' fields turn green with the seedlings of paddy
and mandia while their own fields remained barren. They
had not had a proper meal in months: they were living on
powdered mango or tamarind seed, or roots and leaves
from the jungle. Sometimes, for a change, they would
cook a broth with the larvae of wild wasps taken from
their nests. They had grown accustomed to hunger.

But on market day they still wore their brightest clothes
and their ornaments of brass and copper. They would
wash their faces and smear them with turmeric paste, oil
and comb their hair, stick a bunch of flame-coloured amla
flowers in their plaits, and run happily to the market. They
would linger, as of old, at the stalls where glass bangles
and sweets made of fried-rice and molasses were sold,
though they never bought anything now. It was eight
miles from their home to the market place, but the journey
seemed almost too short. On market day they could laugh

and talk and join in the singing once again; it was good to be alive.

Once the seedlings had sprouted, their services would be needed to help with weeding and later with transplantation. They would earn enough wages to keep hunger away.

But the wound in Jili's heart remained.

At midday, Bagla Jani sat in the yard in front of his new home while Kajodi bathed him with warm water which she scooped from an earthen pot in a dipper made out of a gourd shell. All Paraja wives helped their husbands in this way. Bagla sat on a low wooden seat with legs outstretched wearing only a tiny loin-cloth, and Kajodi, quite unselfconsciously, rubbed his back vigorously.

Jili often witnessed this domestic scene as she walked past the house to the stream. Kajodi would call out to her, using the old terms of endearment: 'Fine Paddy!' But Jili would quicken her footsteps, with Bagla and Kajodi's laughter ringing in her ears. She could not get used to the feeling of emptiness.

Chapter 55

One evening, Jili had a visit from a neighbour, Diptimoni; she wanted to borrow some embers from the fire in order to start her own fire at home. She was the daughter of the Domb Barik, or village messenger. Diptimoni herself was

the village gossip, a frequent visitor in every home.
'Mathia, the Christian preacher, came to visit us today,'
she began.

'Yes?' Jili said, casually.

'He has just come back from Koraput and Lachhimpur',
Diptimoni continued.

'So?'

'He said many people from our district are going away
to Assam. A new road is being built.'

'H'm.'

'The man-eater has made another kill at Lachhimpur and
the Sub-Inspector of Police has gone there for the enquiry.'

'What else?' Jili prompted.

'A bullock-cart full of grain was looted near the Podagad
market.'

'Whose was it?'

'I don't know. I hear the Government is distributing
orange seedlings and radish seeds to the farmers.'

'Really?'

'The rent-collector is coming to Dumbaguda to collect
rents.'

'When?'

'Oh, soon. The highway near the Dharam-Dooar is
going to be repaired. The contractor's agent is going round
the villages looking for labourers to hire and paying them
advances on wages. They say he carries thousands of rupees in a bag.'

'Will he come here, do you think?' Jili asked.

'Sooner than you think,' Diptimoni replied. 'The
women will be paid two annas and the men three annas a
day.'

'But the Dharam-Dooar pass is so far away,' Jili said.

'Could one come back home after work, every night?'

'Why should one? Everyone will be living in camps.'

'And what's the work like?'

'Oh, simple. One has to carry earth and sand in baskets, fetch water and so on.'

'Are people going from our village?'

'Of course. A lot of people in our street are going.' Jili and Bili had many questions to ask now, and Diptimoni had to sit for more than an hour talking to them. By then the burning cinders had turned into cold ashes.

The news travelled quickly: the contractor was hiring labourers, and the wages were good. Two annas – it was wealth! One could gorge oneself on mandia, buy castor-oil for the hair and even soap! And all this in the lean months before the harvest, when most people are content to scratch for roots in the forest. It was too good to be true.

And life in the camp would be one long holiday, with dancing and music and liquor enough to drown in! And the girls would have young men in abundance to pay them court. Money was almost a minor temptation.

One hot afternoon, Jili and Bili were digging for tubers in the forest. The red, pebbly soil was unkind to bare feet, and the loneliness oppressive. The river-bed was dry and the mountainside bare of all but a few withered leaves, the last greying tufts. The ground was pocked with holes that others had dug, searching for tubers – but of the plants themselves there was no sign.

Jili and Bili flitted from tree to tree like a pair of thirsty cranes on a hot day, stalking wearily on flimsy legs, shoulders drooping and long beaks gaping and closing. They would sit for a moment in the shade of a skeletal tree, before moving on again in their search for tubers.

But the tubers seemed to have become invisible that day.
'We've come too far,' Bili said. 'Let's go back.'
'And what are we going to eat?' Jili asked.
'Is it true about the contractor?' Bili said, after a pause.
'How should I know? Jili answered.
'The Barik said he's coming to our village,' Bili went
on. 'Shall we go out and work for him?'
'Why not?' Jili said. 'Everyone else seems to be going.'
'And what shall we do about the house?'
'Lock it up, of course.'
'Yes, but what will father say?'

Just then a jagged piece of stone, grown unbearably hot
in the sun, pierced the sole of Jili's foot, causing her to drop
the crowbar she was carrying. She cried out: 'I don't care
what father will say! What does he care about us?'

They were now near the Bear's Ravine—the place where
the man-eater had killed their mother. The forest was bald
and dry, but they felt afraid. It was said that the spirits of
those who had been killed by tigers roamed through the
jungle at noon. They took the shape of little children –
whether boy or girl one could not tell. Their heads were
red and so were their eyes and lips, and long hair grew all
over their bodies. They uttered strange sounds—like the
moaning or grunting or roaring of wild beasts, or the
crackling of dry twigs—and seemed to delight in chasing
people and frightening them away.

When Jili spoke she felt as if she could hear the voice of
some other person, a hoarse voice that echoed round the
hills. They had indeed strayed too far, and no one else was
in sight. The water of the hill stream seemed to be boiling,
the waves of heat danced over the empty fields, and the
hills were drowsy with sleep.

She mopped the sweat from her forehead, turned round and said, 'Let's go back.'

Chapter 56

At the meeting of the paths in front of the Sahukar's house, the old Barik from Sarsupadar stopped to ask for directions, leaning on his ancient and knotted stick.

'Does Sukru Jani of Sarsupadar village live here?' he asked a child who was playing by the wayside.

'I don't know,' the child answered.

The old man asked several other people and finally reached the Paraja settlement. It was noon. Sukru Jani and his sons had just begun their afternoon meal.

The Barik said: 'The headman has sent me.'

They said nothing, for their mouths were full of mandia gruel, but the expression on their faces was enough.

'Can you hear me?' the Barik shouted. 'You haven't paid your rent for the last two years.'

'I know,' Sukru Jani replied.

'The rent-collector is coming to our village,' the Barik went on, tapping angrily with his stick on the ground. 'The headman says you must pay up—there's no other way. All dues *must* be cleared before the night of the full moon. And remember, I can't come here again looking for you – I'm too old for that. You can either pay the rent or give up the land.'

'And what if we can't? Do you mean the headman will

take our lands away and give them to someone else?' asked
Mandia angrily.
'Certainly he will,' the Barik replied. What else can he
do? Do you think the rent-collector will wait until you're
free to come home again? Why should anyone do you a
favour? You're never there in the village when the Raja's
men come on their rounds; you've never done your share
of unpaid labour. Well, that's the message: if you don't pay
up your rent before the full moon, your land will be
taken.'
The Barik did not wait to see the effect of his words; he
turned and left, grumbling to himself for having been
forced to walk so far in the hot sun.
Sukru Jani and his sons sat in silence.
'I knew this would happen!' Mandia burst out. 'That
land is of no use to us and it's been lying idle for a whole
year. You refuse to mortgage it, and here we are! And now
we're going to lose the land, anyway. All because of you!'
He got up and walked angrily away, followed by Tikra.
The old man sat there, alone, crumpled and broken, looking straight ahead. The fields burned in the sun, and the
wind drove the dust here and there. His eyes looked at
everything, seeing nothing. Presently, darkness came and
hid everything, but he still sat there.

Chapter 57

Jili and Bili sat in the darkness outside the hut, cocooned in
self-pity. Unshared, their store of misery had grown and

grown. The food had all gone, as food inevitably will; their clothes had turned to rags, for it is the nature of cloth to tear, and torn clothes do not become whole again. The many patches on their clothes were witness to the brave attempts they had made to repair their dignity, but the fabric had grown immune to any needle, and the rents appeared again. A garment was more than a covering; it was as intimate a part of one's being as the skin. The bits of torn apparel dropping away each day by the wayside were like pieces of one's own existence being corroded and trampled underfoot; nothing could mend the injury to one's pride.

The village square was crowded. The contractor's men had arrived with a bagful of coins, looking for young men and women to hire. In front of each hut the family sat in conclave, pondering the contractor's offer. Fathers were telling their sons, 'No, you may not go – I don't wish it,' and mothers were protesting that they would not allow their daughters to go, even when the fathers were tempted.

And in front of one hut there were only two young girls to decide.

But another presence was there too, making a third. An entity not seen, but acutely felt, for everywhere he is a part of human existence. He lives in derelict houses, empty cooking-pots, in heaps of tattered clothing; he lurks in the dark of the evening. He fills the minds of men with dreams, wave upon wave; he shows them new paths to follow, pricking them into wakefulness as they lie curled up in sleep by the fireside. He pushes them out of doors and slams the door shut after them. He guides men to the prison-cell or to the gallows. He inspires women to sell themselves in the market-place. In him, all want and hunger are incarnated.

Jili and Bili sat listening to the contractor's agent as he talked to the young men. And an unseen finger kept pointing to the great bag of money.

Jili had made up her mind long ago.

'What is there to consider?' she asked Bili. 'So many of the girls are going. Don't we need the money?'

Bili said nothing, but her eyes revealed her doubts.

'Oh, we needn't wait to tell Father,' Jili said, reading the look. 'The neighbours will tell him. And since there's nothing in the house anyway, we don't need to stay and look after it.'

The night brooded over them and, out of the dark, some unknown impulse came to Bili. The path ahead looked easy now – the boulders on it were hidden by the darkness.

'Very well,' she said. 'Let's go then.'

'We shall start tomorrow. Now go to bed.'

Next morning, several of the houses had their front doors shut and fastened, for the occupants were leaving. The girls went out early to bathe and came back dewy-fresh. Cooking utensils, mostly of cheap aluminium, were packed in bundles which the girls carried on their heads as they set out behind the contractor's agent. Behind them, in turn, came the young men, with their effects slung across their shoulders on bamboo poles. The village was left half-empty and drained of all laughter.

The fields and hills looked fresh with the promise of adventure. No one thought of what lay ahead; they were happy to have shaken off the dust of old habits.

The highway lay far ahead. Quite how far, no one cared to ask.

Chapter 58

Sukru Jani was ploughing the Sahukar's land when the news reached him; Mandia was away driving a bullock-cart, and Tikra was in the forest, herding the cattle.

Sukru Jani listened sullenly; then he began to plough furiously. He pressed the ploughshare deep into the soil with the full weight of his body until his limbs and waist and neck ached; he flogged the two bullocks mercilessly, venting his anger on them, on himself, and on the earth which he was ploughing.

That evening he told Mandia what had happened. Mandia was delighted.

'Well done, girls!' he exclaimed.

Sukru Jani fired off a volley of abuse at his son.

'Why are you so angry, father?' Mandia asked. 'What have you done for them over the last year, since we left home? They've solved their own problems, haven't they?'

'But why didn't they ask me?' Sukru Jani groaned.

'They've done the right thing,' Mandia said. 'Why shouldn't they earn for themselves? What *we* should do now is go to the Sahukar, mortgage our land and get ourselves freed. What use is the land to us now, when Jili and Bili are gone?'

And Tikra said: 'How lucky they are! I wish I could go and work on the highway.'

Sukru Jani lay tossing on his straw bed all night, smoking his cheroots endlessly. A Paraja may work for a neighbour occasionally and get rewarded for it, but he never sells his labour for wages. He felt betrayed by his daughters, and thoroughly confused. All his experience was confined to the land: he knew how to plough, dam a stream, clear jungle; for what was happening now, he was simply not equipped.

The night advanced: sombre and monotonous. The mosquitoes kept pestering him, making it hard for him to marshal his thoughts. He did not know when he fell asleep.

When he woke up the next morning his mind was clear: he would mortgage his land to the money-lender. Jili and Bili had snapped the ties which had bound him to the land; surely it was not more precious than they.

'Come Mandia,' he said to his son. 'Let us go to the Sahukar.'

'Do you really mean that, father?'

'What else can I do?' Sukru said.

A searing pain stabbed Mandia, as though he had been stung by scorpions. When his father had hesitated Mandia had been eloquent; now he was suddenly afraid. Would the land ever come back to them? The Sahukar could not be trusted.

'Maybe we should think it over first,' Mandia said slowly. 'Don't do anything in a hurry.'

'Well! *I* do something in a hurry? Wasn't it your idea in the first place?'

'Yes, that's true. But what if the Sahukar feels tempted to grab our land?'

'Are you mad? He has thousands of acres of his own – why should he want our land? I'm not sure if he will even agree to take it on mortgage.'

Mandia knew that his father would not easily change his

mind once he had reached a decision.

'Very well, father,' he said. 'Let us ask the Sahukar.'

That afternoon Sukru Jani went to the Sahukar and spoke to him again about the land.

The Sahukar said: 'What use will the land be to me? Your village is much too far away! Do you think I have no better use for money than to throw it away?'

Sukru Jani pleaded: 'All of us are bound to you, Sahukar. Who will help us if you don't? Please take the land on mortgage and give us some money.'

'Why don't you sell me the land?'

'I don't want to sell it.'

'What if I don't agree to take it on mortgage?' asked the Sahukar cunningly.

'In that case, I have nothing to say.'

'Very well,' said the Sahukar. 'Go back to work now, we shall talk about it later.'

Sukru Jani felt humiliated; he had offered the Sahukar his most treasured possession and it had been spurned as though it were beneath contempt.

'What does he know about land?' he grumbled to himself. 'After all, he's the son of a moneylender; he can't understand how a farmer feels.'

Sukru Jani told his sons about his encounter with the Sahukar.

'The stingy rascal,' Mandia said. 'What are we to do with him?'

'There isn't another piece of land like ours in the whole district,' Tikra said. 'Where can the Sahukar find land like that?'

Sukru Jani could guess what was in his sons' minds. 'Very well,' he said. 'I shall go to him again and ask him once more.' But now Mandia said, vey softly, 'Do as you think best, father.'

Mandia and Tikra went away, each to his work, and the old man looked at them with eyes that were suddenly moist.

Mandia was like him in so many ways: he never spoke much, but he understood every feeling in Sukru Jani's heart. The father felt very proud of his son: he had not forgotten the dignity of the Paraja peasant working on his own land. Circumstances had bowed him down, but not broken him.

And Sukru Jani remembered that he had promised Mandia a bride before April had passed.

A few evenings later he asked the Sahukar: 'What have you decided, Sahukar?'

'About what?'

'About the land.'

'Which land?'

'The land I had asked you to take on mortgage. Don't you remember?'

'Oh, that land!' exclaimed the Sahukar. 'What exactly did you have in mind?'

'I want you to take my land on mortgage and set Mandia free. Tikra and I will go on working for you. Whatever Mandia grows on the land will be yours, and that way our debt will be paid off faster.'

The Sahukar suddenly grew angry and began to shout at him.

'Oh, I see you're tired of working for me' he said sarcastically. 'I suppose you don't like the food I give you! It's not even a year since you started working for me, and already you're planning to go. You fool, don't you realize

that even your great-grandson will never be able to repay
the debt! And you're offering me a worthless piece of land
and hoping to get part of your debt written off! Do you
think I'm so stupid as to let Mandia go? Try that one on
somebody else!'

And the Sahukar turned and walked into his house, leaving Sukru Jani alone in the darkness.

Chapter 59

The house lay empty. The front door, made of slivers of
bamboo, had been shut and barred; but it hung crookedly
from the hinges, and the tell-tale streaks of mud across the
timber showed that the ravages of white ants had begun.
The thatch-eaves were hung with cobwebs among which
dead insects had been trapped—monuments to emptiness.
The mud-built veranda was cracking, as human lips do in
winter. The thatch was beginning to gape, and the
framework of split bamboo gleamed through the straw
like a skeleton.

May was almost over and massed clouds tumbled across
the sky, driven by the wind. The house seemed to be gaping expectantly at the sky as though hoping to catch the
first drops of rain. Dead leaves and dry twigs lay scattered
around – all that remained of a flourishing garden. Two
old baskets, whose bottoms had fallen out, hung from the
thatch; a little way off lay the broken handle of an axe. In
the courtyard, the remains of the hearth still stood, co-

vered with cold ashes and pieces of half-burnt charcoal.

Behind the house lay the fields where mandia and paddy once grew. Wild spear-grass had sprouted on the land, grown up, withered and died; and the leafless stumps of wild weeds stood in the fields, measuring the passage of hours and days with their shifting shadows. Sometimes, bani birds hopped through the grass looking for insects, and the ghostly silence was broken by their twittering. The birds would fly away and the surviving crickets would set up a funereal chant to mourn their dead. From neighbouring fields came the sound of ploughmen at work and the ploughshares churning up the soil.

But Sukru Jani's house and his fields lay desolate.

Chapter 60

The 'highway' was being repaired.

It was actually a dirt track, surfaced with red clay, winding through the paddy fields on either side, and flanked by jhodi and karanja trees. The air was thick with the red dust raised by the labourers.

People from distant villages had come there to work. The women were mostly Parajas or Gadabas, but the men were drawn from various tribes, with Kondhs predominating, and most of the skilled masons were Dombs. They formed a restless kaleidoscope of colours and patterns: the Paraja women with their necklaces of coloured beads; the Gadaba women, from whose ears hung long coils of brass

wire, reaching below their shoulders; the bright clothes of
the Domb girls mingling with the coarse, matted hair of
the Kondhs and the huge turban of the Kutchee contractor;
the blue smoke from the cheroots and the clouds of red
dust. The young Supervisor strutted about with his pencil
stuck into one of his knee-length socks, while his foot-rule
hung out of his breast pocket.

Large square pits had been dug by the side of the road
and the earth from these pits lay heaped, together wih
mounds of road-metal and brick pounded into powder.
Some of the labourers were breaking boulders into chips,
while others carried sand or earth in baskets on their heads.
They laughed and sang as they worked, their hands and
feet moving together in a natural rhythm. Men shouted at
each other needlessly, making themselves out to be far
more busy than they actually were.

At evening the work stopped; those who lived in nearby villages walked home while the others went to the col-
ony of huts which had sprung up by the roadside. They
washed in the stream, and the women examined their faces
in their cheap mirrors, oiled and combed their hair, and
dressed it with wild flowers plucked from the trees.

Fires would be lit and, while the evening meal was being
cooked, the young men would play on their dungudungas.

But soon the fires would grow cold and the dungudungas become silent; the labourers would crawl into their little huts and fasten their doors. The camp would seem to
melt into the darkness, leaving no trace behind.

And as the day ended the men and women felt themselves richer, for each had earned several copper coins.

The first few days had passed quickly, amid the excitement
of new surroundings; there was no time either for joy or

for regret. But gradually new acquaintances turned into friendships; the surroundings became familiar, and finally intimate. The labourers' huts grew friendly with the warmth of their own bodies, the red road and the uneven hills rose to welcome them each morning. Each day, as the labourers walked to their work, they could see the karanja trees shedding their flowers, and their eyes would grow soft. The little incidents of everyday life began to fall into a pattern, filling them with the expectation of a certain regularity of sequence and interval. They came to know each ploughman working on his little patch of land by the roadside, each tree under which he rested, each tune which he played on his flute.

And at dusk the same two eagles would play among the branches of the neem tree which stood near their huts; they wheeled around, turned somersaults in the air, screamed at each other, flew apart and came together again. They were always there at the same hour each day; if the labourers did not see them they felt disappointed, as though the crust of things had cracked and a deep chasm opened up, through which old hidden wounds began to peep.

And their days were filled with this strange harmony, events moving like the hands of a clock. And though the pageant of events seemed to have no great significance, yet life had a rhythm which echoed deep within. They measured out their days in sweat, and time clung to them like the dust settling on clammy skins. When their work was done they sang; but it was only the prelude to the night and to another day of work.

The days followed each other in procession.

Chapter 61

Pay-day came once every week, transforming the camp·
into a festival. The labourers splashed all morning in the
stream; the women lingered endlessly over their toilet,
teasing their hair into meticulous order, fussing over their
clothes. In the afternoon they all gathered in front of the
Supervisor's hut for their wages. The rest of the day was a
riot of celebration, in which memories of the week's
labour were quickly buried.

Jili's initiation into this pattern was unnerving. She was
strolling through the camp one evening, a little distrait,
and did not notice that she had strayed outside the line of
huts. The evening fires were beginning to glow. Suddenly,
a man rushed at her out of the gathering darkness. He was
obviously drunk; and he seized the end of her sari and began pulling her towards him. She recognized the man: it
was Shama Paraja. 'Come with me!' he panted. Jili broke
away and ran, pouring out a flood of abuse; behind her,
she heard coarse laughter and giggling. She turned to look,
and saw the shadowy figures of women surrounding the
man. He had his arms around two of them; they were enjoying themselves hugely at her discomfiture.

But soon Bili and she had grown accustomed to such
things. As they lay inside their little hut at night, they often
heard the shuffling of furtive feet, whistling and humming, and the meaningful clearing of throats. The sounds
went on all night, and they found their bodies disturbed by
strange sensations.

Quite often, as they laboured on the highway, some girl

would leave her work and walk away, as if she had suddenly remembered something—and it would be quite some time before she came back to work again. A young man might take a fancy to some girl, and the two would be found together always. He would dig the earth out of a pit and fill her basket and help her lift it on to her head, or she might be found standing beside him and talking softly to him as he hammered away at the boulders, breaking them into chips. Such things became a part of the pattern; but Jili and Bili had no share in them, though they observed everything that went on.

The Supervisor and his team were all young men, and as they walked among the labourers inspecting their work they would suddenly stoop over some girl, pat her on the back and say, 'Hurry up now, you're too slow.' Their eyes were restless, and the girls would grow nervous.

And something within Jili and Bili was prompting them to pull down the dykes and let themselves drift with the tide.

Memories of home often assailed them; at times Bili would become restless and say 'Let's go home!' but Jili would remind her that they had to eat. Luckily, there was not much time to brood. They had made many new friends among the other girls, who all seemed far wiser than they in the ways of the world.

One day Kambala—one of the girls—said to them, as they were chatting together: 'My father was ill; he's always ill. He couldn't work, and my mother left him for another man. There was no food at home, so I came here, leaving my younger sister to look after father. At first I was very lonely. Then Philemon, the mason, began chasing me and now we're living together. Of course I shall leave whenever I feel like it, but for the present . . .' She stopped and laughed and pointed at the red sari which she wore, and her heavy gold ear-rings.

Jili and Bili had never heard anyone speak so bluntly before and were a little shocked. On another evening, three of the girls came to them and said: 'The Supervisor is going to play some music for us. Let's go to his hut.'

There was a crowd of girls outside the Supervisor's hut. The Supervisor sat with three of the foremen, playing vigorously on an ancient harmonium; he seemed to be performing gymnastics on the broken keys.

The Supervisor's friends said to the girls: 'Why are you standing so far away? Come closer.' The girls moved closer. The Supervisor continued to play and the girls stood listening, fascinated. A little lantern had been lit inside the hut, but after a while someone put it out. The sounds of scuffling and of bodies being dragged were heard in the darkness.

Jili, Bili and a girl called Jamuna managed to get away; but then Jamuna complained: 'Why did you drag me away from there?'

Jili and Bili laughed and Jili said: 'That's quite enough for today.'

The sisters were finding it increasingly difficult to become angry.

And every evening the young people would dance together and buy presents for each other with the wages they earned: little bells for the ankles of the dancers, bits of steel wire for the dungudungas of the young men, small cakes of soap and bottles of castor-oil for the hair.

The Supervisor was a young man of twenty-five, with a slender moustache that showed up dark against his fair skin. All day he would ride on his bicycle from one gang of workers to another; it was hard work, and by the evening he felt he had earned his relaxation. As he moved among the workmen, he would appraise the girls quickly and observe how they responded to his look. Some of the girls would thrust themselves on his notice; others were shy. Long experience had taught him that a direct approach gave less enjoyment than a pretence of romance, a little game of hide-and-seek which needed cunning and subterfuge.

He frequently employed two old women named Rami and Moti to assist him in these pursuits—much as hunters use tame she-elephants as decoys.

Rami from Champi village was famous for her skills, and in the past she had assisted many officials of high rank. After the evening meal was over, the Supervisor would exercise his vocal chords to the accompaniment of the harmonium and then lie down in bed, surrendering himself to the aches and pains that followed a hard day's work. Then Rami and Moti would come to him and begin massaging his legs and talking softly to him until he fell asleep. He would tell them what had happened to him during the day, everything that had interested and aroused him, and Rami and Moti would assure him that they were making strenuous efforts to meet his wants. On some nights, there would be a girl waiting outside the hut, and while the old women massaged the Supervisor's legs they would call out to the girl: 'I say, won't you come in and help?' Then, when the girl had come in, they would say: 'Our arms are aching, we're too old. Won't you help us and massage the Supervisor's legs?' And they would withdraw discreetly, leaving the girl behind.

Many of the girls received visits from Rami. She would carry presents for them, hidden in the folds of her sari: flowers, small cakes of perfumed soap and necklaces of coloured beads. And she would press these presents into a girl's hands and say: 'These are for you. From the Supervisor! What a gentleman he is! You must come to his hut tonight and listen to him sing.' And she would smile, holding the girl's chin lovingly in her hand and gaze into her face and say: 'How beautiful you are!'

Rami, it was said, had herself once been a charmer. Now she was no longer young but she still nursed her memories. She would imagine herself as the heroine of every play that she stage-managed, and identify herself with each girl. Later, she would admire her face in the mirror and re-arrange the hair over her ears so that the streaks of grey were concealed, and tuck some flowers into it. She would hum a tune, and the face that looked back at her from the broken mirror would seem to be beautiful once more.

After that evening in the Supervisor's hut, Jili and Bili became the objects of Rami's favours. She visited them often, but always when one or other of the sisters was away, and she spoke to them in whispers: 'Why do you sit here and mope, my dear? It isn't right! You must go out and enjoy yourself in the evenings. You're only young once!' She brought them flowers and dressed their hair, unasked. Sometimes the Supervisor would give her a copper coin or two, but she needed no reward for plotting these intrigues; the pleasure of vicarious romance was reward enough.

Chapter 62

Jili and Bili grew more lonely each day. As they watched the life all around, strange tensions arose inside them, particularly in the evenings, when the young men courted the girls with song, dance and drink, A girl would resist her lover for perhaps a week, and then surrender on some wild night when the dance had entered her blood. All this Jili and Bili witnessed. The sound of dungudungas and flutes and the wailing of the Supervisor's harmonium kept them awake night after night. Rami's blandishments became insistent. Each looked to the other for the restraint that no one else would supply; yet the same restlessness was shared by both.

One afternoon, while Bili and the others were at work, Jili lay at home with a headache. Rami, watching her chance, came stealthily to her.

She spoke deviously of this and that, and then said: 'The Supervisor has been asking about you. He'd like you to come and listen to him sing tonight.'

'Why me in particular?' Jili asked.

Rami smiled. 'Why don't you ask him that yourself?' she replied.

Jili felt suddenly faint. 'No,' she said. 'I won't go. It's not good.'

'What isn't good?' Rami said, caressing her back. 'In our tribes it's perfectly normal for a girl to live with anyone she likes, for as long as she likes—there's nothing immoral in that. And anyway, you shouldn't be worrying your pretty little head about such things. At your age the only sin is to shut yourself up the way you're doing.'

Jili could feel herself weakening, but she gathered herself together and said again: 'No, I won't. I'll return home tomorrow.'

'Oh, all right, if that's what you really want!' Rami said. 'Go home and starve, who am *I* to stop you? But remember, one isn't always young. Poor folk like us must take what comes. Virtue won't get you far. Here's this handsome young gentleman eager to give you everything you can possibly want. You're lucky, I tell you. Why, half the girls in the camp have been begging me to put in a word for them; but catch me doing such a thing! He's *pining* for you, Jili. "Rami," he says to me, "get me at least a flower from her hair or I shall die!" '

Rami sighed deeply in commiseration.

Jili sat with downcast eyes, tracing patterns on the mud floor with her fingernails.

'I'm frightened, Rami' she said hoarsely.

Rami hugged her. 'Why, my dear?' she cooed. 'What is there to be frightened of? No one need know. Just leave it to me.'

She got up to go before Jili could say a word. 'I'll come back later tonight,' she said, turning at the door. 'Wait for me.'

And Jili sat alone with her shame and the hungers of her young body.

The first lights were beginning to wink when Rami returned, behaving as if she had just dropped in accidentally.

'Jili!' she called, standing outside the door.

She had brought a wreath of wild roses for Jili's hair. 'It's from him,' she whispered. 'I'll come again, later.'

Night came on. Evening meals were cooked and eaten,

the dungudungas warmed up and eager voices arose. Jili stepped out of her hut, and Rami, who had been waiting, clasped her tightly to herself. She had brought with her a long white piece of cloth, like a sheet. This was draped over Jili's head and then wound round both their bodies. In the dark, they began to walk swiftly, in tandem, towards the Supervisor's hut. Anyone who looked in their direction would have seen a single head and, if he were very observant, two pairs of legs below the wrapping. No one, however, saw them go.

Many hours later, Jili pushed gently at the flimsy door of her hut and entered. Bili was stretched out on the floor, alone.

'Where have you been, Jili?' she asked.

'Oh, dancing,' Jili answered, drunkenly.

'You must be tired,' Bili said. 'Come, lie down with me.'

And Bili laughed bitterly to herself, thinking, 'Well, well. My turn to dance next?' For the first time she felt angry with Jili, though she could not have named a reason for her resentment.

Jili's eyes were heavy with sleep. She was too tired and confused to think, she just lay there, letting her body go slack.

After that it was not necessary for Rami to come to them. The Supervisor would lie in wait somewhere for either Jili or Bili, and neither was reluctant. And sometimes, there were other young men too. They fell easily into the pattern, finding only pleasure, with no aftertaste. They were all alike in their urges, all young.

Sometimes, when the other was not there, Jili or Bili

would gloat over the treasures they had accumulated. There were coins—whole rupees, and two-anna and eight-anna pieces—brand-new saris of different colours, little cakes of perfumed soap, bottles of scented oil for the hair, and beads and rings. They were rich! And life was full: work (when they felt like it), dancing, singing. There was no time to think.

Memories of home still came from time to time, but were swiftly dispelled. All their affection went, instead, to the little hut in the camp. On a tiny patch of ground behind the hut, they sowed seeds of sweet gourd and snake gourd and pumpkin; and they brought a sprig of wild rose and a little malli plant from the Supervisor's garden and planted them near their hut, waiting for the rains to come and make everything bloom.

In the evenings, they would both come out dressed in their best and with their hair groomed and plaited and garnished with flowers. Bili would join the dance while Jili sat listening to the singing. They were their own masters – and fit for any company.

During the day, a crowd of girls might be seen, dragging a roller over the newly built road. They would shuffle and heave and tug, and the roller would inch its way forward. Then, a sudden early shower would drench them to the skin, and the water would run down their faces. Unperturbed, they would form two rows, one on either side of the roller, grip the long handle and sway and rock back and forth, bare breasts swinging, colliding against each other. They laughed and sang as they worked, carefree, each feeling herself reflected in the others, so that she was not one but many.

Chapter 63

When the clouds rumbled in the sky, lost memories returned and pain gnawed at the heart. The rains came—no
longer the sharp, crisp May showers but the long, lingering rains that go on and on and on. The sky turned a sickly
grey-green and the sun disappeared.

The gotis huddled together in their miserable shelters,
shrinking and shivering. They sat on the narrow platforms
running the length of the huts and watched the rain-water
rushing in torrents along the ground. And, as they smoked
their cheroots, thoughts gathered like the clouds in the sky;
and sometimes took weird and grotesque forms, as if re-
flecting the strange patterns made by the eddying water.
The incessant chatter of the rain ringing in their ears made
them long to lie still, without moving a muscle. How far
could one see into the future through the nets of falling
rain? Everything became blurred and confused.

The entire heavens seemed to be tumbling down. The
day was pale and faded, a ghost of a day, when noon and
evening were indistinguishable. All one could see in the
distance was the dance of the rain. Earth and sky were
merged into one, rising and falling in a succession of
waves. The hills that rose on every side were wreathed in
swirling vapour and capped with peaks of cloud that ta-
pered away into the sky. One curtain of rain would come
rolling in from the distance as another curtain moved
away; as it came it would break up into long, slanting
spears of rain. An endless wailing seemed to rise from the
land, the wind sighed and whimpered as if searching for

something, and the raindrops pattered down through the leaves of tall trees.

Even in weather like this the gotis were given no rest. Working in groups on the sodden earth, they had become one with the splashing mud. Their skins were smeared with the oils of herbs and fruits which they believed would protect them from the cold; their bodies cloaked with dried palm leaves, knitted together to form a kind of waterproof covering. But none of this was of any use against the torrential rain.

Their hands and feet moved blindly, their minds had grown muddy and clammy. But sometimes a lingering tendril of pain would clutch at them.

Sukru Jani said to Mandia: 'Look at that terrible rain, my son. Your poor sisters must be getting drenched.'

'What can we do about it, father?'

'I've been thinking, Mandia . Maybe we should speak to the Sahukar once again.'

'About our lands? But we've done that so often! No, I have a better idea: let's brew some liquor out of mahua. It'll do us good in this weather and we could sell some. It's safe enough now – who's going to come here in this rain to catch us?'

'Haven't we had enough of that stupidity, Mandia? If you tried it again one of those Dombs would be sure to inform on you. No, Mandia, only that land can help us out of this.'

'The land isn't everything. Let the land go – let everything go, if only we can all be together in our own hut. What a relief that would be! I wouldn't mind if we had to starve together. But look at us now: here we are, bound hand and foot, while the poor girls are starving. I must go to the Sahukar again.'

'Very well, father.' Neither had anything more to say that night; each was pursuing his own anxious train of thought. Only Tikra was carefree enough to feel grateful for his warm bed of straw.

Next morning, when Sukru Jani went to ask the Sahukar for the maize seeds which he would have to sow that day, he lingered on, hesitant and embarrassed. Finally he blurted out: 'Sahukar, have you decided anything about my land?'

'What land?' asked the Sahukar, squinting up from his ledgers. 'Oh, you mean the mortgage? Why, what's the hurry? And besides, why do I need any more land?'

'You mean you won't accept it on mortgage?'

'I mean I have no time to waste arguing with you. Get back to your work.'

'Then let me go for a couple of days, Sahukar, so that I can talk to somebody else about this.'

'We'll see about that later,' the Sahukar said. 'Get back to work.'

Sukru Jani left with a pale face and a heavy heart. The Sahukar, however, now decided that he had feigned indifference long enough, and that the time had come to go and see the land. He did indeed have land in plenty but he could always do with more. If this land was on a hillside it might be excellent for growing oranges, coffee, or even vegetables.

That evening he asked the Domb Barik to look at the land and report back to him.

The Barik returned and said: 'It's valuable land, Sahukar. Don't let it go.'

So next morning the Sahukar summoned Sukru Jani and

said: 'Look, Sukru, I think I'll go and have a look at that
land of yours. You may as well come along and show it to
me. But don't raise your hopes, because I may not like
your land. And even if I take the land, it will only mean a
small amount taken off the debt each year.'

Sukru Jani was overjoyed. 'Did you hear that?' he said to
Mandia. 'The Sahukar probably doesn't think much of our
land now; but let him look at it once, and he'll surely agree
to write off a much larger part of the debt against the mortgage. And then I can go and bring my daughters home.'

That night the rain was exceptionally heavy, the darkness was dense and close. The wind crept howling into the
little huts where the gotis lived, like jackals in their holes,
and blew out all the fires which were burning inside. The
sparks flew here and there inside the little cells. Sukru Jani
talked eloquently of the happy times that were coming;
then he fell asleep. Tikra began to snore. But Mandia was
kept awake by all kinds of apprehensions. Surely, the
Sahukar would find some means of doing them out of their
land. Everyone was after their land; there was not an inch
they could call their own. They would always be somebody's slaves, whether here or in their own village.

Suddenly he felt as if the night was suffocating him. The
rain and the wind were eating into his flesh. Kajodi was
gone. What would he do with land, or home? On nights
like this he had lain awake in the young men's dormitory,
playing on his dungudunga; and presently Kajodi would
come to him, awakened by the sound, nestle close to him
and hum in tune with his dungudunga. And she would
whisper her complaint into his ear: 'When are you going to
wed me, Mandia? Your promises are false.' What a terrible
night it was! His ears were ringing with a thousand

noises – the whole world seemed to be turning over in a
sleep made fitful by the endless, nightmarish rain – but he
could see nothing. And from the depths of his consciousness Kajodi arose to the surface. He got up, groped for his
dungudunga in the dark and began to sing:

> O my darling jayi flower,
> Slender and sweet;
> My darling malli bud,
> Sparkling and fragrant!
> Your thick, black, glossy hair
> Interlaced with star-white flowers;
> I know you will come to me!

How strange his own voice sounded against the rain! His
eyes crinkled with pleasure and his face lit up in a smile.
And the song brought back happy memories – of lovers'
quarrels, and secret meetings, of Kajodi and himself
together. The song ended and his voice sank lower and
lower in the refrain until it was a whisper: 'Kajodi!' And as
he whispered her name the spell was gone and he was back
in the rain and the inky darkness, with the thunder rumbling outside.

Kajodi had jilted him and was gone.

He sat still and listened to the rain; a great cry rose from
his heart and mingled with the howling of the wind, and
he wept. Kajodi's face reappeared, and she was smiling
that familiar smile; but the more she smiled the more it
hurt, and the more he wept. He thought: 'Let it all go – the
land, our home, everything! Let the Sahukar have it all!'
His happiness had ended, for Kajodi would never be his.

Chapter 64

It was the middle of June when the Sahukar rode out on his nag to inspect Sukru Jani's fields, with Sukru and Mandia trailing along behind. It was a bitter humiliation for them to return to the village where once they had walked with heads held high. Their footsteps were slow; their shoulders drooped and their faces were downcast. But they had come, and they had to go through with it.

Sukru was so anxious to see his house that at the first opportunity he slipped away from the others. The house was empty. There were gaping holes in the thatch, and the mud walls had crumbled in many places. Grass and weeds were growing on the floor.

It was as if a whirlwind had passed over the house. It seemed to be whimpering in pain.

The neighbours saw him and came to greet him.

'Sukru?' they asked. 'But why have you brought the Sahukar?'

As he walked to his land, they followed him curiously, commenting freely. Some said: 'He's not content with bringing trouble on himself – now he wants to bring it down on us.'

The Sahukar walked all round the land, appraising it shrewdly. Yes, the slope down to the rivulet would be excellent for growing oranges; the flat upland would be ideal for wheat; and the deep, wet trough was just right for sugar-cane.

He turned abruptly on Sukru and Mandia. 'You rogues! he roared, 'is this what you've brought me to see? I've been dragged fifty miles for nothing.'

'But the land is good, Sahukar,' Sukru Jani said quietly. 'We haven't lied to you.'

Already the Sahukar had begun his triumphal march through the village, his fingers busy twirling the ends of his moustache into needle-points, his eyes restless, penetrating the very walls of the houses on either side. The women stopped to look at the stranger and he stared back. Curious children trooped behind his pony.

Kajodi came out to see what was happening and almost ran into Mandia. She smiled at him. But he only gaped at her, with no recognition in his eyes. Struck by her beauty the Sahukar stopped for a long look, moistened his lips with his tongue and asked Mandia: 'Who is she?'

Kajodi retreated into the crowd.

The Sahukar had nearly reached the end of the village when Sukru Jani begged him: 'Sahukar, please let me stay on here for a couple of days and attend to my house.' He said this in the hearing of all the villagers in the hope that the Sahukar would find it harder to refuse. But the Sahukar did not relent. The villagers followed them to the end of the village.

The headman told Sukru: 'It's good that you're making an arrangement about your land. But remember, it's you that must pay the rent.'

Sukru Jani replied 'What arrangement have I made? I'm not even sure if the Sahukar will accept my land. Why don't *you* take it on mortgage?'

But the headman shook his head.

Back in his own village, the Sahukar told Sukru: 'Very well, I'll take your land if the terms are right.'

Sukru proposed his terms: the Sahukar should take his

land on mortgage and farm it; he should release one of them and write off ten rupees from the debt each year. The balance would be paid off through the labours of the two remaining gotis.

But the Sahukar only cursed and shouted at him, as though the very idea was absurd.

The evening passed, the next day passed, and after endless hours of argument they came to an agreement. Sukru Jani would be released but his sons would remain with the Sahukar. The land could be redeemed if Sukru Jani paid twenty-five rupees to the Sahukar, but until then it was his. There was no written agreement – it was all done by word of mouth, tribal fashion. There were no witnesses either, though ten other gotis of the Sahukar were present; but Sukru Jani called on Dharmu, the Just One, and the Earth goddess Dharatini to be his witnesses. And, by tribal custom, Sukru Jani ceased to be a goti from the very moment that the agreement was made; and precisely at that moment the land passed into the Sahukar's hands.

Sukru Jani picked up the stout piece of bamboo that was his walking-stick and the split-bamboo pole which he used as a sling for his personal belongings and set off on the long journey home. But his heart was heavy. 'What is this freedom worth,' he thought, 'when my sons are still gotis?'

His land was gone. He was alone, with no one to help him – a lonely old man, helpless and drained of all strength.

Chapter 65

The house was empty, deserted. The rain, coming down in torrents, poured through the thatch and there was nowhere he could keep himself dry.

There was nothing in the house but a few old, broken dungudungas and some tatters of feminine garments, all covered with mildew. There were no voices now—only the moaning in the rain-sodden air as the darkness loomed out of the horizon and swallowed up the sky even in the daytime. Sometimes, one could see his hunched figure stealing through the empty street; then it would be lost in the haze of rain. He lay soaking on a torn mattress spread on the floor, with his head cushioned on one arm, moaning inwardly in despair. If there was a break in the rain, he would rise to light a fire and cook himself a meal from a handful of millets he had scraped together; otherwise he just lay there all day, shivering with cold, seeing no one, brooding, alone with his memories.

Several days went by in this way before it occurred to Sukru Jani that he ought to go and bring his daughters home.

But what could he feed them on? How would they live? Ought he to bring them home to share his hunger and pain?

As he lay there in the darkness of the evening, shadows from the past crept into his mind. Everything he had tried to build had crumbled to dust—why? He could find no reason. He had prayed regularly to the tribal gods, sacrificed pigeons and fowls and goats and fallen full length on the ground before their altars. And the priests had praised him for his devotion and blessed him at every festival. How could he have offended the gods? But they had deserted him now, become deaf to all his cries. He was alone with his fate.

His mind and body were numb. The wind howled. The thatch of his house rose and fell. He lay awake at night as though expecting someone. He could hear the thud of walls collapsing. The storm shook his house—and he felt as if his own existence was quaking, for the house was a shell protecting his body, a part of himself. The wind tore away handfuls of thatch and the holes grew larger as he watched.

Suddenly he sat up, listening intently. Sounds of loud sobbing seemed to float down the wind from far away in the dark, lonely night. He remembered his dead wife—it must be her spirit that was roaming about, weeping. He beat his forehead on the wet mud, and in a hoarse voice broken by his sobs he cried out to his gods: 'How cruel you are!' But the wind only howled the louder.

Chapter 66

For four days Sukru Jani worked as a labourer on his neighbours' lands. On the fifth he walked to the weekly market, where he purchased some sweetmeats made of parched rice and molasses. On the sixth he tied these up into a bundle which he slung over his shoulder and set out to meet his daughters. It was raining steadly, he had no protection and he was soon drenched as he walked slowly through the forest, wading through the flooded streams.

It was nearly sunset before he reached the end of his journey. He was shivering with cold, and wearing only a loincloth from which water was dripping. A gang of labourers was returning to camp after the day's work. They were all spattered with red mud and they carried crowbars and pickaxes over their shoulders. They walked together in a compact group, both boys and girls, jostling each other, laughing and joking. Other groups followed.

But he did not see Jili or Bili among them. He walked up to one group after another, looking closely at the girls. Some of them, seeing the bundles slung at the end of the bamboo pole, asked jokingly: 'Are these things for us, grandfather?' Others said: 'Maybe he's going to meet some relatives in another village. Be careful, old man, don't let the tigers get you.' And the old man asked them: 'Have you seen Jili and Bili? From Sarsupadar village?' They laughed at him and went on their way.

Presently he got tired of searching and let himself drift with the crowd. He came to the rows of huts in which the labourers lived. Darkness had fallen and the cold grew intense. A star would appear, occasionally, out of the dark clouds, as though it had suddenly come to life, and again disappear. He walked, tired and halting, with the load on his shoulders, across the row of huts, shouting, 'Jili! Bili!'

There were many who bore these names, apparently, for they came out of their huts to see who was calling. Each time this happened, he walked up to them, peered closely at their faces in the dark and came back disappointed. And still his cries continued: 'Jili! Bili!'

They had dressed up for the evening and were waiting for Rami to call for them when they heard the agonized cries outside their door.

Bili rushed out. Jili had not finished dressing her hair but she came rushing out too, with the end of her sari dragging on the ground. It was their father! They cried out excitedly, while he just stood there and let his tears flow. He tried to be harsh with them, but his voice betrayed him.

'And so the two of you walked out on me!' was all he said.

They felt ashamed suddenly and shrank back, sobbing.

He stood motionless in the doorway; his feet seemed to be rooted to the spot. The little kerosene lamp inside the hut cast a reddish glow, lighting up half his face. Behind him was the black night. He was gnarled and bony, old—an apparition that had suddenly materialized in a house filled with warmth and joy.

His daughters rushed at him and clung to his shoulders. Then they dragged him inside the hut.

Chapter 67

Sukru Jani wanted his daughters to return with him at once, but they were in no hurry. 'We can leave whenever we want,' they said, 'but what will happen to us afterwards?'

'That's nothing *you* need worry about,' Sukru Jani retorted. 'You're far too young. It's a disgrace that you two should be working to support me – death would be better!'

'But how shall we manage?' they persisted.

'I've always managed quite well so far, and I don't need to be taught by my own children,' was the sullen reply.

For the moment there was no more to be said.

That night the Supervisor himself came to persuade Sukru Jani. He gave him two shining silver rupees and said: 'Look, this is for you to spend as you wish. Stay on here, and I shall find work for you. Why do you want to take Jili and Bili home? You'll only be adding to your worries.'

Jili and Bili eagerly supported the proposal, and for a moment Sukru Jani was tempted. Two rupees was a lot of money, and the gentleman seemed so kind, so modest – why, he did not even mind coming to their miserable hut and talking to them as an equal, even though his clothes showed him to be an official of some standing.

Sukru Jani bowed low to the Supervisor and said: 'Lord, since you are so kind to us, please allow my daughters to go home while I stay here and work. They can't stand up to this hard work in the rain – they're bound to fall ill. Do let them go, Your Honour.'

The Supervisor puffed gravely at his cigarette and said. 'If I listened to you I would have to send all the younger people home and keep only the old ones. Do you think the Contractor can waste his money on old bags of bones like yourself?'

Sukru Jani was stung. 'I may look old,' he retorted, 'because I haven't been getting enough to eat. But which of your young men could match me for work?'

The Supervisor said: 'Still, you'd better go home. Don't

worry about your daughters. Do they look as if they were starving? They'll be all right.'

But the old man's mind was made up and he cut the discussion short, saying: 'I don't agree, sir.'

The Supervisor knew the men of the hills. Once they clamp their mouths shut, nothing can ever prise them open again. He went away, pulling a wry face.

Sukru Jani spoke again to Jili and Bili. He was aware of the difficulties ahead, but it went against the grain to see his daughters working as paid labourers. A Paraja girl works only for her father or her husband. Sukru Jani, grown ripe with years, could feel in his bones the spirit of his ancestors, to whom such a thing would have been an affront. Nor did the life here fit in with his sense of dignity or decency.

'A shame on this life!' he said.

'Why?' his daughters argued. 'What's wrong with the life here?'

But Sukru Jani was unyielding, for he knew how the younger generation loved to argue.

'No,' he said. 'That's final. I don't want money. We'll manage somehow. Let's go home.'

And the matter was settled. Jili and Bili wound up their little household, packed all their belongings into bundles which they carried on their heads, and trudged homewards behind their father, in single file. They were sorry to be leaving everything behind. The tendrils of gourd and pumpkin had begun to creep up the thatch of their little hut, and the malli plants had revealed their first fragrant buds.

Chapter 68

Though Jili and Bili tried to slip into the old groove, life at home was not the same as before. In the evenings they were restless with a vague expectation: they dressed themselves up as they had done in the workers' camp, but as night advanced they would grow frustrated and tired and lie down quietly. They seldom went to the young women's dormitory.

But Sukru Jani was happy. He worked twice as hard as before—he was completely tireless. First he had to repair his house, and this was not easy. For the thatch he had to have either rice-straw, which is difficult to find once the harvest is over, or else long spear-grass from the jungle, which cannot be used until it is ripe and dry. Finally, however, the house was repaired, and Sukru Jani was able to turn his thoughts to the problem of finding food for the family.

He went to the village headman and said: 'You know I've mortgaged my land. Give me some other land so that I can cultivate it and keep my family alive. I shall pay the rent regularly and my children will remember you with gratitude.'

The headman promised to help. He said there was no more land in the village, but there might be an adjacent hamlet which came within his jurisdiction.

Meanwhile they all found work on their neighbours' lands, for sowing was not yet complete and the rice-fields needed weeding. Jili, Bili and he worked all day, and by evening each had earned a quantity of mandia and a few copper coins – enough to keep them alive.

While he worked on alien land Sukru Jani kept remembering his own fields which were lying fallow, but
which the Sahukar would soon be cultivating. And
whenever he had the time he would go and sit beside his
fields. Absent-mindedly he would begin to pluck the ubi-
quitous weeds – until he remembered that the land had
already been mortgaged.

The realization made him feel old. His eyes narrowed to
slits, and he sat there brooding, his forehead creased and
his head was weighed down with cares. And as darkness
fell, he would come to himself, realize that his tears were
flowing, and turn round to see if he had been observed.

Chapter 69

The experiences which Jili and Bili had shared in the camp
had brought them closer together. For some days after
their return home they worked in silence, their faces
glum and tight. Then, one day, they broke into laughter
once again. Occasionally, while working, they would
grow restless, stop and laugh over something they
remembered.

Kau Paraja dogged their footsteps, and they joked about
him often. Jili would order him to fetch flowers and Bili
would say to him gravely: 'Do come to our house this
evening.' His face would light up, and the sisters would
roll with laughter. He was constantly hanging around

them, happy to run errands for them, obedient to their slightest wish.

One evening, as they were returning from work, the sky grew overcast and people ran for shelter. Kau Paraja was with Jili and Bili. They stopped under a sprawling banyan tree and Jili said: 'I can't run any more, my foot hurts.'

They sat down and Jili said: 'Kau, see if there's a thorn in my foot.'

He inspected her foot gravely, holding it up in his hands, trying to squeeze the thorn out. Jili said she felt better.

A light drizzle has started. Jili said: 'Kau, I'm cold Cover us up, will you?'

He took off the cotton sheet he used to wrap himself and draped it over both of them, with himself in the middle. Huddled closely together, the three of them continued on their homeward way.

Jili and Bili began to giggle. Bili said: 'Tell me Kau, which of us would you prefer as your bride?'

Kau was deeply embarrassed. 'No, no,' he protested, 'you mustn't say such things.'

'Oh, come now!' they persisted. 'Don't be shy! Do tell us.'

The girls swayed with laughter, and Kau was obliged to sway with them.

They returned home.

And Kau stuck to them manfully, putting up with all their mockery, never losing hope.

Chapter 70

Sukru Jani finally persuaded the headman to let him have a piece of unclaimed land. It was some distance away from the village, though there was a little hamlet close by. It was virgin land, high up on a hill, and covered with thin scrub. Sukru Jani estimated that he could get about twenty bushels of mandia out of the land if he worked hard. Redgram and chilies could be grown on the upper slopes, where the scrub was thicker, provided he could make a clearing.

All round his land was luxuriant jungle. It looked inviting: he might grow suan millets there – the land was sure to be rich. If only he could cut those trees down! But wouldn't the Forest Guard catch him? Well, what if he did – there was no valuable timber here, no sal or piasal trees, nothing but useless scrub. Surely no one would hang him for clearing the scrub. Besides, why should the Forest Guard come here at all?

But he was alone, and he couldn't afford hired labour. It seemed pointless to think of clearing all that jungle, when he could barely manage the land the headman had assigned him.

There were five Kondhs living in the neighbouring hamlet, and there is no one more skilled than a Kondh in the art of felling and burning timber and reclaiming jungle for cultivation. If only he had a single helper, the two of them could have offered, whenever they were free, to help the Kondhs in their cultivation, and in return the five Kondhs could have helped him to clear the jungle: such an exchange of labour was quite common among the hill tribes and no wages were expected or paid. But there was no one at all to help him and he would never have time to help the Kondhs and so earn the right to ask for their help in exchange.

Chapter 71

For a Paraja father, having an unmarried daughter is as good as owning property, for she will fetch him a bride-price some day. Sukru Jani had two nubile daughters, but no suitor had come for them yet. He began to feel he must give his daughters away in marriage before he could hope to start cultivating his land and stand on his own feet again. But what could he do if no suitor came?

He must do something, or else his two sons would remain gotis for ever. And so he encouraged his daughters to go and sleep in the young women's dormitory and to join the communal dancing. He even escorted them in person to the dances. And he managed to send them frequently to the weekly market on some plea or other—it was 'Jili, will you get me some tobacco from the haat?' or 'Bili, get me some kerosene for the lamp; who else is there to do these things for me now?'

He wanted them to look cheerful and well-dressed when they went out. 'Why haven't you combed your hair, Jili?' he would ask. 'You know your mother would never have let you go out looking so ragged.'

He could get them to do anything by mentioning their mother, a fact which he exploited skilfully. 'Who am I to tell you what to do?' he moaned. 'I am only an old bull that knows nothing about bringing up children. If your mother had been alive she would have taken care of you.'

His voice would grow thick as he mentioned their dead mother, his face would cloud over and his tears begin to flow. Bili would murmur sadly to her sister: 'Father has grown too old!' And Sukru Jani's attempts to cheer them up would be in vain.

Kau Paraja would drop in quietly and ask: 'Why do you look so sad, girls?'

'Can't you guess?' Bili would answer. 'It's because you haven't been coming to see us.' And she would burst out laughing while tears welled up in her eyes.

Chapter 72

The clouds massed in the sky in enclaves all round the horizon, then rushed together to join in an orchestra of rain, pouring incessantly. It was July.

The darkness was uninterrupted by sunshine. Through the gloom one could see little black figures dotting the hill-tops, singly or in groups. They were of the same substance as the sooty darkness, the black, oozing mud, the trees of the forest: from a distance they looked no different from the stones or logs or heaps of mud. They were like grotesque shadows raised up from the mud by the whirling winds. The shifting vapours of the clouds made them look as if they were mounted on invisible swings; at times they would disappear behind one of these swirling masses.

And the drumming of the rain on the hills was answered by the thud of hoe and pickaxe as the men laboured to push the mountains back and turn rock into soil. Below them the terraced fields rolled down to the distant valleys, and here, in the villages and settlements, people covered themselves with varieties of crude rainwear and worked on the land, pulling out weeds or preparing the beds for transplantation. Most of the land belonged to the rich Sundhis or Kumutis, who were money–lenders as well as traders. Few of those working owned their plots.

And on the hilltops the men seemed to cling to the slopes like lizards, each pounding away at the patch of rock he had selected for himself. They were the dispossessed. There was nothing for them in the safe valleys and settlements down below—no prepared land which they could cultivate. But they were cheerful. They were one with the storm; the kite and the mountain eagle were their companions, and the lonely spirits that haunted the hills watched their labours. Those wind-swept heights were like a bridge between this birth and the next, in which they firmly believed. The storm roared in their ears, shutting out all thoughts except that of work, and their hopes grew in the image of the sky. They were free.

Sukru Jani sent his daughters to work in the valley while he himself worked on the mountain. The needles of rain pricking his bare skin sent a thrill through his body. This was the life he knew, though for some time he had forgotten the taste of it. He turned his back on the village and faced the mountains, and as the days passed he seemed to work harder and harder. He was all alone, but he had no time to brood. In front of him the thick clouds were locked in combat. The sky was a blend of blue-green and iron grey, like a field of pulses streaked with katechu; there was no trace of the daylight by which he was accustomed to measure time.

On such a day of cloud and thunder Nandibali Paraja of Dumbaguda village set out to find himself a bride, with the inevitable bamboo sling on his shoulder. He was young and he was alone; he had lost both his parents, his father only the year before. He had no land and he could not be bothered with the cares of a household. He owned nothing but his strong, muscular limbs. When the first rains came he thought he should get married – but paupers cannot be husbands. He decided to leave his village and wander through the hills in the rain, hoping to discover the girl who had been destined for him. And when he found her he would offer himself as a goti to her father and work for him until the bride-price had been paid.

He had four strips of loin-cloth, a drinking-cup of cheap aluminium, and three gourd-shell flasks besides his dungu-dunga, his bamboo staff, and some mandia flour to cook and eat on the way.

Whenever he came to a large village which had some Paraja families, he stopped for a day or two. He would ask the people of his tribe: Does anyone want a husband for his daughter? I can work for him as a goti in return.' And in the evenings he would peep in at the doors of young women's dormitories and, while he stood shouldering his load there, pull out his dungudunga and strum on it, announcing to everyone concerned that a new suitor was available.

But he had had no success. He did not look like a man of substance: he had no tall turban on his head and his shoulders were bare. He had to keep on walking.

When his mandia flour was all gone he worked as a labourer on somebody's land, and when he had earned enough to re-provision himself he resumed his journey.

Some fifteen days after leaving home he heard, in another village, of the two daughters of Sukru Jani. That night he slept in Sargiguda, and next morning he walked to Sarsupadar.

He asked his way to Sukru Jani's house, but when he arrived there no one was at home. He waited on the veranda outside, and presently Bili appeared. She had been working in the fields, and had come to get some food for Jili and herself.

Nandibali and Bili eyed each other closely from head to foot. He laughed and took out his dungudunga, which was hanging at the end of the bamboo sling, and twanged on it lightly with his fingertips.

'Who are you,' Bili asked, 'and what do you want?'

'I have come in search of you, my dear,' he said, 'and I am your bridegroom.'

She seemed displeased and, turning her back on him without a word, she walked into the house. Having collected her lunch, she came out again and started back to the fields. Nandibali followed her, shouting: 'Listen, my girl, are you angry?' Then he came right up to her and said: 'Shall I carry your bundle for you?' He pointed to the bamboo pole from which all his bundles were hanging and said: 'Look at the load I am carrying already – what difference will your little bundle make? Come on, give it to me! Where is your father?' And, very meaningly, he added: 'Won't you call him to me?' Bili laughed, and Nandibali struck up a Paraja tune:

Come, let us join hands
And play our games.

'Do you know,' he asked, 'how far I've walked in this rain for you?' And he opened a bundle and offered her sweets. She took them: for a girl is a girl anywhere and sweets are sweets, whether they be chocolate candies or fried-rice dipped in molasses. After this, she lost all her shyness and told him where to find her father. 'I shall come back with more sweets for you,' were Nandibali's parting words.

As Sukru Jani was working on the hilltop Nandibali came up to him and said: 'Two men are better than one. I don't have my pickaxe with me, or we could have worked side by side. But give me your axe while you rest, and you shall see how fast I can dig.' And before the astonished Sukru Jani could answer, Nandibali had removed his raincoat of palm leaves, put down his bundles, taken the pickaxe from him and started to dig the earth. The muscles on his bare body bulged as his shoulders moved in an easy rhythm. He did not look even once at Sukru Jani. The latter chewed his tobacco and smiled as he observed the young man, who seemed to grow more enormous and formidable as he continued to attack the rock with quick, vigorous blows.

Sukru Jani said: 'Yes, I can see you're really good with that axe. But let me have it back – you can't work for me all day.'

Nandibali said, without pausing in his work, 'Why not? I am your goti.' He threw the words at him casually, over his shoulder.

'What did you say?' Sukru Jani exclaimed.

Nandibali put down his axe, came close to the old man and looked him straight in the face. Then he told him who he was, about his lineage and ancestry, how he had come to find a bride and had been directed to Sukru Jani's village, how he had met Bili and chosen her for his bride, and how he planned to serve as a goti because he could not pay the bride-price. His words were direct and simple.

The old man heard everything and said: 'But shouldn't you rather have Jili for your bride? She's the elder.'

Nandibali became grave. 'I have said all that I have to say,' he answered. 'It's for you to decide. I met Bili first and liked her. I've given her my word. It must be Bili or no one.'

Sukru Jani's face was wrinkled in thought. The old man and the young one stood on the hilltop, facing each other. On one side of them lay the forest, on the other a deep valley, flanked by a line of mountains that curled and twisted away into the distance, like an endless series of heads and shoulders. And now Sukru Jani saw a smoking cloud stretching out towards him across those heads and shoulders; faster and faster it came, like a rolling sea of milk, and Sukru Jani felt the world around him shrinking and shrinking until it was a single point of thought.

He stretched out his hand, Nandibali gripped it, and they embraced. Gifts of tobacco were exchanged. Neither spoke. Nandibali picked up his axe again and went to work, while Sukru Jani sat on a boulder and watched. The floating cloud poured water over their heads and drifted away, followed by thick vapoury smoke which hid everything from view.

Chapter 73

In many tribes a younger sister may not be given in marriage before the elder, but among the Parajas there is no such restriction. Jili adjusted herself easily to the new member of the family—for though Nandibali could not formally be accepted as Bili's husband until he had paid the bride-price he became a part of the household, and at night he slept beside the old man. Whenever he was asked, he introduced himself as the new goti, but when Bili and he met, at the dance or elsewhere, they were like any other girl and her lover, totally spontaneous in their behaviour. As for Jili, she was the favourite sister-in-law, with whom he could joke and laugh as though she was an equal.

Jili paid him back with interest for all his pranks, but her jokes and gaiety were only a front. In reality she felt withdrawn from everything. Her heart overflowed with tenderness for Bili, for they had come very close during those days of loneliness and neglect; but often she found herself unable to speak to Bili, even about things which were of interest to both of them, such as Kau Paraja or Kajodi and Bagla. When they sat together now, she merely listened, or let her thoughts wander, while Bili talked.

And though Jili still dressed her sister's hair lovingly and adorned it with flowers, it seemed as if she had lost all interest in her own appearance. If Bili urged her to dress up for the dance, she usually found some excuse for not doing so.

Sukru Jani and Nandibali worked away as though they had worked together all their lives. Nandibali was invaluable: he repaired the house all by himself, cleared and fenced in a patch of ground near the house, where vegetables were planted and were soon growing profusely, and helped Sukru Jani to work for the Kondhs, so that they, in return, came and ploughed Sukru Jani's new land on the mountain. And soon Sukru Jani's plot of land had grown, until it stretched from the higher slopes to the foot of the mountain. And the harder they worked, the more their appetite for work grew – and so did the fantasies which they wove around the land. They worked and talked and dreamed, and the days were always too short for them.

Chapter 74

Most of the farmers had begun sowing, and some were transplanting the seedlings of rice. But Sukru Jani's land still lay fallow. Then one day the Sahukar arrived, accompanied by three of his gotis and a swarm of other labourers who carried his belongings slung from bamboo poles. The Sahukar's bag of money swung at his waist for everyone to see. A handsome tip to the headman secured him the

exclusive use of the young men's dormitory. He hired bullocks, and his gotis ploughed Sukru Jani's land. The Sahukar was eager to extend his possessions, and he went about
the village asking: 'Does anyone have any land for sale?'
No one was particularly interested in the Sahukar's proposal, however, for there was plenty of work in the fields
and no one needed his money now. The Sahukar would go
out of his way to talk to the young girls, staring at them
and calling them by the names which only their
sweethearts used: 'Sweet Spring Rice!' or 'Sweet Spring
Flower!' When he met the elders of the village he twirled
his moustache and said importantly: 'I have taken some
land in this village on mortgage and I intend to have an
orchard. I shall set up my warehouse here and give loans of
paddy and mandia to the villagers to help them in their
need. And I shall also give them loans and engage many
labourers. I shall lay roads inside the village and ask my
labourers to dig a tank so that there will be enough drinking water for everybody. You will see how I change the
face of the village.'

When the evening grew dark, the Sahukar walked up to
the young women's dormitory and squatted on the ground
in front of it, with four or five of the villagers to keep him
company. There was a light drizzle and a distant rumbling
of thunder. Presently the Sahukar began an oration. First,
he spoke of himself: of his wealth and possessions, his
power and his influence with the officials, through whom
he could get anything he wanted, get anyone punished or
released from jail. Then he spoke of his high ideals and his
deep love for his fellow men. He told them how kind and
merciful he was to his labourers, how gentle and unselfish,
and how pious. He told them how little he cared for

money; he told them of gotis who had died before they
could repay a single penny of their loans and whose children had been released from debt and helped in rehabilitat-
ing themselves. He named persons and villages that no one
had heard of before, and nobody could disbelieve him. He
smoked one cheroot after another as he chattered on and
the people sitting near him joined in the conversation. He
could see the lantern burning dimly inside the young
women's dormitory and a group of young girls slowly
moving forward, arms linked together, attracted by his
talk. As they drew nearer he could hear them giggling or
whispering, see them nudging each other with their
elbows. From time to time they would break into sudden
laughter—which made the Sahukar pause in the middle of
a sentence and cast a swift glance into the dimly lighted
room, the roots of his hair tingling with a strange sensa-
tion. He strained his ears to hear what they were saying.

As the night advanced, some of the people sitting near
the Sahukar rose and moved away. At this point the Sahukar addressed himself to the girls and said: 'How about a
dance and some songs, my dears?' The only reply was a
peal of laughter; and somebody said from inside the room,
'How can we dance when there is no one to play on the
dungudunga?' To which the Sahukar replied: 'Well, begin
your dance and I shall find a young man to play for you.'
The dark night grew heavy with clouds and the pattering
of the rain alternated with the croaking of frogs. There
were some exchanges, and then the Sahukar said in a
hoarse voice: 'Girls, if you need anything, let me know.
You can have anything you like—clothes, ornaments,
sweets, anything. I only want to see you happy.'

In his excitement he got up and took a few steps towards

the door of the young women's dormitory. The young women giggled and scampered away into the room, chattering excitedly, like a flock of birds suddenly taking off together in alarm.

Isak, the nephew of the village Barik, and Madhu, a young man of the caste, who were among the Sahukar's companions, said to him: 'Let us go to your hut. It is getting late, Sahukar.' The Sahukar heaved a sigh and rose reluctantly to his feet.

The night was intensely dark: not a single star could be seen. Hundreds of fireflies glowed among the trees, so that they stood out against the darkness. Everything else— houses, hills, the sky, the forest—was lost to sight. Sometimes a gust of wind would come roaring through the drizzle of rain, chilling one to the marrow. As they walked, the Sahukar suddenly felt very lonely; he tried to recall the excitements of a life full of pleasure and triumphs, but could remember nothing. All he could feel was frustration; he had nothing and he must have more of everything, more girls, more land and more gotis.

Isak left him at the entrance to the young men's dormitory and went home, but the Sahukar asked Madhu Ghasi to stay. He was a sturdy young man with thick lips and pink eyes, and at eighteeen he was already a hardened criminal.

The Sahukar lit a match in the darkness, pulled out a bottle of liquor and gulped the fiery liquid down. Madhu Ghasi sat outside the door sniffing the fumes of liquor. The Sahukar lit a cigar and came closer to Madhu Ghasi.

'What a dismal night it is!' he said. 'Everything is so sad! I wish there was someone here to talk to. Could you help me, Madhu? There's a rupee for you!'

'Why, that's easy!' Madhu Ghasi replied. 'I wish you'd told me earlier. It's not possible to find anyone in this village but there are other villages. There are beautiful Pali girls in Bhitar Garh not far from here. It's rather late now and everyone must be fast asleep, but give me the money and I'll see what I can do.'

The Sahukar lay down to sleep, but no sleep came. He tossed from side to side, fidgeting impatiently. He pictured to himself some delightful experience that was about to be-fall him, but as each moment passed he gradually lost hope. He lay still, listening to the sound of the rain and growing more and more restless. At last he thought he could hear knocking, whispering, and the sound of a giggle. Trembling like a palm leaf in the wind, he ran quickly to the door, flung it open and stood there waiting expectantly. But there was no one there. While he stood and waited, even the slow pattering of the rain stopped. Suddenly, the night was cracked open by repeated flashes of lightning. He came back into the room and threw himself on the bed. Again he strained his ears, for sleep would not come to him. Several times more he got up and went outside and came back again, until at last sleep overpowered him.

The next morning Madhu Ghasi met him near the young men's dormitory. He had his excuse ready. 'I was walking half the night for your sake. *And* I hurt my foot, stumbling in the dark. Look!' He raised his foot close to the Sahukar's face for him to see and continued: 'I searched everywhere—never mind about your foot, I said to my-self. I went to the street where the Dombs live, and I went to the Parajas, and I asked any number of girls but not one of them was willing. Then I remembered a young girl in Kalar village. She's newly married, but her husband is lame and he drinks, so I went to her and asked her to come with me. At first she wouldn't, but I pressed her and she agreed. But she said, "Give me a rupee now and another rupee later." I had to agree. She went inside to get dressed and I waited outside for her in the rain. Then, just as she was coming out, her husband woke up and shouted at me. He's a foul-tempered man, so she slipped out quickly and told me, "I can't come tonight but I'll come tomorrow"; then she ran back into the house and I had to come back alone. But I didn't like to disturb you in your sleep and so here I am.'

The Sahukar heard the story. He did not believe a word of it but there was no use complaining. He only said: 'Well, see that nothing goes wrong tonight.'

Madhu Ghasi promised that nothing would, but before leaving the Sahukar he said: 'This has been a lot of work for me. Can't I have another rupee?'

The Sahukar answered: 'Later—after tonight.'

Chapter 75

All day the moneylender was busy looking after the land he had taken from Sukru Jani. Sometimes he would meet other people who owned land and attempt to persuade them to entrust it to him. He would say, for example: 'I hear you have a grown-up son and haven't found a wife for him yet; what's the matter? Is it because you have no money to pay the bride-price? How much money do you need? I can give you a loan on your land.' But he also found time to speak to the unmarried girls as they went about their work in the village. In particular, he haunted the path leading to the pool where they went to fetch water, and the places where they used to go to gather grass for the cattle. He would sigh and look longingly at them and offer them money to buy clothes and whatever else they wanted; and sometimes a girl would smile back encouragingly and he would follow her for a long distance.

The villagers saw all this, but regarded it with indifference. In their society an unmarried girl was free to talk to anyone she liked and to choose her own friends. The village was like the Sahukar's second home and no one questioned his movements.

And sometimes at night, when the rain was pouring down, Madhu Ghasi would steal into his room with a woman in tow. On these occasions the doubtful pleasures of the night were invariably succeeded by the smouldering dissatisfactions of the morning, when the Sahukar's anger would rise up against Madhu Ghasi. He would get up, bathe in the women's pool—how was he, a stranger, to know there was a separate pool for men?—and while he bathed, reciting the holy mantras, his eyes would rove over the bathing women and he would curse Madhu Ghasi for his lack of taste and enterprise.

His bath over, he rose from the pool and went to his quarters in the village, where, watched by the villagers, he anointed his body with sandalwood paste like a holy sadhu. Then he produced a little prayer-bell which tinkled merrily while he said his prayers, and the children gathered round him looking on curiously. He plugged one nostril with his finger, breathing through the other, and after he had drawn five long breaths he closed the other nostril, practising the yoga which Garaja Sundara, the Revenue Inspector, had taught him; and he twisted his fingers in strange gestures and rolled his eyeballs upwards and downwards repeatedly, making peculiar grimaces. Then he shut his eyes and tried to see within the darkness of his own being the spark of light which his guru had told him to expect, and on which he was to concentrate until it took the form of a god; but all he could see was the scene at the bathing-pool. The ceremony over, he opened his eyes and picked up the ripe banana which he had kept on the floor as an offering to his god. Ants had already begun to swarm on it and he threw it disdainfully to the children. The children fought for the prize, shouted and went away. Then he thrust out his hand towards the god, holding in it, as a devotional offering, a pipe full of ganja; the next moment he withdrew it and puffed greedily at the pipe; and as he went on puffing and belching out smoke, strange thoughts raced through his brain.

Chapter 76

The colour of the sunlight changed constantly: from ashy-grey to a sickly pea-green, back to grey again and then to blue, while all the time great clouds went floating across the sky. These clouds had white and reddish streaks at the edges and were flecked with bands of every conceivable colour. It was as if someone had set to work with brush and paint and then forgotten himself, so that all his fantasies had found expression in a variety of forms, strange and familiar. In places where his brush had lingered while he was lost in thought there were dabs of black; elsewhere the sky was grey with the seething rain which looked like smoke in the distance. Sometimes the scene was of unrelieved blackness, harsh and forbidding. But it was never still; it was perpetually breaking up and re-forming. From time to time, the sun peeped briefly through the gashes in the clouds, its face strangely grey; in those moments a soft melancholy light played over the panorama below. The rain-water eddied over the paddy fields, while every hill was laced with silver threads – rivulets which had once been footpaths. Sunken roads had likewise turned into rushing yellow torrents. Water was everywhere. Mountain streams roared as if vying with the thunder. Lower down, kadamba trees stood shivering on the brink, gazing nervously at the reflections of their newly opened blossoms, which looked like human heads with the hairs standing erect. Suddenly, there came a sound from the stream as of water boiling, and patches of foam appeared; these were the signs of the approaching flood – a swirling chaos of water, uprooted trees, and the bodies of animals that had been taken unawares.

The sun, looking more dead than alive, brooded over the scene. Then it set; the last rays found their way through chinks in the clouds, and the coloured shafts turned the muddy water into a burning flame. The red light faded and grew faint, playing on one side of the hills, while the other was in darkness, turning them into dabs of green and red mixed together. There were also patches of black: trees and boulders transformed by the uncertain light into the weird shapes of wild animals.

Peacocks screamed as they settled for the night in the branches of great trees. Black and white ducks, their long necks laid side by side and wings spread out close to each other, flew across the sky in continuous formation. A hush spread over the land as the sounds of the rain grew fainter and fainter. Suddenly, the giant kullu ducks which stalked the paddy fields sent out a loud and piteous wail. And from the hilltop, at intervals regular as clockwork, came the cry of barking-deer, as the light faded and another day moved to its close.

In the gathering darkness, smoke from the various houses merged and rolled in waves over the thatched roofs and the patches of garden. A mist rose from the flooded paddy fields and spread over the village and its surroundings. Gradually the night closed in from all sides, swallowing up one object after another. The fires in the village died out. Valleys, mountains and sky were buried beneath the sooty darkness, and the air was heavy with the feeling of desolation.

Chapter 77

Tikra tended one of the Sahukar's herds of buffalo. There were several hundred animals in each herd, and they were left deep in the jungle to graze, with one or more gotis in charge. Some of the grazing-grounds were marked by little huts of mud and grass which the herdsmen had put up.

They were scattered through the jungle, far from any other human habitation, and most of the time they were unoccupied. The doors, of slivered bamboo, stood wide open; inside, there might be large earthen jars full of milk or curd, dangling from the ceiling, or a few utensils for the herdsman's use, or some of the heavy metal bells which were hung round the necks of the buffaloes.

Each herdsman carried an enormous palm-leaf umbrella as a parasol, with the handle cunningly hooked round the left shoulder and tied fast so that the hands were left free—and there was plenty for them to do. Across one shoulder was balanced a staff from which were slung assorted bundles and gourd-shells full of mandia gruel; the other shoulder supported the herdsman's axe, from which hung two large buffalo horns. When he blew on these horns the buffaloes came running for the lumps of salt which they had been trained to expect at this signal.

The herdsman was a quaint sight in his huge turban, more like a canopy, but still quite overshadowed by the parasol, with the buffaloes prancing behind. He knew each buffalo by sight: by the number of whorls on the back, or by such distinguishing marks as a branded flank or a clipped tail or a notched horn. And as the buffaloes milled around him, waiting for their lumps of salt, he checked on their number, counting always in scores, for he had never learned to count beyond twenty. As soon as they had had their lick of salt, the buffaloes scattered again; some strayed into the jungle, others wallowed in the mud of some shallow river-bed, but the herdsman never lost track of them.

When evening overtook the herdsman, he would blow his horn and round up his herd; then he would gather some brushwood and light a fire, beside which he would plant

his umbrella and stretch himself out for the night. The fire
would smoulder while the herdsman and his herd slept
under a thick, living blanket of mosquitoes. The man
would occasionally stir in his sleep and hit out at the blood-
thirsty insects.

Chapter 78

The jungle, which had been sparse and bald in summer,
now grew lush with the rain. There were varieties of wild
grass, some of them six feet tall, which the tribesmen used
to thatch their houses. The bushes and weeds grew so high
and dense that travellers walking along the paths could get
completely lost among them. Trees, vines and bushes were
matted together so thickly that in some places no sunlight
could filter through. The rain produced a tremendous
howling noise, and long after a shower was over, drops as
big as plums dripped from the living leaves down on to the
dead ones lying on the forest floor, drowning the foot falls
of wild animals, so that it was difficult to track them as
they moved through the dim forest. The herdsman had to
clear a path through the jungle with axe. Thorny clusters,
flowers and creepers hung down from the trees and
swayed from side to side, scratching and tearing the skin
off his back and limbs.

As he moved through the jungle, the herdsman was constantly on his guard against roving tigers. Their pugmarks
in the mud were frequent, and the narrow passes were dot-

ted with heaps of their dung, some of which were quite fresh. Sometimes the herdsman could even smell the tiger, and hear the sound of its movement through the bushes along the bank of the ravine. When the mountain paths were covered with mist the herdsman grew apprehensive, for man-eating tigers were known to creep up on their prey under cover of the mist. Whenever the sky was cloudy and there was a light breeze the tribesmen said it was 'tiger weather' and never moved out of their houses. It was said that in such weather the man-eater grew ravenously hungry and was filled with a mad urge to dance in the jungle with its tail in the air. If it saw travellers in the jungle at such a time, it would charge them even if there were twenty men in a group; it would attack them even during daytime and carry one of them off. The unfortunate victim would be eaten up within a few hours, and the tiger, intoxicated with its feast, would lie down to sleep beside some stream. It would rest for a day and then make another kill in some other village. It would prowl through the jungle all day, and lie crouched by the side of the road as evening fell, and as night grew it would move to the outskirts of some village. It could easily cover thirty miles in a single night.

In some villages ten or fifteen people were killed in a single year and the surviving inhabitants moved away in terror, leaving the village deserted. The traveller might find a few houses still standing, with their orchards of fruit trees, but the jungle would have invaded the neighbouring fields which had once been farmland, and be creeping up on the abandoned village. Several of these villages had the word *bagh* (tiger) affixed to their names, to mark the ravages of some man-eater. As the rains begin each year the man-eaters become active, and until the coming of spring there is no safety in the jungle.

But the goti had to tend his herds even in the worst tiger weather. There was no escape for him; and if a single buffalo was missing from the herd the money-lender would recover its price by making him work longer without payment. It was easier to face the man-eater.

Tikra had another goti to keep him company in the forest, a wizened old man named Milku Paraja, who had grown deaf and slightly lame. He had no wife or children, yet he was always afraid the tiger would carry him off. He would cajole Tikra into leaving him behind in some village while he went out alone into the jungle with the herd.

As a rule, Tikra took comfort from the thought that no tiger would dare to come near a herd of buffalo, but sometimes the buffaloes caught the scent of the tiger and then they would crowd together into a solid wall and the bulls would stand on guard, their nostrils distended, ears sloping, heads bent and horns pointing straight ahead, ready for action. Tikra would stand in the middle of the herd, waiting in suspense. The buffaloes would stay huddled together until the scent of the tiger disappeared, when they would again move out to graze. On these occasions Tikra felt nervous even after the danger had passed. He would stay close to the buffaloes and speak to them in a soothing voice; sometimes he would ride on the back of one and stroke its head affectionately.

Occasionally he would catch hold of a hanging creeper and swing himself up in the air. There was a kind of creeper known as the guluchi, which lay coiled around the trees like a great net. Its tendrils hung in the air like thick ropes.

Tikra would catch hold of one of these strands of guluchi
and swing himself forward as far as he could go, then catch
hold of another tendril and swing from that in turn, so that
he travelled for quite a distance without his feet touching
the ground. But sometimes he thought he saw a fluttering
movement among the dense leaves of some creeper, and
then he would go cold with fear of the unknown danger
lurking among those leaves. When he walked with his herd
in the jungle he sniffed the air to catch the scent of wild
animals, scanned every bush for signs of movement, and
strained his ears to catch the slightest sound. If he had any
suspicion of danger he would raise his axe and blow on his
horn until the entire herd surrounded him, and he felt
afraid no more.

He remembered stories of men who had been carried off
by tigers: the headman who had vanished near the Black
Ravine; the jhodi tree near Mahul Kana where a tiger had
carried off two people in rapid succession; and, of course,
the fate of his own mother, Sombari. The memories of
these incidents made him shudder, and in cloudy weather
the image of a tiger pouncing on a man was never far from
his mind.

Tikra had to milk the buffaloes and make curds out of
the milk. He worked hard and honestly, but the Sahukar
always suspected him and frequently called him a thief.

At times, the forest would suddenly grow black with the
clouds overhead and the rain would come down in torrents. The brushwood would soon become much too wet
to burn; and Tikra and Milku Paraja, drenched to the skin,
could not even light a fire to dry themselves. Milku Paraja
would cough all night, and Tikra would get no sleep. On
these dark, rainy nights fear could assume a thousand

shapes. Sometimes Tikra would see a solitary light in the distance and would wonder if it was a goddess of the jungle or an evil spirit, or merely the glowing eyes of a tiger. At other times, a strange wailing would come to their ears, and Milku Paraja would crowd closer to him and whisper: 'Do you hear that? It's a tiger-spirit!' And Tikra would find himself sweating.

There were times when Tikra lay thinking of the happy life he had enjoyed at home, and feeling that somehow it was the buffaloes who were to blame for all his troubles. 'What silly fools these creatures are,' he would say to himself. 'Why can't they graze near the village? Why must they make me run after them through the endless jungle, where tigers are thick as mosquitoes?'

Next, his anger would shift to the Sahukar and a string of curses would follow. How the Sahukar made him work! What a cruel face he had! The Sahukar's eyes seemed all the time to be saying: 'You're only my slave, bound to me for ever and for ever; you can never be free!' And then Tikra would feel happy that he was in the jungle, where the Sahukar could not follow him. He need not look at those glowing eyes or that puffed face, more like a monkey's than that of a human being; those bristling, pointed whiskers which seemed to pierce him like needles; those thick, blubbery lips. Life in the jungle had its joys: the birds chirped in the trees, the peacocks grazed, undisturbed by his presence; a she-bear shuffled through the bushes, a wild goat bounded from rock to rock. Spotted deer peeped shyly from the cover of bushes and quickly disappeared. Jungle fowl played in the undergrowth, and herds of wild boars looked for roots in the mud on the river banks. Chameleons nodded gravely at him from the trees and he could watch the changing of their colours. Flying squirrels with their little black and white and chocolate bodies jumped from tree to tree.

There were rich perfumes in the damp jungle, and amusements in plenty. Tikra could leap over waterfalls, chase monkeys, pluck the beans of the siali creeper, roast and eat them, blow experimental combinations of notes on his horns and lie on the back of some buffalo as it slowly bore him through the shade of the trees. Sometimes, when he met a young girl in the forest, he would sing love songs and pursue her, half playfully and half in earnest.

Sometimes he was obliged to halt in a village which was unfamiliar to him. He would spend the night in the dormitory singing and dancing with the other young people, and the next morning the herd would lead him on to new places. All in all, it was a happy life; but he could not quite shake off the shadow of the Sahukar, which brooded over him like an evil thing, giving him no rest.

Chapter 79

Mandia and Tikra shared a room in the row of huts where the gotis lived. It was more like a cattle-shed. The grass thatch, unchanged for years, had rotted; in addition, it crawled with snakes which had nested there. The cracks in the mud walls swarmed with scorpions; white ants had built huge nests, and weeds and fungi grew luxuriantly. The gotis had no time to clean or repair their huts, for the

Sahukar kept them constantly busy. And if someone complained to the Sahukar about the huts, he laughed and said:
'Am I expected to build palaces for my gotis?'

The seedlings of rice in the Sahukar's fields were about a
foot high. Some of the fields were covered with knee-deep
water, and the gotis had to ensure that the water could
flow everywhere without obstruction. The uneven fields
had been cut into terraces, and the ridges between them
looked like the steps of a ladder.

To protect the young plants from cattle, the fields had to
be fenced all round with thorny branches which the gotis
had to fetch, together with firewood, from the jungle. It
was a risky business, for wild animals prowled through the
forest in the afternoon.

The Sahukar could never bear to see a man idle: if there
was no other work he would send him away on some un-
important errand to a distant village. Every evening he
would check to see how much work had been done, and if
he was not satisfied the gotis would be abused and
threatened with reduced rations. And after his long stay in
Sukru Jani's village he was particularly anxious to make up
for the time he felt sure had been wasted in his absence. So
now there was more work for the gotis than ever before.

One day while Mandia and Tikra were returning from
work they saw a man running towards the Sahukar's
house, crying pitifully as he went. It was Dasru Paraja,
another goti who had been told to look after the herd of
buffalo in the Kendu Adora forest. They followed him.
The Sahukar was sitting on the veranda and the man stopped in front of him.

'I am killed, Sahukar!' he wailed. 'The tiger has carried
off my brother Sania. We were tending your herds in the

jungle when it rushed at us and carried him away.' He was shaking all over and could barely give them the details. He rolled in the dust, his body convulsed with sobs.

The money-lender jumped down from his veranda into the yard. 'What!' he shouted. 'Is he gone? And my money with him? Now stop that, you idiot'—Dasru Paraja had started hysterically recounting the virtues of his dead brother—'and tell me what's going to happen to my money? Never mind about your brother—I must have my money back. You must repay your brother's debt, or I shall take you to court and have your lands and your oxen sold.'

'Sahukar, it was *you* that sent my poor brother to the forest,' said Dasru Paraja. 'Can you give him back to me?'

The Sahukar flew into a rage. 'You rogue!' he cried. 'How dare you speak to me like that! I shall have you beaten with shoes. Did I set the tiger on your brother? If you don't like working for me you can pay up your debts or you can go to hell. Meanwhile you'd better go to the police station and report your brother's death to the Sub-Inspector, or you'll be in trouble.'

Dasru Paraja went away weeping bitterly. The money-lender continued for some time cursing poor Sania Paraja, who had managed to escape his clutches. Then he ordered Tikra to go next day to the Kendu Adora forest and take charge of the herd which the dead man had been tending.

Tikra and Mandia protested, but the money-lender said: 'You'll have to go. If you refuse, others will also refuse. I cannot allow all my buffaloes to be killed. If you don't want to obey me you can repay my debt with principal and interest and go home.'

Mandia said to the Sahukar: 'Very well, then *I* shall go

and not Tikra. But I must have five or six other people to keep me company. I cannot go alone!'

There was a fierce argument. The Sahukar shouted and cursed but Mandia Jani held firm. A crowd of people collected and finally the Sahukar had to yield. Some of the other gotis said to Mandia: 'It is not wise to argue with the Sahukar. He may be forced to give in now, but he will only create more trouble for you in the future.'

Mandia Jani waved his arms and said: 'What do I care? What more can he do to me than he has already done?' At that moment some of the old fire seemed to burn in him still. But much of his spirit had been crushed by the life of a debt-bound slave, and he went about his duties with bowed head and downcast eyes, obsessed with his own suffering.

Chapter 80

That night Mandia and Tikra lay awake in their hut for a long time, and all they could talk about was tigers. As they talked they seemed to hear the roar of tigers all round them – now like distant thunder, now like an infant's plaintive cry. They talked of the way the tiger's eyes gleamed in the night – like two green stars set close together; and as one continued to stare at them it seemed as if doors were opening, and beyond them lay twin caves of fire, and the closer one went the deeper those caves became. It was said that the tiger could make its body grow or shrink at will; as it lay in wait beneath some bush, it could camouflage itself as a striped blanket spread out on the ground, or it could swell up to the size of a large buffalo. How beautiful it looked sprinting through the jungle like a playful kitten, its belly rocking and almost grazing the ground, and the striped body shining as if glazed with wax! But seen from the rear, didn't it look more like a gigantic monkey? As for the way a tiger attacked a man – rushing at him like a whirlwind, sending him flying with one blow, picking him up and holding him in the crook of one foreleg, squeezing him against its ribs; carrying him off to a distance before puncturing his neck and drinking his blood. And if the victim was a woman she would be raped first! Mandia knew of a woman in Kutinga village, the wife of Kodru Kondh, who had been mauled sexually but had managed to drag herself away, and the tiger had been scared off by the shouting of the villagers. It just went to prove that if you were fated to live nothing could harm you, not even a tiger. What about Dihudu Saonta, the Kondh headman of Toyaput? The tiger had carried him off as a cat carries a mouse, but suddenly he came to his senses and gave the tiger such a blow with the crowbar which was still in his hand that it dropped him and ran. And then there was Muska Kondh, of Thotaguda: the tiger had sprung at him barely a hundred yards from his own hut, but he had a long spear in his hand and just managed to thrust the end of it into the beast's mouth; the tiger had bitten so hard on the iron spear-head that it still bore the tooth marks, but Muska had got away! It was strange, wasn't it, that tigers seemed to have a weakness for Kondhs, but seldom attacked a Paraja? The reason was, of course, that the Kondhs were eaters of monkeys, which made Kondh flesh

particularly toothsome; whereas the Parajas were snake-
eaters, and the tigers knew better than to eat *them*! So Man-
dia and Tikra were safe, really. At last Mandia fell asleep and began to snore, followed a
little later by Tikra. Tikra had a dream: a thick jungle, in
which there were two hills separated by a ravine, thickly
matted with scrub; and a single sal tree growing on one of
the slopes. And there he sat, Tikra, among the highest
branches, and Mandia was beside him with his ancient
muzzle-loader – waiting for the man-eater. At the foot of
the tree lay the mangled corpse of some victim, pegged
down to the ground and secured with strands of siali. The
dead man lay in a patch of faint moonlight, but everything
else seemed dark. Tikra's heartbeats sounded like drums.
Suddenly the man-eater appeared, dancing; and it was as
big as a buffalo! It sniffed at the corpse and licked it, and
the corpse raised one arm and pointed straight to the spot
where Mandia and Tikra sat hidden. The tiger looked up,
and its eyes burnt through Tikra like red-hot coals. He
broke into a sweat, and felt as though he were being
choked. Then the tiger turned to the corpse again; it gripped an arm between its teeth and wrenched it off with a
sickening crunch. It darted off to a distance, prancing
happily, chewed up the morsel, opened its mouth wide
and laughed, its teeth gleaming white in the moonlight.
Then it bounded back to the corpse, and kicked at it so that
the strong ropes of siali which tied it to the ground snapped like string. The tiger licked the corpse all over, sniffed
at it and caressed it with velvet paws, moaning softly as if
it were coaxing and pleading. Then it bit off more mouth-
fuls with horrible tearing sounds, tossed the pieces into the
air and caught them again as they fell, rolled the corpse

over, licked its lips and beat the ground with its tail. Throughout this performance, it was growing bigger and bigger, until Tikra, terrified, rolled off the branch and fell – down, down through unending space, never touching ground, falling and falling until he woke up.

Chapter 81

The earth was one expanse of green, which covered the jungle and the fields of rice in equal measure.

As the rice plants, now waist-high, touched one's body they had an extraordinarily soothing effect on the mind, straightening out whatever had been warped and twisted, and making one look forward eagerly to what lay ahead. The fragrance of the rice fields was as heady as the first puff from a cheroot. As for the hill slopes, the various pulses, gourds, pumpkins and cucumbers grew so luxuriantly that anyone walking through the fields was frequently caught, as if the creepers were unwilling to let him go.

When Sukru Jani saw the crops bursting forth out of his newly prepared fields, all regret for the old lands was forgotten. He and Nandibali would pick up their crowbars and spades at the end of a day's work and turn to look at their fields and their vegetable garden. No matter how hard they worked, there always seemed to be something more to be done: some gourd creeper trailing pitifully on the ground because it had no proper support on which to lean, some plant needing more earth around its roots, patches of shrub to be cut or cleared, some destructive insect which had gone into hiding under the leaves and could not be found in the dark – it would have to be rooted out in the morning. From every hilltop came the sound of young Kondh boys and girls singing and answering each other in song; and sometimes Nandibali would join them. But Sukru Jani would look on in silence, puffing at his cheroot, and thinking only of the work which still remained to be done.

As he gazed at his lands he felt like a brother to the forest and the crops, for, like them, he was born of the earth and belonged to it. But, at the same time, he could not help hearing sounds from another, distant world which threatened to snatch him away. Against this other influence he struggled hard, clutching at all the beauty around him, unwilling to let it go, continually finding something new in familiar scenes.

There was, for example, the hour just before sunset when solitary trees stood silhouetted against the fading light as if lost in a dream. On either side, a tangled chain of hills stretched away into the distance, those nearest to him sharply etched and glowing with a wealth of varied colour, while further away the details were lost in the darkness.

Below him lay the thatched houses of Sarsupadar, the thorny bushes that encircled them looking blue in the distance. On the slope above the houses, peaceful-looking paddy fields competed for a foothold with patches of wild banana – some lost in shadow while in others the broad leaves flickered in the last play of light. Here and there stood a solitary banyan tree, dark, domineering and proud; or a mahua, whose pendant branches looked like long tapering fingers with shining nails.

Gradually the shadows grew darker and the scene was blacked out. It was time for Sukru Jani and Nandibali to return home.

With the coming of darkness the old man grew sad and lonely. He would sit brooding – he could feel his days coming to a close, and as yet he had accomplished nothing for the children. His sons were still in bondage and he did not know when they would be free. They were also still unmarried. If he should die now, his spirit would never find rest, for it is the hope of every Paraja to be born again as the child of one of his own sons, so that he may live with his children again and share their joys and sorrows. Then he remembered his dead wife Sombari – and consoled himself with the thought that perhaps she was waiting for him somewhere, so that he would never be lonely.

Chapter 82

The Sahukar returned to Sarsupadar with his ploughmen and his oxen. It was high noon. The girls from the village were going down to the pool to wash; most of them were chewing on little twigs from the trees, which served as toothbrushes.

Madhu Ghasi heard of the Sahukar's arrival and went out to welcome him. There were whispered consultations: the Sahukar would point at various people and Madhu Ghasi would brief him about them. When girls passed by, the two men made a pretence of indifference, but followed

them with greedy eyes; then there were more questions
from the Sahukar which Madhu Ghasi had to answer.

No one could say just what took place between them,
but presently Madhu held out a palm and the Sahukar
dropped a rupee into it, not without some reluctance. A
moment later Jili came down the path. Madhu nudged the
Sahukar to signal that here was something which deserved
close scrutiny – and the Sahukar gazed at her admiringly.
As she advanced Jili called out: 'Is that you, Madhu?'

'Yes,' he shouted back. 'Will you come here for a minute, Jili?'

'No, I can't,' she replied, 'It's getting late.'

She walked away, chewing on her twig, but once or
twice she turned round to look at them; and each time she
did so, the money-lender raised his hand, with the thick
bracelet of gold around his wrist, and beckoned her to
come. His mouth opened as if he was about to call to her,
but no sound escaped his lips.

'You'll never get her to come just by waving your hand,
Sahukar,' Madhu Ghasi told him. 'She wants fine clothes,
and perfumed soap and oil, and maybe a garland of flowers
and some money.'

'Well,' said the Sahukar, 'have I ever said no?'

'Ah, but this one is special,' Madhu replied. 'So she has a
higher price.'

The Sahukar did not speak, but his mind was hard at
work. With deliberate insolence, Madhu broke in on his
thoughts: 'You need a new woman every day, don't you,
Sahukar? But it's risky, you know; you might catch something that you'd regret. One can't be too careful. Why
don't you pick a few nice ones and stick to them?'

No one had ever spoken like this to the Sahukar, and he

felt his anger rising. Controlling himself, he whispered to
Madhu, almost pleadingly: 'Oh, Madhu, I know I can
count on you. Don't let me down.'

The rain had stopped and he went to the young men's
dormitory, which had again been reserved for his use. His
servants had to fend for themselves.

At dawn next morning he took his gotis to Sukru Jani's
fields and the ploughing began. There was much work to
be done and his men were kept busy. The sun rose higher
through the clouds. Presently Sukru Jani and Nandibali
appeared.

Sukru Jani was effusive. 'Greetings, Sahukar;' he
shouted. 'So you are ploughing the land? Didn't I say it
was beautiful soil? See how easy it is to plough.'

'Anything is easy if you have the money,' replied the
Sahukar.

But Sukru Jani continued: 'Are you going to sow rice
here? What kind of rice do you plan to have? Oh well, any
kind will grow on this land, it's so rich. Here's where I
grew paddy. And on the other side I used to grow mandia.
Olsi there. And there, red gram. Is that how you plan to
do it, or have you something else in mind?'

He rambled on; from time to time the Sahukar would
interpose a caustic comment. Nandibali grew restless.
'Shall we go now?' he asked. 'Yes, yes,' Sukru Jani said, 'in
a minute. Let me just give them a few tips. It's important
to select the right crop for each part of the land, or else everything will go wrong and the soil will be ruined. What
does the Sahukar know about this? And what does he care?
It's my land after all, and it's I who'll suffer if the soil is
ruined.'

The Sahukar heard this and said 'Yes, it's your land, so

you ought to know best how to plough it. Why don't you come and give us a demonstration?' The idea seemed to amuse him. 'Yes, come and plough,' he went on, roaring with laughter. 'I'll pay you wages; take that load off your shoulder and start ploughing.'

Nandibali dragged the old man away, saying, 'We must go. There's much to be done.' As they went they heard the Sahukar shouting after them: 'Silly old fool; only the other day he was my slave, and look at him now – standing there preaching at me instead of doing as he's told; Paraja dog. And look at that household pet, his son-in-law; strutting around like a turkey – who does he think he is?'

Nandibali said to the old man: 'You mustn't go near your old lands again.'

'Why not?' he demanded, furious.

Nandibali answered him with a proverb: 'What a man spits out, he cannot lick up again.'

'What do you mean?' Sukru Jani shouted. 'I haven't sold my land.'

'That makes no difference. It's his land until you can re-deem it. If you go there again, he'll only insult you again.'

Sukru Jani felt the truth of this, and fell silent. 'Yes,' he thought, 'I am nobody there now. An outsider.' His be-loved land was being ravished by an alien, and if he so much as looked at it he would be abused, perhaps kicked. He hung his head and walked with halting steps, his eyes staring fixedly at the end of his nose as if at the pain which was seated there.

But the south wind laid soft hands on him and the sha-dow lifted. Yes, better times would come – he could wait. Jili would fetch him such a price that all his debts would be paid, his land redeemed and his sons released. He drew a deep breath. But what bitterness; to have to pass by one's own land, in which the history of generations lay buried, without being able to look at it; he had betrayed himself, been false to the Earth. It would never forgive him. He could see his ancestors rising up from beneath the memorial stones and pointing at him, accusing him. He burnt in shame.

What if the Sahukar did not agree to give him back the land, even when the debt was paid? The thought was torture. But surely, such a thing was inconceivable. Besides, was it not better to let the Sahukar plough his land than to keep it fallow? And even his sons had wanted this. But Sombari? Would she have approved? Had he not bartered away the Earth from selfish motives, just to escape from his debt-bound slavery? Yes, his ancestors were right to condemn him.

As Sukru Jani stood on his new land, buried up to his chest in the rippling rice plants, visions of his own helplessness continued to visit him. There was the Sahukar, tearing at his land with his talons while he stood by and watched. The Sahukar's plough seemed to be carving up his own flesh. It was more than he could bear. Sukru Jani realized that his endurance of the injustices – which he had represented to himself as magnanimity towards his tormentor – was nothing but weakness.

One day, Bili took Nandibali aside and said: 'Have you noticed, father is becoming thinner every day and eating less and less? I'm worried; are you making the old man work too hard?'

'No,' answered Nandibali. 'I try not to let him work too much; most of the time he is hardly doing any work in the

field, he merely stands with his hoe on his shoulder staring
at something straight ahead – I don't know what.'

'Don't tell me you can work harder than my father,' Bili
said.

'Perhaps not,' Nandibali rejoined. 'Maybe *you* can work
harder than I. Shall we see how strong you are?'

And he broke into a Paraja song:

> Are you as strong as the veranda of the Sundhi's
> house?
> Come, my girl, let me test how strong and young you
> are.

Both of them laughed.

Bili said: 'No, Nandibali, I'm serious. I've been watching him. He sits alone on the veranda, smoking, and
doesn't even remember to eat the mandia I've cooked for
him, and he never speaks to anyone. I wonder what's
wrong with him.'

'I shouldn't worry,' Nandibali answered. 'Anybody
would feel tired after working all day in the fields. You
girls wouldn't understand that – all you can think of is
dancing and singing in the evening. You don't know what
it is to be out in the rain all day. No one wants to talk after
a hard day's work. Look at me, do I talk much?'

'Can you never be serious? Something is terribly wrong
with father. He simply sits and broods.'

Nandibali said: 'Yes, I know, he does seem to grow
more and more forgetful. He stands there in the field staring at nothing and doesn't even notice the rain or the hail.
And sometimes I find him muttering to himself.'

Bili added: 'And he keeps harking back to my mother

all the time. Otherwise he never says anything to me – just
stands silently beside me and strokes my back.'

'Don't cry,' Nandibali consoled her. 'I shall look after
him and nothing will happen. You can depend on me.'

Chapter 83

Madhu Ghasi came often to Jili. She knew what it was all
about, but she thought of the whole thing as a game. It was
amusing to see the money-lender panting for her, ignoring
all the other girls in the village. She felt very sure of herself. It would be a malicious pleasure to make the Sahukar
wriggle and squirm. She took care to keep her hair well
combed, with a big bunch of flowers tucked into it; and
while the Sahukar was loitering near the stream she would
pass by, swaying her hips idly.

Madhu Ghasi would detain her in talk, and the Sahukar
would stroll up to them whistling bravely, and when his
eyes met Jili's he would break into an enormous smile.
Sometimes Jili smiled back, but she never stopped for him
and she walked down to the stream quickly. As she walked
back to her house, she laughed within herself and said:
'What a ghastly grin! How he seemed to be suffering!' And
she would say to herself· 'Why doesn't death come to
him?' But the contempt in the words of abuse which rose to
her lips was mingled with something very like affection.

There were times when Madhu Ghasi did not come to
Jili for two or three days at a time, and she would grow

restless with a vague persistent itching. The intervals were deliberately planned by Madhu Ghasi, for he knew how to play a girl. And when he finally met her he would begin: 'The Sahukar sent me to the Kumuti's shop to order a jacket for you. What, have you never seen one? I thought as much, Well, you are going to have a beautiful one soon, with an embroidered border. And that's not all – the Sahukar is buying you some saris, a box of soap and a bottle of perfumed hair-oil.'

'That miser give me presents?' Jili exclaimed. 'He's never given a penny to my brothers.'

'Well, you'll see,' Madhu Ghasi replied. 'Your presents are coming. But why don't you speak to him? That's all he wants; and you could have anything for the asking. Shall I tell him?' But Jili shook her head and said hurriedly: 'No, no. I can't.'

'Why do you keep on saying you can't? Just think of those presents. I'll go and tell him you're willing to meet· him.'

Jili's face took on a cunning expression as she said: 'First let me see what he can give me.'

Madhu Ghasi went away. Later in the day he returned and gave Jili four annas.

'What use are four annas?' Jili said.

'All right, here's some more,' Madhu Ghasi said, giving her another four annas.

She clutched the coins and hurried away.

Eight annas! Four day's wages! What should she spend it on? Or would it be better to save the money? Lifting up the end of her sari she wrapped the money in it and fastened it with a knot. Then she remembered the highway and the young Supervisor, and felt a pang of nostalgia. She kept turning over Madhu Ghasi's proposal in her mind, but it was as if she were hiding something from herself, from some other part of her being to which it could not be revealed. Suddenly she wanted to throw the money into the stream. She untied the knot in her sari, laid the coins in her palm and stood gazing at them. Then she looked quickly round to see if anyone was watching, and replaced them in her sari.

Next day Madhu Ghasi was back with an eight-anna piece, but this time she sent him away, saying: 'No, I won't.' He was back again, the next day, with a sari which he had hidden among his own clothes. He gave it to her surreptitiously, saying: 'Put it on this evening. There's a jacket to match; I shall be back later.'

Jili stayed at home that evening, lying on her bed and telling everyone she had a headache. The headache became real, and she could not sleep. Around midnight she went out into the street and looked around nervously. There was no one there. She felt relieved. 'How lucky for me that Madhu Ghasi hasn't come,' she thought. 'I wonder what would have happened if he had!' Breathing more easily, she turned towards the house and was just going up the steps to the veranda when she felt someone tugging at the end of her sari. She turned round and it was Madhu Ghasi. 'Come,' he said softly. She went with him, tottering as if she were drunk. She did not speak. He took her to what had been the young men's dormitory, pushed her softly into the darkness within, and vanished.

Chapter 84

Day after day Mandia and Tikra accompanied the Sahukar's herd of buffalo through the jungle in a haphazard
wandering that seemed as if it would never end. Mandia
accepted his younger brother as an equal, and they talked
freely to each other, without any reserve.

Once Tikra said: 'Mandia, do you think father was wise
to give Bili away to some pauper who can't afford the
bride-price? If she had found the right man our debts could
have been paid, and we'd have been free by now.'

Mandia said nothing, and Tikra went on: 'But it's useless talking to you; you'll never say anything to father, will
you? You're too busy thinking about yourself, like everyone else. I've a good mind to eut and run – maybe I'll find
work somewhere.'

'So that's the kind of scoundrel you are', Mandia exclaimed angrily. 'I'd have expected better of you.'

Thus snubbed, Tikra became silent and morose. After
some time Mandia said: 'Tikra, I can understand how you
feel. I'll tell you what – let me go to the Sahukar and ask
him to release you. I'll take on your debt as well as my
own. It will mean I'll be here most of my life, but what
does it matter?'

'Do you really think I'd leave you alone here?' Tikra
asked. 'Still, don't you agree that father should have demanded a higher bride-price for Bili?'

Mandia said: 'Yes, but from what I hear nobody can
work as hard as Nandibali. He seems to have been manag-
ing everything. It's he who looks after the land – it's he

who looks after father. And after all, there's still Jili – I'm sure she'll get a good bride-price.'

'I wonder! Jili doesn't seem to be too lucky where men are concerned.' He thought for a moment, then added: 'Mandia, will you do me a favour? Let me stay behind at Dhamanjodi today while you take the herd into the jungle.'

'I don't mind, but what will the Sahukar say?'

'He needn't know. I want to spend the day looking for a bridegroom for Jili and, perhaps, a sister-in-law for myself.'

Mandia laughed and said: 'What about a bride for yourself?'

'I'm not worried about that. Do let me go – and maybe I'll find a bottle or two of liquor somewhere.'

'Very well,' Mandia said – 'but don't be too long. I might want to go myself and find a bride for *you*.'

Chapter 85

For three days there had been no sign of Jili; after that one night, she seemed to have decided to have nothing more to do with him. She worked all day in the fields and went straight home in the evening, avoiding everyone.

But when she was alone in the house she would open the box in which she kept the clothes and money she had received, and the sight of them soon dispelled any feeling of guilt. It was only the fear of discovery that kept her at home.

The Sahukar cursed Madhu Ghasi roundly and accused him of bad faith. 'But why blame me?' Madhu Ghasi protested. 'Maybe you did something to scare her off.'

'Indeed!' the Sahukar retorted angrily, 'I suppose the clothes and money I sent her scared her away. I should never have trusted you!'

'You don't understand,' Madhu Ghasi said. 'Different fish need different bait. I told you this girl is special, you can't expect to hook her with a few trinkets; you'll have to convince her that you're really in love with her, and for that you may have to spend some money. My advice is to build her a house. If you think only of the expense I'm afraid I can't help you.'

The Sahukar felt he was being fleeced but he was powerless. It was a new experience to meet someone capable of rejecting him. After brooding for a while, he made his peace with Madhu Ghasi, and fresh plans were laid. Madhu Ghasi settled all the details including his own fee. Not for the first time, the Sahukar told himself that he had never felt this way about any other woman. And not for the first time, he deceived himself: he was an animal, to whom nothing mattered except the moment.

Chapter 86

Life at home was without pattern or meaning to Jili. Her father seemed to live only for his land, his work, and his thoughts. Bili was totally wrapped up in her love for

Nandibali. There was nothing for Jili to share and she felt that nobody wanted her. Sometimes Nandibali exchanged a joke with her, but it was no more than the splash of the oars which the boatman leaves behind as he rows straight ahead, looking neither left nor right. Presently he would retire with Bili, and Jili would be left brooding in silence, thinking: 'What is Nandibali to me?'

It was August, when evening set in early, amid the steady wailing of rain and storm. Jili sat alone near the hearth after the fire had gone cold, with her cheek resting on her palm, thinking of nothing except her own loneliness. She felt herself growing old without having received anything from life; she had gathered nothing, saved nothing, and there was no one to call her own.

Somehow Madhu Ghasi always came to her while she was in such a mood; he had come twice already. She would hear the meaningful cough which signalled his approach, and her heart would jump. He would speak to her softly, soothingly, while she said nothing. After he was gone she would sigh. She could feel the change working within her. What was there so wrong about the suggestion which Madhu Ghasi was making to her? Why must she feel lonely and miserable? What sin had she committed to endure this penance? Whom had she wronged? She must cut the ropes and free herself. She had a right to be happy like anybody else. The starless night whispered to her that she could find a new life for herself. As a Paraja girl she had the right to choose any man that she liked and to cast him off and take another if she wanted to; she had the right to make her own home, to break it, and to build another. She was young, and she needed laughter and joy, not tears.

That night, Madhu Ghasi came again. Thunder was

rumbling in the distance and a chill wind blew in great
gusts. Jili rose quietly and went out with him into the
dark.

Chapter 87

The Sahukar had already stayed in the village for about ten
days but he felt no desire to leave. He liked the rich land,
which he felt would be ideal for his gardens and orchards.
There were fine sturdy Paraja youths who could become
his gotis and work for him; and there were the girls.

He untied his purse-strings, speaking to everyone who
looked as though he might be in need of a loan, offering
them money on the most attractive terms, sympathizing
with them in their troubles, propounding excellent
schemes for enriching them. Soon he had negotiated mort-
gages on six more plots adjoining the land that he had
taken from Sukru Jani. Several villagers needed loans to
purchase bullocks for the plough; the headman needed
money to pay off his arrears of rent; Tinphalia Domb
wanted a loan to start a trade in hides; there was the usual
crop of young men wanting money to buy themselves
brides.

The Sahukar wanted more gotis, more land and more
interest from his money. Twice a day, and with fervour,
he said his ceremonial prayers. He sat in the villagers'
assembly and smoked ganja. Some of the old men gathered
round him to learn the charms which he was reputed to

know. Nandu Jani's cattle had been dying mysteriously;
Buti Paraja had remained childless. He promised to accept
them ail as his disciples at the proper time.

The Sahukar felt pleased with his successes and grateful
to his guru, Garaja Sundara, the Revenue Inspector.

Chapter 88

When Jili came back no one ever asked her any questions.
Her excursions with Madhu Ghasi now became frequent;
on some nights he did not come and she went by herself.
As she walked through the darkness feeling neither happy
nor miserable, she would listen to the sounds which came to
her from behind closed doors; a husband calling affectionately to his wife, or a mother lulling her baby to sleep.
She grew bitter. She too would find happiness in her own
way. She would live her own life and revenge herself on
the world for everything it had denied her. She would no
longer be a nobody.

But each night as she walked back home, she felt de-
feated and miserable. The wind moaned in her ears and she
felt something gnawing like a worm at her heart. Sometimes the moon would emerge from behind a bank of
black clouds and light up her path, but it only made her
loneliness more vivid.

Her life had become an unending journey along these
solitary paths; the only sounds that she could hear were the
rustling of her own clothes and the jingling of her bangles.

As she drew nearer home her mind would be full of misgivings. If only she could melt into the darkness and escape from it all.

Sometimes she would wake at night and hear in the distance the drone of a dungudunga and the husky voice of the singer. More absorbing were the sounds within the house itself: less the snoring of her father then certain urgent whispers and sounds of suppressed laughter. She would toss and turn, and cover up her face with her arms, as if to block out the sounds; or she would draw up her legs and huddle against the wall as if she wanted to creep inside it and never be seen again. Her eyes burned and she closed her eyelids tightly. The pain became unbearable.

But when day came she would inspect her new clothes and her money, and things would again seem much brighter. She felt she could afford to flout the world. Soon the Sahukar would pay the bride-price for her and arrange a feast for all her relations such as they would never forget! She would dazzle them with her finery and her gold, and all their insults would be stuffed down their own throats.

She was like a child, clutching at what little comfort she could find, trying to reassure herself that her suffering would come to an end. Everything was happening as fated: there was nothing that she could have done differently. And gradually, with the help of such arguments, she was growing used to her new life, to ganja fumes and the smell of stale liquor in dark and solitary rooms.

'Where do you go at night, Jili?' Bili once asked her.

'To the young women's dormitory, of course.'

'No, you don't – I know where you go.' Bili laughed.

'Then don't tell anyone.'

But Bili did not know, nor did she have time to indulge

such curiosity as she felt – she was too engrossed in Nandibali.

Someone started a rumour that the Sahukar was planning to marry one of the girls in the village. Several names
were mentioned, Jili's among them, but the tribesmen
were never greatly interested in discussing other people's
affairs, for fear of getting involved. The whispers became
faint; then one day the Sahukar left the village, and they
died away completely. But Madhu Ghasi and Jili knew that
the Sahukar would return. He had given them his word.

Chapter 89

It was September, and the Parajas were observing one of
their many festivals. The Sahukar had returned to the village several times. Most of the lands which he had taken
had been cropped, but nothing was planted on Sukru Jani's
land. The sides of the hill were heavy with suan and paddy and maize, but Sukru Jani's land remained bare,
although the Sahukar had dug rows of pits and filled them
up with manure. Sukru Jani wondered what the matter
was.

His new land had borne a rich crop of paddy, chilies and
red-gram and his hopes were high. In a couple of months
the harvest would be ready for market, and he would be
able to repay a part of the Sahukar's debt as well as provide
food for his family.

He asked the Sahukar why nothing had been grown on

his land. The money-lender laughed and said: 'What do you know about farming? Let me first prepare the soil and then you'll see what I grow on it.'

Sukru Jani spoke to Nandibali, who said: 'Maybe he'll plant sweet potatoes in those pits. You can never know what's inside a money-lender's head. Let us wait and see.' Sukru Jani was not satisfied. He went again to the Sahukar and said: 'I can't understand what you intend to do with my land. Are you going to plant bananas?' This time the Sahukar swore at him and said: 'Mind your own business. If you're so worried about your land, you can pay your debts and take your land back right now.'

The rainy season was coming to an end and everything was green. The jungle was more luxuriant than ever and the fields were full of ripening crops. But Sukru Jani was still morose and depressed. Things would never be right for him again, he felt.

Mandia and Tikra has come on a short visit, when Nandibali and Sukru Jani had taken them round the new fields and proudly shown them the crops. But neither Mandia nor Tikra seemed interested. They looked at each other and laughed.

'And how much money do you think this will fetch us?' Mandia asked.

Nandibali said derisively: 'It's a pity you weren't here to help us, or you would have turned the soil inside out.'

'Just listen to him!' Mandia said, half in jest. 'Listen to this beggar from some unknown village! It was lucky for you I wasn't here, or I'd have taught you a lesson.' Then both brothers pleaded with their father to work less hard. 'Otherwise you will fall ill. You need some rest.'

Mandia took a stroll through the village and had a look

at their old land. 'When are you going to get the land
back?' he asked his father. 'Have you thought about it?'

'When we can find the money,' Sukru Jani answered.

'Yes,' said Mandia, 'but make sure you tell the Sahukar
in advance so that he can make no excuses when the time
comes.'

Sukru Jani was surprised to hear Mandia talk as if the
money was growing on some tree, waiting to be plucked.
But his sons told him nothing more, and shortly afterwards their visit came to an end.

Blossoms had appeared on the plants of rice, mandia and
maize, and the wind played gently with the flowers. In the
mornings the ground would be thick with dew, which
rose in a curtain of mist as the sun appeared from behind
the hill and began to climb the sky, dissolving the clouds as
it did so. The call of peacocks and wild fowl mingled
with the happy shouts of girls from the village as they
walked up the slope into the jungle to collect young
sprouts of bamboo.

Sukru Jani felt the glow of the fresh sunlight on his face,
and his thoughts danced and trembled with the mist, with
the crops in the fields, with the dew and the sunlight, all of
which had melted together and become one. And he said
to himself: 'What did Mandia mean?' But in the afternoon,
when the sky grew dark with clouds, he decided it was
only the prattling of an irresponsible young fool, and
meant nothing.

Returning home from his work, he would walk past his
old field, with its empty pits like pockmarks. He could not
understand the meaning of these empty pits.

But a few days later the mystery was solved when a
number of the Sahukar's gotis arrived, bent double under

loads of orange seedlings, which they proceeded to plant in the pits. As soon as they heard what was happening, Sukru Jani and Nandibali went out and remonstrated with the gotis, who shrugged their shoulders and said: 'We're only doing what the Sahukar has ordered. You'd better keep away or there'll be trouble.'

By now the village was in an uproar. Most people took the view that if the Sahukar planted his orange trees there he would never part with the land again, and it would be lost to Sukru Jani for ever.

'It serves him right,' said some. 'And after all, the land was his only in name.'

But others were sorry for Sukru Jani and shook their heads sadly.

Meanwhile, the Sahukar arrived. When he learned what the commotion was about, he laughed and said: 'Do you really think I will rob the poor man of his land? I'm not such a brute. I am planting orange trees to improve the land, and he can have it back, orange trees and all, as soon as he clears the debt. I only want you people to be happy and prosperous. Do you know, the Konds in Narayanpatna have become rich by growing oranges on their land? Why don't you do the same? I am only trying to show how it can be done.'

'But the orange trees will suck all the juice out of the soil, and leave my land barren,' Sukru Jani protested.

'Well, if you don't like it, you can give me back my money and get your land back,' the Sahukar retorted.

Sukru Jani flew into a rage. 'You know I can't repay your debt now,' he shouted.

'Then keep quiet and don't argue. If you get angry, there will be a curse on the fruit of these trees and the oranges will be sour. Don't you see that oranges will fetch you at least ten times what your paddy and mandia could? In three or four years the trees will bear fruit and it will be *your* gain, not mine.'

Sukru Jani said quietly: 'I have nothing to say, Sahukar. Do as you please, and may God be the judge between us.'

The Sahukar said reassuringly: 'Don't worry, Sukru. I'm not after your land. You can have it back the moment you pay off your debt.'

Chapter 90

'Have I lost the land for ever?' Sukru Jani kept asking himself. His mind was full of apprehension.

If only he had had the money he would have flung it in the Sahukar's face and told him: 'There! Count it up! And now take your cursed orange trees and go! Off my land!' But this would remain a dream. The clear, moonlit nights mocked him; the fragrance of jungle flowers mingled with the scent of the ripening grain – but he remained all alone in his dark hut, while his thoughts swarmed and buzzed around him.

The chanting of a pair of crickets under the thatch-eaves caught his attention, and he became aware also of the rustling of the wind outside. For a time he was lifted out of himself. But the misgivings came back. Everything was gone: his wife, his money, his freedom, everything; nothing remained. His thoughts were as monotonous as the

drone of the crickets, or the whistling of the wind. Everything was passing away, away, in the same unchanging
rhythm, endlessly, into the same oblivion – the moon, the
stars, the bits and pieces of cloud, himself, everything.
The wind fell, its rustling ceased and the crickets were
quiet. He lay sprawled on the veranda, his stick beside
him, and the half-burnt cheroot dislodged from behind his
ear. By imperceptible stages he fell asleep, his meditations
merging into a dream – a happy dream, in which a great
boulder came rolling down a hill; inside a deep gorge a
rivulet was flowing and flowing. He too was going somewhere, walking very fast; it was as if his limbs had been
separated from his body and were flying away at a dizzy
speed. Suddenly he woke up to the sound of scampering
mice. He opened his eyes wide and looked around him.
Uneasily he called out: 'Jili! Bili! Nandibali!' There was no
answer.

Chapter 91

Mandia and Tikra had determined to rid themselves of the
Sahukar, whatever the cost. There seemed to be three
possible roads to freedom. They could take to crime –
there was a gang of Dombs that they knew about – and
thus find the money to pay the Sahukar; but this was something no Paraja would stoop to. Or they could abscond to
the Assam tea plantations; the recruiting agents were everywhere, with their breathtaking accounts of life in those dis-

tant hills – unlimited liquor, girls for the asking, money to burn. Tikra had tried to talk his brother into it, but Mandia would grow so gloomy at the mere thought that it was all Tikra could do to cheer him up again. The suggestion was not repeated.

There was one other way, and, predictably, this was the one favoured by Mandia: the distilling and sale of liquor. 'Only this time we'll be more careful,' he said. 'One of us must always stand guard while the other is brewing, and at the slightest sound we must drop everything and run!'

It would not be difficult to sell the stuff – they need only wait at some spot where the paths crossed in the jungle.

'The season is right,' Mandia pointed out. 'In September we have the festival when cooked rice is fed to the cattle. Then there's the Dasahara festival when people will travel in crowds to Jeypore for the dancing. 'We'll sell enough liquor in a month to pay off the Sahukar, and then – goodbye to all this!'

This was why they now led their herd into the jungle almost without fear. Each day they followed a new path through the jungle. Deep in the forest, the villages amounted to no more than four or five huts – crumbling remnants of some more prosperous settlement. But even here the young folk followed the pattern of the dormitories, and the three or four unmarried girls dressed as brightly, combed their hair as smooth and laughed as challengingly as their sisters in the larger villages. For Mandia and Tikra there was never a dull moment, all day they herded the buffaloes and distilled their liquor, while every evening was passed among new companions, with much ribald laughter and jingling of coins.

One day Mandia announced: 'We've saved three score of

rupees so far; we only need another two. By the end of October, if the gods wish it – '

'– we can both afford to buy ourselves brides,' Tikra interrupted.

'Why, you idiot! Is this the time to think of marriage? First we have to free ourselves.'

'No, no; first the girls. I can't wait.' Tikra was not, in fact, particularly eager to marry; this was just his joke. He laughed until his sides ached and tears came; even Mandia smiled.

'Do you know, Tikra,' he said, 'I nearly told father eveverything the other day, I felt so sorry for him. But if anyone gets to know, we may find ourselves in jail this time.'

'You talk too much, Mandia. So you nearly told father everything! And just now you told me your plans. Did I ever ask you for accounts? Why did you have to tell me? If you tell me, what's to stop you from telling it to everyone?'

'You needn't be afraid of that. Why, I've even given up drinking for fear it might loosen my tongue.'

'Given up drinking indeed! I suppose it's only water from the mountain springs you're drinking nowadays!'

'Do be serious, Tikra. You can't imagine what may happen if someone finds out.'

He could visualize it, though: the crowds of people being led away, hands roped together, guarded front and rear by angry, red-eyed demons with stout rods of bamboo, herded through the single opening into the tiger's den. Did any breath of wind from the outside world ever enter that dungeon? Was one allowed any tobacco there? Or a drop of mandia beer? It was pitch-dark inside, with only a faint light glowing in the distance. In the villages the women would be tearing their cheeks hysterically with their nails, sobbing uncontrollably for their men; and they would wait for days, hoping that the wind would carry the sound of a familiar footstep. But no one ever returned.

Horror of the law is rooted in the marrow of the tribesman, and Mandia was haunted by nightmarish visions of desperate flight and unrelenting pursuit.

Sometimes it was Tikra who reminded him of the danger in which they were living. 'If people knew, you'd never be able to find a bride,' he would say.

'What does it matter? I shall take all the blame myself. No harm shall come to you, and with the money that we've earned you'll be able to find a bride for yourself as well as pay off all your debts. And if I go to jail you must all do your best to forget me.' And Mandia would swell with his own imagined generosity.

Washed by the rain, the jungle glistened and grew fragrant. It was just the atmosphere to conjure up thoughts of girls bathing in sparkling pools with the light playing on their bodies and wet hair. But Tikra had no time for dreams. He would stare at the girls who walked through the forest on their way to the market carrying milk or firewood on their heads. He would chat and joke with them, and this would put him in such high spirits that he would pluck bunches of flowers in the jungle and hang them round his own neck or the necks of his buffaloes. He would collect shining pebbles from the beds of the streams and fill up the folds of his garments with his collections. He lived from moment to moment; he was in no hurry to build a nest.

But Mandia was different; every experience made a deep impression on him, as on a patch of loam. Kajodi was gone but still he carried her image in his heart, hidden from the whole world and even from himself; and it made him happy. Not all the icy waters of the mountain streams could wash away those memories. In his conscious hours he could feel anger, and his face would become hard and grim; but there were times when he dozed off under the shadow of a tree, and in his dreams his heart was filled with tenderness, so that his lips curled into a smile as he lay there. And, as he slept, the wind sang, the waterfall boomed, flies and mosquitoes and bumble-bees droned in his ear, and small birds peeped at him through the leaves and trilled.

Chapter 92

Everyone knew the Sahukar and his habits. But, as the tribesmen say, there is no ladder to help you climb up to heaven, and there are no words to criticize those who are rich and powerful. However much a tribesman knows, if you ask him he will tell you, 'I know nothing.'

Everyone knew the Sahukar – everyone, that is, except Jili. She never guessed that the spider's web which had been woven for her was also meant for other butterflies. As the Sahukar's influence grew, Madhu Ghasi became more and more energetic in his pursuit of girls. The people in the village saw everything, but chose to ignore what they saw. They were afraid of the Sahukar. They had seen him coming out of the house where the Dombs lived, on days when all the men were either working in the fields or busy buying and selling in the haat. Everyone suspected his neighbour's wife or daughter, though no one was ever willing to believe that the women in his own house were under the Sahukar's evil eye.

The net of suspicion tightened and closed around a single hunted deer, and that was Jili.

Even now, however, the suspicion remained vague; no one had discovered the exact pattern of her relationship with the Sahukar. Every night she would walk out of her hut, wrapped from head to foot and with Madhu Ghasi shadowing her, and by waiting until the village was sure to be asleep she managed to avoid the prying eyes.

Gradually, the middle-aged Sahukar became a part of her solitary life. Her nocturnal flittings were by now almost routine, but the need for secrecy prevented her from becoming bored, while he for his part found her very different from the Domb girls who were always trying to force themselves on him, inviting him brazenly into their homes. Jili had far more spirit: she would never be anybody's puppet or slave. There were moments when he felt inclined to laugh at her; but more often he felt humbled in her presence. She had her fits of temper; sometimes she would even lecture him in high moral tones. He admired her and wanted her.

He would say to her: 'Why don't you come and live with me? Or we could go to my village!'

She would twist her body languidly, roll her eyes and reply: 'What will people say?'

'Who can say anything if the bride-price is paid and the wedding feast given? Is this game of hide-and-seek necessary? But have it your own way.'

One day she told him she was tired of him and would

not be coming to him any more. Whereupon he threw himself at her feet and begged her not to leave him. He was a little drunk and drowsy with ganja, and at such times she could do what she liked with him. She would scold him for getting drunk, but in her heart she felt sorry for him. The more he grovelled and cringed, the closer she felt to him. The mighty Sahukar who had taken away her father's land and made her brothers gotis was transformed into a helpless creature whom she only wanted to comfort and lull to sleep.

When he was drunk he became garrulous. 'Why don't you shut the door when you come in!' he would shout. And then the next moment: 'I will make you my queen! I will leave you all my land and everything I have. Oh! you are a treasure and no Paraja knows your worth. No one can love you as I do, neither your father nor your brothers. There is nothing I would like better than to lie here and gaze at you for ever. Promise me that you will never leave me!'

At times his drunken maunderings became tedious, and she would ask herself whether things might have been different if she had found herself a young man of her own tribe. And she reminded herself that any young Paraja would have been penniless and would have expected her to work for him; at least he was rich and expected nothing more of her.

Any Paraja youth would have courted her with the same words of love as the Sahukar, because these were the stock words that all men used. What was the difference? And did it matter what other people thought? Besides, she could hardly sink further in public estimation than her family had already fallen.

But however hard she tried to convince herself with these arguments, she never quite suceeded; there was one fact that could never be argued away. She had gone searching for romance and found only a skeleton; the pride of youth had been denied. She recoiled from what she had done, but there was no way out, and she could only clutch at the golden trappings in which the skeleton had been laid out.

She tried to imagine a future which would include the Sahukar's devotion and generosity but not even the shadow of his physical being.

Chapter 93

Meanwhile, Kau Paraja had never ceased to be Jili's slave. She laughed at his uncouth ways and he knew that he was despised, for he had no illusions about himself; but he continued to follow her and worship her from a distance. He had been slowly gathering the bride-price; and as the time came nearer when he would have enough to claim her hand, he became more and more nervous and could not even look Jili in the face. He was as shy as a young girl.

Bili would shout to him from the bathing-pool, 'Why don't you come to see us any more, brother Kau? Have you forgotten us?'

Kau Paraja would laugh, and try to hide his embarrassment by busying himself with his master's bullocks, making clicking sounds to call the animals to him.

Gradually he became a little bolder and he would stand by the side of the path as Jili walked about the village, gazing at her with adoring eyes. Sometimes he carried gifts of flowers in the folds of his dress, but he was still too shy to offer them to her and he would content himself with questions about her welfare.

But when he was alone with the cattle in the forest he would become a dashing lover, bold and adventurous. The monkeys would screech at him from the tree-tops, the hornbills would wail, and Kau Paraja would slap his thighs, tie garlands of flowers round his head, and whistle gaily to himself. He would lie on the ground and kick his legs in the air, turn cartwheels and roar out in his harsh and broken voice:

Oh my Jili, Jilli, Jili—
She wears rings in her ear-lobes.

And the monkeys would join in the chorus, crying 'Khakako, Khakako, Khakako' from the trees. Kau Paraja would laugh and throw stones at them, feeling immensely proud of his strength and his marksmanship. And, as the monkeys ran, he would chase them shouting 'Ha, ha, ha . . . ' On other occasions he would run up steep hills and jump across narrow ravines. Or he would catch a young calf by the horns and wrestle with it, delighting in his own strength and agility. Misshapen and ugly as he was, he never ever looked at his own reflection in the water. The age at which he should have married had long since passed, and he could no longer remember how old he was. But his thoughts were only of the future.

He bought a Kondh flute from a young Kondh boy,

with whose help he taught himself to play on it. He learned everything except the art of blowing through it so as to produce a musical note. A Kondh flute is nearly three feet long and has six holes; it is held horizontally, touching the shoulder. Kau Paraja held his lips to the blow-hole to pour out the music in his heart, but only a few screeching notes came out. He tried and tried, swelling out his cheeks and puffing with all his might, as he had seen the flute-players do, determined to persevere with his flute until he could coax it to produce at least two notes: 'Ji – li.' His head swam and the sweat poured off him. Even when the rain came down in torrents he continued with his flute, protecting himself against the rain by rubbing kusuma oil on his body.

The jungle was full of flowers. There were wild marigolds and cornflowers that looked as if they were made of paper, and tiny scarlet flowers growing profusely on the dhatiki bushes. There were flowers of the 'tiger's paw', with five curved, brightly-coloured petals; there were flowers of wild arum growing in pungent-smelling spikes. The ground was covered with grasses and creepers, the bushes and trees grew luxuriantly, and the crops in the fields were nearly as tall as a man. The wind was soft, and the sky had been washed pure as an emerald; only the sound of the flute was out of tune. In the evening Kau Paraja would return home with his cattle, wading knee-deep through the slush of the village paths. The pits around the cowsheds were full of cowdung and the rich smell of dung and the urine of the cattle came to his nostrils and brought a sense of completeness.

He began to take his relationship with Jili for granted, and to discuss it with Bili and Nandibali, or with his old

mother; when there was no one else available he discussed
it with his flute. Nandibali refrained from comment, as if
he had not heard. Bili pulled his leg. His mother would get
irritated and say, 'You have lost your head! I wonder what
will happen if she *does* become your wife. I suppose you'll
have no time for me at all!' As for the flute, it made its
usual screeching noises, and kept slipping off his lips.

He passed his days in expectation. The moon appeared
again in the sky and he could get no sleep. He longed to
take Jili to some lonely spot in the forest and whisper everything that was in his heart; and the very thought quickened his pulse. In his excitement he would go out into the
night – a misshapen shadow, bent beneath some unknown
load. He would slowly circle the village – once, twice,
three times – before coming stealthily to a halt in front of
the young women's dormitory, where he hoped that Jili
might be.

One night, as he was standing there in the darkness, a
girl almost ran into him. 'Who's there', she exclaimed.

'It's me, Kau.'

'What are you doing here alone, brother Kau? You gave
me a scare.' The girl hummed a tune, went on up to the
veranda of the house and said: 'I'm still trembling; come
and feel. It's very cold outside; come in and we'll light a
fire and warm ourselves.'

'No, no,' Kau Paraja answered hurriedly, 'I was only
taking a stroll.' He moved away and was soon lost in the
thick mist rising from the swampy ground. He could hear
the girl laughing.

Many a time he returned from the young women's
dormitory without having seen Jili. He would toy with the

idea of walking to her house to see her; but he was afraid of meeting Nandibali, the old man or Bili, for if they asked him what he was doing there he could not answer them.

One night, a few days before full moon, Kau Paraja found himself roaming aimlessly close to Sukru Jani's house. He sat down quietly in the shade of a tree hoping to catch a glimpse of Jili if she came out. He stared at her house and thought: 'She is there—inside that house.'

Time passed, the shadows of the houses grew longer in the moonlight, and the mist crept up close.

Suddenly, the door of Sukru Jani's house opened and someone came out. He could see the figure in silhouette, and knew it was Jili. He gazed at her as if trying to absorb her entire being through his eyes. She stood there for a moment, wrapped from head to foot, looked quickly around and hurried away. Kau Paraja was stunned. He had heard of people walking in their sleep. He believed also that on moonlit nights evil spirits woke people from their sleep and drove them out of doors. He felt himself sweating. Once or twice he thought of calling out to her but he was unable to speak. Frightened as he was, he followed her at a distance, never taking his eyes off her, telling himself that he would protect her from the evil spirit even if it should eat him alive.

A night-bird screeched; jackals howled. He felt as if he were in a dream. They walked across a patch of swamp, where frogs croaked and grasshoppers chanted. Jili was walking fast, ahead of him. As she approached the familiar hut he asked himself: 'Doesn't the Sahukar live here?' She paused and looked around. Then she knocked three times, and the door opened and closed again behind her.

Wild with anger, he lurched forward as if to break down

the door. But he had not even a stick in his hand. 'Let her go to the devil!' he thought.

His flat ugly face was contorted with a peculiar expression; he felt tears in his eyes and a lump in his throat.

As he made his way back he looked even more monstrous than before, like a gigantic frog that pauses every now and then between bursts of ungainly movement.

Chapter 94

It was the morning after.

'Your daughter has been going every night to the Sahukar's hut,' Kau Paraja said, and walked away. He never spoke much, but all his hatred was put into those few words. He wanted to end the ugly business as quickly as he could before retiring to nurse his wounds.

The old man turned round, rushed after him and shouted: 'What's that you say?'

Kau Paraja did not reply.

'Answer me!' the old man repeated, seizing him by the wrist. 'What was that you said?'

'Go home,' Kau Paraja said. 'I have work to do; I can't stop now.'

Sukru Jani looked fiercely and intensely into his eyes and repeated 'What did you say?'

'I only told you what I have seen. Ask the Sahukar – ask your daughter,' Kau Paraja said sadly and continued on his way.

He had already arranged a loan to complete the bride-price for Jili. But all that was over now.

After seeing Jili going to the Sahukar's hut he had been unable to sleep. Now that he had spoken out, he felt a little better.

He had created an idol on whose altar he had laid offerings of flowers, incense and everything that he possessed. Now the ceremony of worship was over, and only the last ritual of casting the goddess's image into a stream remained.

He wanted never to see Jili's face again. He thought of revenging himself on the Sahukar, but the unconscious fears which he had inherited from his ancestors stopped him with arguments of undeniable logic. He thought to himself: 'Why dash my head against a mountain?' Instead, like a child that has been slapped, he went sulking and complaining to one person after another. But people only laughed at him. Very soon the entire village knew. The mystery was over.

Sukru Jani was grim as he walked home. 'Jili!' he called out. But she was not there.

He sat on the veranda, his eyes bloodshot, his head reeling. A hundred incidents which at the time had seemed trivial suddenly took on a new and ominous meaning. The honour of his tribe had been outraged. He had lost face. The Sahukar had robbed him of his last possession. But how could Jili do such a thing? If only he had been younger and stronger he would have cut the Sahukar down with his axe! But was it true? He could not believe it of his own daughter. Kau Paraja must have told him a lie. He remembered how Kau had once come to him as the Forest Guard's pimp, and he had beaten him black and blue and driven him away. Or maybe Kau Paraja had mistaken someone else for Jili. But the more he thought of it, the more confused he grew. There was nothing he could do to prove or disprove the charge. Suddenly he was seized with panic. 'Suppose it's true!' he said in alarm. 'We shall have to face the elders of the tribe. Jili will be there too. What a humiliation! And if they impose a fine on us we shall have to pay!' He looked wildly around him, as if people were watching him from every bush, waiting to jump on him and tear him to pieces.

Next, he began blaming himself. It was all his own fault. He had neglected his family. He had been like a guest in his own home, receiving his share of mandia every morning and evening, but taking no interest, leaving his daughters to manage the household. And what a mess they had made of it! Everything had turned into ashes. Yes, it was all his fault.

Suddenly he rushed into the house and pulled out the box in which Jili kept her things. It was unlocked and contained three new saris, still folded the way they had been by the maker; a small bottle of red hair-oil whose perfume seemed to fill the house; and cakes of scented soap. He had never seen these things before, and they told their own tale. He rose to his feet in a frenzy, scattering the contents of the box around the floor, beating his chest with his hands, and pulling at his hair.

Jili returned from her bath in the stream, in her most cheerful frame of mind, knowing nothing of what had happened. As she stepped into the room she saw him and stood there as if transfixed. The old man was trembling all over. 'Jili!' he screamed, raising his fist above his head, 'You . . . with that Sahukar!'

Jili's breasts heaved and fell; her eyes rolled wildly from side to side. A flame seemed to burn and then splutter out. She saw and understood everything. As she rushed out of the house he shouted: 'Don't show your face here again! If you do . . .'

But she was gone.

He stepped out on to the veranda. Restraining an impulse to go at once and have it out with the Sahukar, he squatted on the floor, smoking his cheroot and spitting.

He was alone. Overhead, the sun was hot; it was almost time for people to return from the fields. Bili and Nandibali would arrive soon. He could hear children shouting in neighbouring houses; others were outside, chasing brightly-coloured butterflies, chewing cucumbers or stalks of maize. Hens scampered down the street with their broods of chicks, pecking at the ground. A calf mooed to its mother. His eyes rested on a little patch of grass which looked like molten fire in the bright sun. The sun felt unusually hot; the tobacco in his mouth tasted bitter, and he spat it out again and again.

Chapter 95

All doors were closed to Jili except one; there was nowhere she could go except to the money-lender. So far she had seen her relationship with him through a romantic haze; now she was compelled to see it in the harsh light of necessity. The face of the Sahukar rose up before her and she saw it for what it was – the face of an old lecher, whom she could never love. The whole affair was sordid and ugly; but there was no choice for her, she must go back to him and beg him to let her have a place at his feet.

The same day, at noon, she went to the hut in which he lived and stood before the door, pale and expressionless.

The money-lender was alone. He looked at her in surprise, laughed and said banteringly, 'This is a real honour! What has brought you here at this hour? Come in and let us talk.'

'Father knows everything,' Jili said, and she burst into tears. He stared at her in amazement. 'Who told him?' he asked.

'I don't know,' Jili said. 'But he has found out.'

'Well, let him – who cares?' shouted the money-lender. 'What can he do to me? Don't cry. Let them ask the bride-price and I'll pay it.'

He caught her and pulled her into the hut. As she looked at those fierce moustaches and the stern expression on his face she felt overpowered by his strength. She sat down; she could not think.

The news caused a great commotion in the village. Towards the afternoon, the headman and the other important persons in the village, together with Sukru Jani, came in a body to the Sahukar. He saw them coming from a distance and sat waiting for them.

As soon as they came near, he began to speak, firmly and with confidence. 'Ah, headman, you have come at just the right moment,' he began. 'I have something to ask you: tell me if I wanted to take a Paraja wife, how much would I have to pay for her? And you, Sukru, why do you look so sullen and sour? I see you're angry with me. Well, be careful what you say, or I'll go to the police station and report you to the Sub-Inspector. Do you understand? You should feel thankful. How many Parajas could boast of a son-in-law like me? From now on all your worries will be over. Well, what do you all say?'

Perplexed by his impudence, they looked at each other and said nothing. Sukru Jani felt his blood beginning to boil and he suddenly burst out: 'You cheat! you liar! You have stolen my daughter, you devil!'

The Sahukar shouted back even more violently: 'So! How dare you abuse me! Be careful! Did I go to your house and carry your daughter off, or am I keeping her here against her wish? If you don't want to settle things peacefully you can go and do your worst; I don't care!'

Others went up to Sukru Jani and whispered to him: 'What has happened has happened. It is not wise to annoy the Sahukar.'

Someone suggested: 'Let us call the panchayat and ask the girl what she has to say.' And the Sahukar said 'Yes; that's much better. Ask her yourselves. Jili, come here!'

'How did you come to be here, Jili?' the headman asked her.

She glanced nervously at the Sahukar and murmured: 'I came here of my own accord.'

There were gasps and exclamations. Sukru Jani attempted to rush at her but was held back by the others. Jili went back into the hut.

The Sahukar said loudly: 'Now listen, all of you. I have asked this old man to name the bride-price and he has not done so. So I shall give him what I think fair, and I shall not listen to any protest. All of you are my witnesses.'

They listened in silence as he proceeded with his lecture,

rolling his great red eyes, and generally acting as if someone had done him an irreparable injury.

'You people make me laugh!' he shouted. 'Have I stolen
any man's money or land? There are men who marry a
thousand wives, and all that *I* have done is to take a second
wife to work for me and look after my land. What wrong
have I done? I have helped the people of this village in a
thousand ways and this is how they repay me. They call a
meeting of the panchayat and threaten me; the whole village is against me! It's a regular rebellion! Very well, I'll go
to the police station tomorrow and file a report. I'll get a
petition written, put a stamp on it, and present it to the authorities. What do these fellows here take me for? Let the
officials come and learn the truth.'

The headman tried to placate him. 'Don't be angry with
us, Sahukar; who would be so foolish as to offend you?
Only, you should have informed the village elders and
asked the girl's father; that's the custom of our tribe. But it
doesn't really matter. You can pay the price now and give
us a wedding feast later, and that will settle everything.
Isn't that fair, Sukru?'

And everyone said: 'Yes, yes, it is true' or: 'If the girl has
chosen him what more is there to say?' or: 'The Sahukar is
the incarnation of justice. Every word that he says is true.
The father cannot bind his daughter, it is not our custom.'
The Sahukar took notice of everything, studied the expression on each face and calculated the effect of his words
to see how strongly he was entrenched. He saw that his
medicine was beginning to work and that the villagers,
alarmed by words like 'petition', 'report' and 'police', were
preparing to leave Sukru Jani to his fate.

The Sahukar beamed at them benevolently and said:

'Who could have known when I first came here, that I was
going to marry into your tribe? But now I am one of you; I
shall call some of you 'father-in-law' and others 'brother-
in-law'; I shall share your feasts and your cheroots. And
maybe I shall have to build a house here to store all the gifts
which you will be giving me!'

They laughed. Sukru Jani did not speak; he was stupid
and helpless with anger.

The headman said: 'Be kind to us always, Sahukar. We
can discuss the bride-price later. We trust you not to run
away; and even if you did we could always catch you.'

There was more laughter and they went away in a body,
as they had come. Jili, watching them through a chink in
the door, was relieved when she heard them laugh, but
when she saw the blank look on her father's face, and his
head bowed low as he departed, she yearned to run after
him and touch him. But the gulf between them was too
deep. Or rather, he and her brothers were on the further
side of a whirling current, into which she had been
thrown, and which was carrying her, tied hand and foot,
into an unknown future.

The Sahukar came in and said: 'Well, that's over. They'll
sting me for a heavy bride-price – but you're worth it.' He
advanced with arms outstretched to embrace her; she was
lost in her own thoughts and, at his touch, she pulled
away. He came closer, and she looked at him and thought:
'He's old, too old. But how strong and fierce he looks –
like a tiger, or a police constable.'

He grabbed her, and this time she did not struggle. But a
cloud passed over her face and wiped away, perhaps for
ever, the smile which a little tenderness could have drawn
from her very soul.

Chapter 96

Sukru Jani sat with what was left of his family, talking in undertones.

'I suspected it,' Bili said, 'but I held my tongue.'

'And has your wisdom blossomed now?' Nandibali rebuked her. 'No, the fact is, none of us knew anything.'

Sukru Jani went on muttering to himself, pausing only for breath: 'They are all rascals, every one of them! They sided with him! Asked him for a wedding feast! He's a sorcerer. He put a charm on my poor child. And there's no one to do justice, no one!'

Nandibali and Bili tried to comfort him.

'After all, father,' Nandibali said, 'he's the man she chose. She *had* to find someone sooner or later; a daughter can't remain in her father's house for ever. Don't be sad. Can a daughter, or even a son, carry you to heaven? Let us all go to the Sahukar and make him pay four score of rupees, or even five. He's a rich man, so why shouldn't he pay?'

'What daughter?' Sukru Jani burst out. 'She's not my daughter! I can't ask a bride-price for her!'

'You mustn't say such things,' Nandibali said. 'It will bring her bad luck. Be patient; we'll wait a little, then get her to leave him and find her another husband – a good one.'

'Will she ever come back?' he moaned. 'If her mother had been alive . . .' He could not go on. Nothing more was said about the bride-price.

Bili looked at Nandibali and her eyes filled with tears.

'What's the matter?' he asked gently.

'I've never been separated from her,' she said. 'Never, since I was a child.'

'Oh, is that all?' he said. 'Every son builds himself a new home, and every daughter has to find a husband. The Sahukar has taken Jili; and who knows, if I hadn't come along, he might have taken you instead! Lucky for you I was here first!' he said, puffing out his chest. 'And so the Sahukar is your brother-in-law? And your father's son-in-law? Good! We'll have someone to buy seeds and bullocks for us, and sweets for you! You can get anything you like out of him; only don't let Jili catch you flirting with him, or she'll brain you with the heavy bangles that he's bound to give her!' He tickled her, and they both laughed.

Chapter 97

That evening the villagers sat around a fire, discussing the events of the day.

'I know that some of you are angry,' the headman said. 'But the Sahukar is a big man and we are small men; and he knows all the big people. Can we fight him? Besides, this may be a blessing for all of us. Let's hope that the beast will stop prowling after our wives and daughters now! And as we all know, there are government officials who come to our villages and take our women and keep them and throw them out again when they're tired of them. We know nothing about those men, but we let them have our women.

At least we know the Sahukar; he belongs to these parts, and he's taken a girl of our tribe as his wife. We are lucky he wants to become one of us – a rich man like him! That old fool Sukru Jani doesn't understand a thing! But he'll get used to it in time!'

The others nodded in agreement; they were used to obeying the village elders.

Sania Paraja said: 'Well, now I can get my bullocks!'

'You'd better speak to the Sahukar's wife first, if you want him to give you a loan,' was the Barik's advice.

Someone said: 'Bagla, wasn't she betrothed to you once?'

'To me?' Bagla said. 'No such luck! Why, look at her, and look at me!'

The villagers bore the Sahukar no grudge. In the dormitory, too, the girls were talking.

'But he's an old man!'

'And he has a Sundhi wife at home. And lots of children.'

'Well, he may be old, but he's not too old to run after girls. He's worse than any young man.'

'And that Jili! She looked so innocent!'

But Jili was gone, leaving them to rub their eyes and talk.

Chapter 98

Jili made herself busy in her new home, sweeping, arranging, cooking. As she sat tending the fire, she kept asking herself if this was happiness, and if it would last.

That morning she had walked boldly into the house, neither hiding nor tapping stealthily on the door. She put the pot on the fire. The money-lender sat a little distance away, smoking ganja. What a mess! he thought – it was as if a dustbin had been emptied over his head. It was fortunate that he had kept his wits about him. If he hadn't humoured the villagers there would have been no end of trouble – they might even have killed him.

Well, he would have to pay about seventy rupees to the old man and give a feast to the people in the village; he didn't like the idea of having to spend so much money, and he intended putting it off as long as possible. He would have to move the girl to some other place as she would never agree to live in this village now. Naturally, he could not take her to his village; his wife would never tolerate that. He had a farmhouse in Kadamjholla, about four miles away from this village, where he had several gotis working for him; he would have to keep Jili there.

He was still fretting about the problem, and about his seventy rupees, when Jili told him that dinner was ready.

That night Jili was like a block of wood when the Sàhukar caressed her. She lay whimpering and sobbing, and he could not console her.

'How can I show my face in the village now?' she kept repeating. He was puzzled by her behaviour. When the storm had been at its height she had been brave and had come to him of herself, ignoring what other people might say; but now, when things were quiet and there was no further need for secrecy, she was frightened and tearful. Women were difficult to understand, and he did not propose to try too hard. He sat up and drank some liquor.

Outside, a light shower was pattering on the damp ground. Inside, the only light was the feeble twinkling of glow-worms trapped in spiders' webs. A lizard chirped. Jili lay beside him in the bed, keeping him awake with her sobs. He took another swig at his liquor.

'Don't worry, my darling,' he reassured her. 'At dawn tomorrow I shall take you to Kadamjholla. I have a farm-house there, and nobody will disturb us.'

'No, no, no,' she sobbed.

'Stop saying no and go to sleep.'

At last they both slept. The tears had dried on Jili's face, her eyes were closed, and with sleep came a forgetting, as dreams rose from the depths of her consciousness and transported her back into a happy past.

Chapter 99

The month of Aswina came, bringing showers that were silvery and light as a feather.

Everywhere edible roots and green fruits were plentiful. In the fields the standing crops danced in the wind, row upon row, balancing basketfuls of food on their heads. The hillsides were festive with colour: light grey-white clouds, blue peaks in the distance and greens of every shade. At the foot of the hills lay the village, its cluster of roofs covered with vines of pumpkin and gourd, all loaded with fruit.

The village paths, beginning to dry after the heavy rain, had been churned and pitted by human feet and the hooves of animals. Discarded spikes of maize, thrown away after the seeds had been eaten, littered the ground like empty honeycombs. Cucumbers, too, had been chewed and the remains thrown here and there by the wayside; piles of paddy and suan straw harvested from the terraced lands higher up on the hills lay everywhere. The dirt and the disorder announced the profusion of Aswina.

Dreams came floating in the air, fragrant with wild kurai flowers and the blood-red flowers of dhatiki. The intoxicating perfumes of wild malli and niali flowers brought memories of sleek shining blobs of hair and high firm breasts. One could never grow tired of the sights and smells. The clusters of smooth, round amla fruits looked like crowds of smiling faces; the slender vines were like hands twined together with tapering fingers, and within their folds the flame-coloured petals waved like little tongues of fire. The tall, full-blown grass symbolized the ripe, sensuous grace of Aswina, and the winding rivulet had become its flowing tresses. Desires flitted by like the coloured butterflies – as gay and as evanescent.

But Aswina wore another face too, for this was the month when the fierce Mother goddess, Durga, takes up her sword to do battle with Evil. Beauty was armed: fragile leaves turned into sword-blades, and flowers into sharp stones; the awful cry of Bhairava, the god of destruction, echoed among the hills.

The spirit of the goddess was abroad, and the soothsayers and the witch-doctors, the kalisis and shamans and begumis, possessed by the deity, danced wildly; buffaloes were sacrificed, their blood spurting out in lurid jets to mingle with the mud; drums throbbed – small drums, bigger drums and gigantic drums six feet wide; trumpets shrilled and the hills echoed. There were flags and processions, displays of swords, battle-axes and spears, and always the shouting and roaring and grunting for blood, more blood. It was if a ghost had appeared out of some forgotten history, rousing them to the excitement of a remote warlike past, when mighty warrior-kings had summoned their chieftains to pay them homage during the Dasahara festival, and armies had marched through these mountains to the rhythm of war-drums. Now all that remained was the echo of distant thunder, and the blood of a chicken sufficed to propitiate the god of war. There was still a 'king' at Jeypore, the seat of the old kingdom, but his glory had dwindled into that of a rent-collector. However, he still held court during Dasahara; his agents sent out a summons to every village headman, and the crowds still collected at Jeypore. They gathered in procession in an open field; authority was present in the shape of the king's Dewan or minister, the managers of the king's Sugar Factory and his Tile Factory, his Chief Forest Officer and other dignitaries. Between them they made a colourful show of puggarees and brocade and satin robes, displayed once a year; there were elephants and horses and vehicles of all kinds.

And then the main event would begin. A brinjal – the fruit of an egg-plant – was speared on the end of a bamboo pole and raised high in the air while, watched by the tribesmen, the various dignitaries took it in turns to fire at the target. The winner was greeted with shouts of acclaim and a victory dance by the assembled tribal girls. Next came a fireworks display. The rockets and squibs and catherine wheels roared and traced bright patterns in the sky, followed intently by thousands of awed faces.

Then the king would hold his ceremonial assembly. First the poets were invited to recite their compositions; there were learned pundits of Sanskrit with heavy gold pendants hanging from their ears, and strings of ornate polysyllables filled the air. Sometimes a poor rustic would ask someone for an explanation, and a knowledgeable neighbour in the crowd would tell him that the king was being compared to the Sun, the Moon, to Brahma and Vishnu, and that the poet was sure to be rewarded for his magnificent verses; and sure enough, there was the jingling of coins, which made the tribesmen gape in wonder.

Such was the festival of Dasahara: the fruit of an egg-plant was shot down, a few plantain trees were ritually felled, fowls were heroically slaughtered, and women danced. But the ghost walked again, war-drums rang out and the earth ran blood. It gave the tribesmen something to talk about and chew over and digest for days.

In the heart of the forest, at the entrance of a narrow mountain pass, Mandia and Tikra sat beside a stream flowing through a ravine and talked. It was two hours before sunset.

Mandia said: 'It's a good thing we didn't go to Jeypore to see the Dasahara festival, as you wanted us to. We've earned another twenty-five rupees. But now we must stop for a while.'

'Why stop now when we've almost got what we wanted? Is money so cheap that one should kick it aside?'

Mandia looked sadly at his brother and said: 'Now that the rains are over, the excise officers will be out on their rounds again. They can smell liquor a mile off. Why take chances?'

Tikra sat thinking for a while. Then he said: 'When we go to the money-lender and hand him the money, where shall we say it came from?'

Mandia flew into a rage at the mention of the Sahukar's name. 'That devil! He seduced Jili! I'd like to . . .'

Tikra laughed and said: 'Why, could he have taken her if she hadn't wanted to go? Anyway, he will have to pay the bride-price, and we need the money.'

'Yes, that we do indeed!' Mandia said bitterly, unconsciously sharpening the edge of his knife on a stone. 'And he has a wife at home too! He's already an old man.'

'But what can you or I do?' Tikra asked. 'It's for Jili to decide what she wants.

Mandia was silent and grim.

Tikra remembered Mandia's rage when he had first heard about Jili and the Sahukar. He had wanted to go after them with his axe at once, and only been restrained with difficulty. Anger could make him pace restlessly up and down for hours, touching no food – a different person altogether from his usual docile self.

Tikra felt angry too. When he saw her, he told himself, he would teach her a lesson. He would glare at her and make her cower before his anger; she would clasp his feet and beg forgiveness, but he would not weaken. And the thought of chastising her added inches to his stature.

Then he felt the absurdity of it. Imagine Jili being frightened of *him*! She would probably tweak his nose and laugh in his face. Everyone in the family treated him as if he were a baby! And Jili had always carried her head high. You couldn't frighten her: she was too big. It pained him to see her shrunk in this way; suddenly he felt protective towards her.

He hated the money-lender and he felt he should have nothing to do with him or with Jili. But how could he cut himself off from his own sister? Was it so wrong to marry someone who did not belong to your tribe? Wasn't he capable of doing the same thing himself? Many of the girls he had seen and courted in the forest had been from other tribes. No, there was nothing wrong in his sister choosing a Sundhi.

But a money-lender? Could there be anything in common between Tikra and him? It would be a meeting of fire and dry grass. Tikra could never accept him.

Whenever he brooded, his anger rose again. But it was not his nature to brood for long; there were too many things to interest and delight. Something would tickle him to laughter; his feet itched for the dance and his hands for work. He would start humming a tune, or pluck some flower that had caught his eye, or chase a monkey up a tree; or he would sniff the fragrant autumn air, dilate his nostrils, and bound away into the forest like a barking deer.

Chapter 100

Kadamjholla was only four miles away from Sarsupadar, but to Jili this was enough; she could forget everything here. She lived in the farmhouse, surrounded by granaries, barns, cattle-sheds and clumps of banana. Only Kondhs lived in this village, and Jili couldn't speak a word of their

dialect. The hills even hid the path by which she had come
to the village; she turned a corner and came to a different
world altogether.

Each morning she would grow apprehensive, thinking
her father might come to demand the bride-price. How
could she face him? Undoubtedly, they were all jeering at
her, thinking she had come running to the middle-aged
Sahukar from sheer greed. But no one came. She felt relieved, and at the same time deserted.

She was alone with her Sahukar.

He was old, and his mind had grown dull with years of
sensual indulgences. He needed his pleasures, but he had
neither taste nor discrimination, and once the novelty had
gone everything became tedious and meaningless to him.

For the first few days he played the infatuated lover,
reaching into his own lost youth to answer her childlike
tricks. But he was too old to be weaving garlands for her
hair and singing traditional songs. It seemed a waste of
time.

He was annoyed with himself. The gossip didn't worry
him, but he resented having to pay good money for the
girl. Now that he had possessed her, it hardly seemed
worth all the trouble. True, she would look after the house
and after him, and it was good to know she would be there
when he needed her; still, seventy rupees was quite a sum.

Several days passed and no one came to see him. He
grew restless and impatient; there was much to attend to
elsewhere, and if Jili's folk wanted him they could look for
him. He had waited for them long enough.

He decided to leave Jili behind. She wouldn't like that;
she would probably cry and make a scene, but it wasn't dif-

ficult to bring a woman round; a little flattery and a few caresses would do the trick. As long as she *looked* happy, it didn't matter what she felt. He had never bothered to think deeply about such things.

Having made his decision, he realized it was time for his evening puja. He sat down cross-legged, plugging first one nostril and then the other, working himself up into a mood of devotion. His god was pleased with him, he felt certain; and his house would overflow with gold.

Two days later, he left. 'Take good care of everything,' he told Jili. 'It's yours as well as mine.' This made her feel important.

Jili could not understand the Kondh dialect, and the only people in Kadamjholla she could talk with were the old Domb Barik and his daughter Sukumani, an intelligent girl still in her teens. Sukumani had been engaged by the Sahukar to help Jili. He had warned Jili that she was a thief, but they soon became friends, even if Jili did keep a wary eye on her companion.

Alone in her unfamiliar surroundings, Jili would only look around her and brood. The hills rose sheer from the valley. On the upper slopes, the streaks of cultivation looked from a distance like a pair of green snakes coiled around each other and looping down; lower down was a chequerboard made up of light green squares of suan and darker fields of mandia. At dusk the peacocks swarmed into the suan fields and danced – three or four hens in a group round each male; and Jili remembered how she and the other girls had formed a ring around the young men and danced. In one field lay a huge boulder, black and mis-shapen, on which the peacocks perched; and it reminded her of Kau Paraja. She shouldn't have spurned him, she

thought; he wasn't so bad after all. And then she found
herself thinking of Bagla with a mixture of tenderness, anger and humiliation that made her ears burn and her eyes
fill with tears.

A light shower of rain fell on her. It was time for the cattle to return home. The smells of evening mingled with the
voices of people talking loudly in the Kondh village. She
felt lonely and unhappy. Memories of the workmen's
camp returned. Were they still working on the highway?
And the Supervisor? The past was full of pain and accusa-
tion, and it was almost as if she raised these memories to
add to her suffering.

The Kondhs were a cheerful crowd; the laughter in their
village never ceased, and the flutes which accompanied the
singers trilled away all night long. But the Sahukar's house
was wrapped in silence.

Sometimes, as Jili lay asleep, the moonlight would seep
through the leaves of the banana trees, penetrating and
rearranging the shadows in the Sahukar's courtyard. It was
as if her pent-up sufferings had found an outlet.

Chapter 101

The Dasahara festival was over and the crowds drained
away from Jeypore Mandia and Tikra had missed all the
fun in order to concentrate on the job in hand. It was quite
a sacrifice – but every act of renunciation is rewarded, and
their profits were huge. That they might be doing wrong
was something that never occurred to them; such ques-

tions were too big for them. A tribesman's life is so hemmed in that he seems to be in danger of breaking the law
each time he sets foot outside his home. And so he does
what he regards as necessary and if he is caught he looks at
you as if to say: 'Very well, I'm beaten again. Do what you
like with me.'

Mandia had determined to cut himself free from the
Sahukar, even if it meant breaking the law. The law! He
should never have paid the magistrate's fine in the first
place; it was this which had made him the Sahukar's goti.
As for jail, he had seen hundreds of Kondhs serving out
their sentences and then returning home as if nothing had
happened; they shaved your head when you were inside,
but your hair grew again. You also lost your caste, but for
an unmarried man was that so terrible?

As their savings grew, Mandia and Tikra became more
and more restless. It was essential to pay off the entire debt
at one fell swoop; otherwise the Sahukar would find some
way of manipulating the accounts so that they were no better off than before. By the end of Dasahara they had put by
four score and three rupees and, by their reckoning, that
should be enough. They counted the money over and over
again, stacking the coins in five-rupee piles on the ground
to make sure there would be no mistake.

They began making their plans. 'Jili must be brought
back home and another husband found for her,' Mandia
said.

'And what about a bride for yourself, brother?' Tikra
asked.

'That can wait. The first thing is to pay off the Sahukar.'

It was exhilarating to think of the future; they felt at
peace with the world, and when they slept there were no

dreams. A few days later, however, they heard that officers of the Excise Department were in the area. Cherenga
Paraja had heard the news from Bhursamunda Domb,
who had come to buy some pigeons; and Cherenga Paraja
told Mandia while the latter was selling him a drink. Mandia and Tikra smashed their distilling apparatus into tiny
fragments and moved on with their herd of buffaloes.

'There is nothing to betray us,' Mandia said, and Tikra
added: 'Except your wagging tongue,' but Mandia only
laughed.

The hills were ablaze with golden olsi. Mandia remembered that the olsi flowers had been in bloom when his
father had first gone to serve as a goti. That was when all
his hopes had crumbled, like the new house which his
father had begun to build for him and Kajodi.

Three days later they were joined by another herd of the
Sahukar's buffaloes, tended by two more of his gotis. The
four of them spent a few happy days in a neighbouring village, laughing and chatting with the young folk in the dormitories. Then Mandia and Tikra persuaded the other two
gotis to take charge of both herds – they themselves *had* to
go home immediately and settle a dispute over some land.
They would inform the Sahukar, but it would be two or
three days before he sent anyone to relieve them. And, for
their pains, Mandia would send them some tobacco!

'Is it really necessary to tell the Sahukar?' Tikra asked
Mandia.

'Indeed it is – otherwise he'll hold us responsible if anything happens while we're away.' And Mandia told his
brother the story of Harguna Kondh, who had four of the
goats in his charge killed by a leopard one night while he
was having a meal; the Sahukar had fined him twenty-five

rupees and made him serve for two years as a goti.

The Sahukar was not at home when they arrived, but they informed his clerk, asked two of the other gotis to relieve them in the forest, and rushed off home.

Chapter 102

Sukru Jani was gazing at the stars.

How vast the sky was! Somewhere in that vastness lay the home of Dharmu, the Just One. Dharmu saw everything, but he never showed himself; he saw everything but he never spoke out – he was as silent as Pandramali mountain, above whose crest shone a particularly bright seasonal star. Suffering left the god unmoved, but if he did not receive his sacrifices of goats and pigeons his anger could be swift and terrible.

Could anything escape the eye of Dharmu? It was Dharmu that killed, Dharmu that brought the dead back to life again. If a man had done wrong in a previous birth, Dharmu would kill him quickly and cast his spirit into another womb so that he would be born again. Was the soul reborn of its own choice, or was it Dharmu who willed everything?

And Sombari? Had she been snatched away so soon because of her misdeeds in an earlier birth? Impossible! She had been too good a soul, too much at peace with herself. And as he remembered her he began to mutter as if he were talking to her, and he complained to her of the aching in his legs, which there was no one to soothe.

It was cold. He must ask Bili to fetch some coals for the brazier. His cheroot had fallen unnoticed and lay smouldering on the ground. How still everything was – even the dogs were asleep!

How much longer must he endure the cold and the darkness? He felt as if he were falling apart.

'Father!'

He started, and sat up; old age and fatigue had dropped away at that sound.

'What brings you here on a night like this?' he asked. 'Have you had something to eat?'

'We have eaten,' came the reply. 'It is not so very late. Tikra, go and wake Jili and Bili. They can't go on sleeping comfortably when *we*'ve been walking all day.'

'Jili is not here, Mandia,' Sukru Jani said quietly. 'Haven't you heard?'

'Yes, yes, I have,' Mandia said quickly. 'Call Bili then; and where is Nandibali?'

Father and sons sat talking half the night. The old man was amazed at how quickly the money had been raised; but it was not a dream. He counted the money himself and hurried away to bury it safely in the ground. There was a short length of hollow bamboo which served as a cash box; into this he dropped two or three coins at a time, and when he heard them jingling he stopped and looked nervously around. He leaned over the kerosene lamp with his cheek almost touching the flame; but he felt nothing. His hands shook and his breath came in quick, short pants. Finally the coins were all hidden away and the lamp put out. Then he came back to read a sermon to his sons. 'It is very wrong to brew liquor,' he said gravely. 'If you had been caught you would have been sent to jail, and then no one could have helped you.' His voice took on an anxious tone. 'Are you sure nobody knows? Have you destroyed the evidence?'

The more he warned and rebuked them, the lighter he felt and the more he wanted to go on talking. His sons sat quietly and heard him through. They knew that the words of reproach came only from the lips.

'Where can we find the Sahukar, father?'

'He is expected here tomorrow.'

The discussion was over. They went to bed and were soon fast asleep. Sukru Jani did not need to count stars any more; the darkness was over and a new day seemed to have dawned.

Chapter 103

The sun was already high, but the mist had not yet fully cleared when the money-lender came riding into the outskirts of the village. He had developed a fondness for this village and felt as if he owned it already. Then he remembered that Jili was no longer there and felt a touch of sadness.

His holdings of land in the village were increasing all the time and soon he would need to build a granary to store all his paddy. He would grant loans of paddy to the villagers during the lean months and his store would increase. The orange trees were growing splendidly. Their leaves had turned a rich dark colour and he could see that they would yield a rich crop soon, for the soil was good, and there was plenty of water. Over the years he would plant more and more orange trees and his profits from the land would increase.

He got down from his horse in order to gloat more fully over his orange orchard, whose young trees were like the promise of first love, and to congratulate himself once again on his choice of a spot.

The mist lifted and the sun welcomed him into the village. It was the bracing sun of October-November, which is the season of the Festival of Lights. He camped as usual in the young men's dormitory, but this time he fretted at the thought that it did not belong to him. Why not build his own house and granary on the land which had been mortgaged to him by the widow Randhai? Admittedly the land did not belong to him as yet, but she was an old woman and she had no family. And in due course the land would come to him.

After he had eaten, he sat on the veranda smoking ganja. Presently he saw a group of villagers coming towards him; among them the headman, the Barik, Sukru Jani – and Mandia and Tikra. The sight of the last two made him wild with anger and he thought, 'How dare they come here and leave my buffaloes in the jungle! They are becoming more and more disobedient.'

The villagers approached hesitatingly, talking to each other in undertones as if to build up their courage. Were they coming to ask the bride-price? He decided he would agree to pay whatever price they demanded, up to eighty rupees. After all, he would only be giving them a promise – and promise and performance were two different things.

'You there, Tikra and Mandia,' he shouted, 'what do you mean by leaving my buffaloes in the forest for the tiger to eat? Your backs seem to be itching! And you, Sukru, a fine pair of gotis you gave me to replace you! I want all of you to witness this thing.'

'Chitam Paraja and Dami Nadu Paraja are there to guard the buffaloes,' Mandia replied easily, 'so you don't need to worry about the tiger. We came here because we had some urgent business with you. We have informed your clerk.'

The villagers squatted on the ground below the veranda. Sukru Jani pulled out a bundle from the folds of his garment and opened it out before the villagers; it was full of coins. He counted out the rupees one by one and placed them on the ground in neat piles.

'Sahukar,' he said, 'here is the money we owe you. Take it, release my sons and leave my land.'

The Sahukar sat speechless for a time. Then he said: 'Where did you find this money? It must be stolen; I shall go to the police station and make a report.'

'Where did I find the money?' Sukru Jani repeated. 'I borrowed some from my friends, sold my new land, and took some money from Nandibali as bride-price. What is there to report to the police? Well, do as you please, but first let us settle the matter of the debt and my land.'

'Wait a bit,' the Sahukar retorted. 'The matter can't be settled as easily as that. I have ploughed that land twice, and each time I had to spend about fifty rupees. The land was mortgaged to me for thirty years; you yourself put your thumb-print on the deed. And now you want me to leave!' He turned and addressed the villagers. 'Maybe you people don't know this; and how could you, since I never told you about it. Not only these two, but the old man here, Sukru Jani, were my gotis, and he mortgaged his land to me for thirty years and got himself released and came here. And he told me, 'Enjoy my land for as long as you wish, even beyond the thirty years; only, write off a part of my debt each year.' And I believed him, for I always thought a Paraja is true to his word. And I spent so much money on his land – I put in manure, and fertilizer, and planted orange trees, and the trees cost me eight annas each – and now he comes to me and demands the land back at once! Was there ever such a scoundrel? Someone must have put him up to this!'

His words unleashed a furore of protest and counter-protest. The village elders who had come to mediate said: 'We never knew this!' while Sukru Jani and his sons indignantly denied the Sahukar's allegations. The money-lender said he could produce witnesses, and the Revenue Inspector himself would support what he said; if they wished they could see the papers on which Sukru Jani had put his thumb-mark.

Some supported the Sahukar, others supported Sukru Jani; others again, fearful of getting involved in all this, slipped quietly away. Sukru Jani, Mandia and Tikra abused the Sahukar for a while; then they too returned home. Nothing was settled.

Back home, they tried to decide who was responsible for the land being mortgaged. Strong words were exchanged, with the father blaming his sons and they him.

'Why did you go felling trees in the jungle and getting into trouble with the Forest Guard?' Mandia shouted at his father.

'And who asked you to brew liquor and get caught by the excise people?' Sukru Jani retorted.

'I was always against the idea of mortgaging the land, but you wouldn't listen to me. Well, do what you think best now.'

'What a dutiful son you are! So eager to accuse your own father!'

They felt that the land was slipping away from them and that there was nothing they could do. Powerless to hurt the money-lender, they fought and quarrelled among themselves. They were still shouting at each other when evening fell, and Sukru Jani went to bed without eating his food.

Chapter 104

The morning was bitterly cold; a heavy fog lay over the houses like the smoke that rises from burning straw. Large drops of moisture fell from the thatch-eaves. Inside Sukru Jani's hut, the family sat huddled round a fire, wrapped in thick cotton sheets, and speaking in subdued voices. The quarrels of the night had been forgotten. Nandibali said: 'You know what money-lenders are; you can't make him give up the land with mere words.'

Mandia said: 'Well, we tried to do things the proper way; we offered him money and he refused to accept it. Why don't we just go and plough up the land? What do you say to that?'

But Sukru Jani knew what could happen if that was done: heads would be called in and people would be arrested.

'No, no,' he said.

Nandibali said: 'The only thing we can do is go to court.'

'But that costs money! Where are we to find it?'

'Oh, it can't cost that much, or else how could people ever go to court? Let's go and find out.'

Sukru Jani beat his forehead with his fists and moaned: 'The land is gone, and now we shall have to see the inside of a court! God alone knows what will happen.'

But his sons reassured him and said: 'Don't be afraid. We must do as Nandibali says; it's the only way.'

But how did one 'go to court'? They knew nothing about these matters; they had only heard that people 'went to court' and 'fought cases', and either won or lost. They had seen from a distance the world of law courts, packed with buzzing crowds of clerks, peons, policemen, and lawyers carrying thick books under their arms, and it was a nightmare world for them. In the court there was always someone growling at you: 'What are you doing there?'; 'Who asked you to come in?'; 'Who is that smoking?'; Stop that noise!' And people asked you not only your name but also your father's name and the name of his father and his father, back to the fourteenth generation; and everything that was spoken was written down in the books. The tribesmen lived in terror of the court, and the stories that they heard only added to their fear.

From time to time, papers were sent out by the court to tribesmen even in the most remote village, and these were known as the 'summons'. The peon of the court sent out these papers together with a red chili or his bamboo walking-stick or the brass badge of office which he wore over his uniform; these things became symbols of the court's authority, and anyone who was handed the papers would have to carry them to their destination, and anyone who received the 'summons' was obliged to attend the court.

They had no idea how to start a case, so they went to the headman, without whose help nothing could be done. The headman told them they would have· to give him five rupees; he would then gather others to help them, and go to court on their behalf when the moment came.

All the important people in the village had to be propitiated. Yes, they would go to court for him and give witness when required, but they would need a little something for food, cheroots and drink. Some said they had no clothes, and some wanted this and others wanted that. In short, it was obvious that they would help Sukru Jani only when their requirements were fulfilled. The old man hesitated, but Mandia and Tikra and Nandibali were ready to go to any length.

It was not long before the Sahukar heard that Sukru Jani was going to court against him and canvassing support from door to door. He at once decided to fight the case. The land was fertile, and he had no intention of giving up his orange orchard; above all, he had his position to uphold. He would start his own suit for recovery of his loan and for enforcing the contract which his gotis had made with him. 'The court does not exist for Parajas alone,' he said to himself. 'The rich are entitled to justice as much as the poor.' He too would canvass for the villagers' support.

Sukru Jani, his sons and Nandibali went to the disari and asked him to tell them the most auspicious hour for going to the court. He said: 'Leave the village just as the first cock is crowing; that is the auspicious moment.'

Since they would have to be away from home for four
or five days, they prepared enough mandia for themselves,
and firewood, and all the other things they would require.
And since it would not be proper to meet an official of the
court unless they carried gifts for him, they procured a
heavy bunch of bananas and a dozen eggs. Thus equipped,
they were ready to start.

Chapter 105

Sukru Jani must have dozed off towards the end of the
night, for suddenly he felt that he was wide awake, but
that his body was gone. He felt very weak without it, and
when he coughed he made only a hollow sound. Gradually
he became conscious of other noises – the sounds of chattering and thudding. This made him angry. He wanted to
lie there in silence, listening to something, and someone
had burst into his room and was shouting and disturbing
him. Then he felt his limbs returning to him, followed by
the rest of his body. But this was still more annoying.
Strange pains were all over his body, and on top of that
there was the thudding and chattering. He shivered, drew
up his legs and closed his eyes, but almost at once all the
cocks in the village started crowing together, and Mandia
shook him and said 'Shouldn't we be making a move?' He
tried to open his eyes and look around him, but his eyelids
were glued together after his sleep. He no longer felt the
pain in his body. The Sahukar was trying to cheat him and
he must go to court; remembering this, he stopped shiver-

ing and rose to his feet, his head instantly clear.

At the auspicious moment they started. It was a long journey across the mountains. Wherever the narrow tracks crossed each other in the jungle, the crossings were marked by cinders and ashes—where people had rested under the trees and cooked their meals—and flat stones on which they had sat. At some of the crossings, they met strangers and Sukru Jani asked each in turn what they knew about courts and the filing of cases. He stored all the information in his head and slowly built up a plan. He would walk into the court-room where the magistrate sat and place the bunch of bananas and the dozen eggs on the magistrate's table, fold his hands and say: 'Great lord, I have been wronged by the money-lender'; and his sons would stand behind him, repeating whatever he said. They would fall at the magistrate's feet again and again and the magistrate would be obliged to listen.

Mandia said that this was not what had happened when he had been tried. But Sukru Jani told him that a case concerning the land was bound to be different from the trial of someone who had been caught brewing liquor. He was determined to prostrate himself without fear at the magistrate's feet and tell him everything, and not to return home until he got justice. One who spoke the truth had nothing to fear. The court was the dwelling-place of Dharmu, the Just One.

Hunger and thirst, pain and fatigue, were all forgotten in the desire for revenge.

At times their path led through fields of olsi, whose characteristic smell of fresh earth reminded them anew of their beloved land. Hope mingled with fear as they plodded on.

By the evening of the second day they had reached Bada Chendri, not far from Koraput. Here they lodged in a wayside inn run by a man called Daniel.

Next day they joined the crowd of gotis and coolies who travelled to Koraput every morning. On the way they asked more questions about the court and the magistrate, but received only vague answers.

The town lay high above the valley and as they climbed the slope, the roofs of the buildings kept looming up through the mist. They cooked their food under a tree; stray dogs pestered them as they ate, and had to be driven away. Here and there under the trees were other groups of Kondhs, Parajas and Dombs, who had come to town from distant villages. Most of them had business in court and had time only for a few routine questions: 'How are the crops in your village?'; Are your cattle troubled with the sickness?'

The court had not yet opened, but under the mango trees in front of the magistrate's house there was already a crowd of people, some of them peering anxiously through the gate. Presently the magistrate's orderly came out in his dazzling uniform and chased them away, telling them to go to the court-house.

Sukru Jani and his sons covered the bunch of bananas with a rag and Sukru Jani tucked the eggs into the folds of his loin-cloth for safety. The bunch of bananas was large and a part of it remained exposed to greedy, inquisitive eyes.

On the veranda of the court-house they met a man dressed in a shirt and a flowing dhoti. He wore spectacles and a short, folded sheet of cloth draped over one shoulder like a scarf. He had a long hooked nose, like a parrot's beak. This was the Petition-Writer. He looked them up and down, nodded his head a few times and asked them to follow him, with the air of a trusted friend. They started telling him their story, but he interrupted saying: 'Leave everything to me!' Then he poured out a stream of incomprehensible advice. As he talked, he kept looking at the bunch of bananas. Noticing this, Sukru Jani covered it up more carefully while Mandia stood between it and the Writer.

'Now listen,' the Writer concluded, 'you must get a petition written, and engage a lawyer.' By this he meant himself. He wanted them to pay him in advance; but this put them on their guard, and they decided to try and manage for themselves.

By now the court was in session. Through the window they could see the magistrate at his table. The court-room was thronged with people, in various dresses and postures. Near the door, at one end of the hall, two men held a cow by a rope; the cow was trying to break away and rush with lowered horns at the seat of judgement. There were jars full of liquor and earthen pots and pipes used for distilling, which had been confiscated in raids. Inside a wooden enclosure and guarded by policemen stood two men with their backs pressed against the wall. But above all, it seemed to them the court-room was full of officials. They were eager to enter, but they were afraid of all these uniformed peons with their red turbans and bands of authority. The magistrate might be annoyed.

At last they plucked up their courage and entered the court-room; but they still did not know what to do. They stood there stupidly. The hours passed; the cow was taken away; the pots and jars of liquor were removed. The policemen clicked their heels and led out the two men who had been inside the dock, the iron chains clanking as they went. From time to time the magistrate spoke: 'You are sentenced to rigorous imprisonment for six months.'

'You are sentenced to pay a fine of two hundred rupees.'

Such words filled them with terror. Sukru Jani would edge his way backwards, pushing his sons behind him. At the entrance stood a peon who shouted out names, whereupon the people who were summoned came in. Lawyers kept coming and going, and the court-room resounded with voices. But the three of them merely stood there, with staring eyes and mouths agape. As the hours passed, the bunch of bananas on Mandia's shoulder grew heavier and heavier.

Finally the court rose and the magistrate walked out of the court-house. At once Sukru, Mandia and Tikra rushed after him, surrounded him and fell at his feet. 'Great lord, take pity on us or we shall be ruined,' they wailed.

The bunch of bananas was laid bare and the old man pulled out the bundle of eggs, but Mandia was clumsy in untying the knots of the bundle and Sukru Jani shouted at him: 'Hurry up! Hurry up!'

The magistrate was irritated. 'Why have you come now? And why do you stop me on the road?' he said. 'Go away now, and come back tomorrow.'

He continued on his way, but the old man ran after him with the bunch of bananas held aloft, saying: 'This humble gift from us, great lord!'

The magistrate growled in anger and Sukru Jani backed away. Pale and shaking, they returned to their shelter under the trees.

Mandia said: 'We must go and ask the Writer to help us. We can't do anything by ourselves.' The others agreed, and in the evening they went to the Writer's house. The Writer took the bananas and the eggs and made out a list of all the items for which they would have to pay in order to file the case.

'The paper will cost you two rupees, plus five rupees for the stamp that has to be fixed to your petition; I shall give you details of the other costs when the time comes.'

Next day their petition was written and filed. The Writer told them they should wait for another two days until a date was fixed for hearing their petition. 'You are bound to win,' he told them. 'Don't be afraid of the cost; you'll get back everything when you have won your case.' They had to part with fifteen rupees but their fear of the court was gone too. The Writer filled them with confidence. He told them how the wicked money-lender was going to be punished, and they were so happy when they heard all this that they forgot how much money they had paid. They took shelter behind his beaked nose and thick spectacles, and in their imagination they hurled stones and sticks at the money-lender to their hearts' content. They thought nothing of spending the winter night under the tree; the words of the Writer kept ringing in their ears and gave them warmth.

Chapter 106

Long, long ago, the people belonging to a certain tribe built a hamlet in the jungle: the tribe bore the name 'Kara' or 'hare', for this animal represented their totem; and in their dialect a hamlet is called a 'put'. Thus 'Kara-put' was born. Over the years this changed to Koraput; today it is the name of the largest district in Orissa as well as of the town.

The Kara tribe has almost disappeared, but its name remains. What could be more satisfying to the liberated spirits of those distant ancestors? Man is not a lone traveller who has come from nowhere, but a wave that has been rolling on and on from time immemorial. Sometimes even the names are forgotten, but the ancestral spirits live on, and no man can shake off his ancestry.

And attachment to the soil becomes a part of the link with one's ancestors. Thus Sukru Jani would never find peace, living or dead, unless he recovered his land from the Sahukar.

The plaint was filed and a summons served, ordering the Sahukar to appear in court on an appointed date. The Writer told Sukru Jani to be present in court on that day. Meanwhile he and his sons could go home. On the way, Mandia and Tikra tried to persuade their father to file another case against the Sahukar, and claim the bride-price for Jili.

'No,' Sukru Jani said sadly. 'I couldn't touch that dirty money. But soon I shall be dead; then you can sell your sister to him and enjoy the money.'

Mandia said: 'Then let's bring Jili back! He has taken our land – why should he have Jili as well without paying the price?'

Sukru Jani said nothing, but his heart was filled with sorrow when he thought of Jili. He had forgiven her long ago: anyone could make a mistake, and he knew she must be suffering. To accept money from the Sahukar would be

to close the door on her for ever. What did these boys
know about it? .

Chapter 107

Jili had grown accustomed to her life with the Sahukar; she
almost liked it. Only, when he drank himself stupid and
ran after her on tottering legs, dripping saliva, and shouting 'Jili, Jili!' or when he was full of ganja smoke and his
eyes grew red like hibiscus flowers and the veins stood out
on his forehead, only at such times did she find him repulsive. More often she pitied him; his old age gave her an
edge over him, a feeling of superiority. Sometimes he
would work hard to please her, combing his hair neatly,
parting it in the middle, waxing his moustaches stiff and
hanging garlands round his neck. Then he would come to
her and talk to her in loving words, but she knew of the
cracks beneath the edifice of words, and was hard put to it
not to laugh in his face.

She could see that he was an important man, and she felt
proud of the position which he had given her. The people
of Kadamjholla looked upon her as the head of the village,
waited for her orders and came to her with all their troubles. The headman of the village said: 'Since you have
come, the Sahukar comes here more often. We can tell him
of our difficulties. It is good for us.'

She would have liked to draw a blind on her past; but
she could not help feeling hurt and humiliated that her
father and brothers had never come to visit her. 'So they

don't care whether I'm alive or dead,' she said to herself;
'Very well, then!' She was going to be happy in spite of
them. It did not matter that she was only the Sahukar's
kept woman and not his wife. Sometimes she became curious about his wife. 'Have you seen her, Sukumani?' she
asked the girl. 'Does she ever come here?'

'I only saw her once when I went to his village,' Sukumani replied. 'She is not like you; she is ugly and old.'

Jili smiled. 'Take some of those ripe bananas, Sukumani,' she said graciously, 'or else they'll go waste. Now, tell
me more about her: is she fair or dark? Dark, you say?'
She laughed with pleasure.

She sat leaning against the wall. She had combed her hair
into a shiny ball and dressed it with flowers. The sky was
clear; the fields looked fresh. Hundreds of bees were
swarming around the olsi flowers. Flights of parrots came
to feast on the ripe paddy in the fields and wild ducks,
white cranes and wood-pigeons flew across the sky in
formation. The billowing hills rose on either side. The
Kondhs were singing. But suddenly she remembered her
home and the smile died on her lips.

'Listen, lady, how they sing!' Sukumani said. She could
catch the words of the chorus but they meant nothing to
her.

Jeita Nilasama Baile, Baile,
Jeita Talasama Baile, Baile.

'Do you understand the language, Sukumani?' she
asked.

'A little. That's because I've been here since I was a
child.'

The Kondhs' song rose and fell and echoed round the hills, sung by thirty or forty voices together; a group of young men standing on top of one hill would sing a couplet, and the girls on a hilltop half a mile away would sing another couplet in reply. Though the words meant nothing to Jili, the song brought several images to her mind. She felt she was flying like a solitary bird, high above the earth, and the sky was pure and open; but she felt sad and lonely. Then the music changed, and her mood changed with it. The melody seemed to be tossing about and turning over and over again, trying to woo the cold earth into excitement.

From joy the music changed to pathos, and Jili felt as if a mountain stream which had been leaping and gurgling among the rocks had suddenly entered a dark ravine where it was muffled by dense jungle. This time she saw leaves drooping under a blazing sun and wood-pigeons lamenting in the jungle, crowded together in a circle, the neck of one bird lying on that of its neighbour.

'Listen to the song,' Sukumani whispered. They both listened.

'What does it all mean!' Jili asked. 'I hear the words 'Lembara', 'Dambara', 'Nilasasa', 'Talasa' over and over again.'

'Those are the names which the Kondhs give to their sweethearts,' Sukumani explained. 'The young men sing: 'We called you again and again, but you never answered. You have forgotten us; and why should you care for us? – you are the daughters of rich parents, who live in whitewashed houses. The ceilings and walls of your houses have been so thickly plastered with lime that the lime dust is always falling from the ceiling.'

Sukumani laughed, but Jili sat silent and pensive. The songs did not interest her any more. Thoughts came crowding. She was a concubine; he was old, had a wife and children. Bagla. The young men's dormitory. Her father's anger. Her brothers never come to see her. Her mother. Her dead mother. Her old father. Bagla. Her mother. Bagla. Bagla. She could utter his name, but without him her life was nothing. She had no right to utter that name, and for that reason it was always uppermost in her mind. She had lost him.

The Sahukar had told her that he would be building a house as he was getting more and more land in her village, on which he intended to grow oranges, wheat and sugarcane; that he would build a house for her there, and that when it was complete he would take her to live there; she could go back to her village in triumph with her head high, and not in shame as she had left. Jili was waiting eagerly for that day. Nobody from the village came to see her, and one day the Sahukar told her that her father had sued him in court. He gave her his own version of the case, making it appear as if he was the one who had been wronged.

When Jili heard that the land had been mortgaged by her father for thirty years, she exclaimed 'Impossible! No one ever told me that before.'

'Ah, that was your father's secret. How could he have told his children? His sons would have killed him if they had known. You can't blame him, the poor old man! He was too old to go on working as a goti, and this was the only way he could free himself. Mandia and Nandibali must have made him go to court; he would never have started this case on his own. It's false! I told them that if they wanted the land back they should pay me the money they owe me – and what I have spent in improving the land and planting the orange trees. Wasn't that fair? And now, because I'm simple and innocent, they drag me to court! Well, God will be the judge.'

Jili could not feel involved in the land. All the old ties had snapped.

The money-lender caressed her and said: 'Should my own relations treat me in this way? Am I not his daughter's husband? But none of them ever come to see you! Why should they be angry with you? It was I who brought you here. But Mandia and Nandibali never stop abusing you. I can't even repeat the words they use; and when I told them it was wrong for families to quarrel, they let fly at me. They are fools! If they were in difficulties they could have asked me for help, or they could have come to you; why not? But no – they only want to fight.'

He tried hard to win her sympathy and was grateful for any word of comfort that she spoke. He would draw himself up, full of righteousness, and say: 'Don't you worry, my pet, they can never snatch away your land from you. Don't be afraid; and trust in God.'

He stayed with her for two days and he bought her a sari and two necklaces, one of aluminium and the other of brass. She had never received such attention and care before. Her heart softened towards him and she discovered new qualities in him. She was sure that he had never loved anyone except her. She no longer found him repulsive.

The future seemed to be shaping itself. She would have a position – she would not be brushed off like something which had been blown by the wind and left clinging to the money-lender. When she thought of the dispute over the land she could not wholly sympathize with her father and

brothers; she began to think of her own interests. Her
doubts and fears had vanished.

Chapter 108

The Sahukar rode to Sarsupadar, opened his money-bags
and waited.

One by one the headman, the barik and the other village
dignitaries were summoned to the young men's dormitory
by Madhu Ghasi. They would arrive after dark, sit in the
unlit room – only the ends of the cheroots glowing – and
talk in whispers, while Madhu Ghasi guarded the entrance.
No one wanted the Sahukar as an enemy; but he could
make a useful ally. After all, Garaja Sundara, the Revenue
Inspector, who could change black into white, was his
friend.

The money-lender appeared to plead with them; but no
one could miss the underlying threat. 'You may do your
worst,' he told them, 'but the court will never accept your
word against all the documents which I have; the Revenue
Inspector will give evidence in my favour and you will be
exposed. And you mustn't blame me if the court punishes
you for giving false witness. Don't come to me when you
are ruined, it will be too late.'

And to the headman he said: 'Don't forget, it was the
Amin and the Revenue Inspector who made you the headman of this village. And they are my friends.'

They listened to him in fear and awe, and the words

burned into their hearts. They weighed the Sahukar's threats against Sukru Jani's promises. And they told themselves: 'If Sukru Jani's cause is just, he will certainly win, no matter who helps him or opposes him. Dharmu, the Just One, knows everything and will understand the circumstances which compel us to side with the Sahukar. He won't blame us.' The headman was the first to go over to the Sahukar; and he was soon followed by the Barik and all the big tenants. Everyone was ready to give evidence in favour of the Sahukar even if they were called as Sukru Jani's witnesses.

'And now, Sahukar,' they said to him, 'you must always be kind to us. We are simple farmers who don't want to get into trouble. It is not for us to judge whether you are right, or Sukru Jani; that is for Dharmu to decide. We only want to cultivate our lands in peace.'

When ten people join in shouting a slogan, they begin to believe in it. While convincing each other they begin to convince themselves.

The village headman explained the position to his friends. 'You see, he is a big man, and he can always do what he wants to do. Let him have the land; we shall find another piece of land for Sukru Jani somewhere. After all, he is one of us and we must look after his children.'

Sukru Jani, knowing nothing of all this, remained confident. The Writer had taken his money and given him hope, and there were others who reinforced what the Writer had said – and were paid for doing so. Sukru Jani went about telling people how the Sahukar was going to be taught a lesson.

The crops of mandia, olsi and chili which he had grown on his new land were plentiful, but he did not feel he could depend on land about which he knew so little. If he got back the old land there would be no dearth of men to cultivate it, and his granary would be as full as before. He lay huddled on the earth with the chill November wind blowing around him and heard his land positively calling to him. There were such memories in that land! He *must* get it back.

He would get bullocks to plough the land from end to end. His fingers itched. But he had become weak; his joints ached and his head swam if he worked even the tiniest bit too hard. It must be due to his worries and the lack of good food he told himself; but he knew in his heart that he was old, and the knowledge depressed him. He must save his strength for the day of the lawsuit. Then, perhaps, with his land restored he could sleep in peace. But no, Mandia and Tikra had to be married; he must bring Jili back and find a proper husband for her – he would build his house again, right from the foundations up. He forgot that he was old: he must live to see his grandchildren – the shouts of young children had not been heard in his house for ages.

Suddenly he was filled with self-pity. He bowed low and beat his head on the ground in deep obeisance to his gods and prayed: 'O Dadi Budha, Soul of my first ancestor; Almighty Dharmu; Dharatini, Mother Earth: have pity on me! Do not trouble me any more, and I will sacrifice as many pigeons and fowl as you wish.'

Chapter 109

The lawsuit 'Sukru Jani versus Ramachandra Bisoi, Sahu-kar' came up for hearing before the court at Koraput. Sukru Jani had no proper lawyer; there was only the Petition-Writer and a friend of his, who was a Pujari or priest, who waited outside the court-room. They had taught him what he should say. Ramachandra Bisoi had engaged a lawyer and filed a written statement. Two dates of hearing passed and on the third day the magistrate explained to both parties that they should produce their witnesses. He told Sukru Jani: 'You should bring your witnesses on the sixth day of the coming month; that is the next date.'

Sukru Jani pleaded: 'Great lord, I am an ignorant man and I do not understand what is meant by a date.' The magistrate consulted a sheet of paper and said, 'Today is a Tuesday. Come back on the fourth Tuesday from now.'

Sukru Jani and his party left the court-room, bewildered by the complexity of dates. They would have to ask the Writer. Outside, in a corner of the premises, they saw the Sahukar surrounded by a crowd of people, among them the Writer and the Pujari. Seeing Sukru Jani, they hurried up to him. 'We were giving the Sahukar a piece of our mind,' the Writer said. 'He is frightened, even though he has engaged a lawyer.'

The Pujari said: 'I hope you remember the next date of hearing. If you don't turn up on that date your case will die and after that nobody will be able to help you.'

The Writer said: 'Of course he'll remember. Is he such a fool that he will forget and let his case die?'

'So, remember the date,' the Pujari said again. 'Get it by heart. The next date of hearing falls on the sixth Tuesday from today. Count five Tuesdays in between and come on the Tuesday following, and remember to bring your witnesses.'

'Now come with me,' said the Writer, 'and I shall instruct each one of you what you should tell the Court.'

Sukru Jani could hear the Sahukar shouting to his men at a little distance: 'Come, let us go. Today is Tuesday; we have to come back here on the sixth Tuesday. Don't forget!'

Sukru Jani and his group went one way and the Sahukar's party another.

That evening the Pujari went and met the Sahukar secretly. Even his enemies could not accuse him of being partial to anyone; he regarded it his duty to help everyone who was engaged in a lawsuit and asked him for assistance.

The next morning Sukru Jani met the Writer and the Pujari once again. They assured him once more that his victory was certain, and the Pujari said: 'You should have heard how I insulted him yesterday outside the courtroom. His liver must have dried up!' Money changed hands. Then Sukru Jani and his party set out for home across the golden olsi fields.

Chapter 110

The chain of Tuesdays seemed to be endless.

The harvest began and bald patches appeared here and there in the rice fields: the mandia and suan were cut and

the hillsides lay bare; the olsi flowers began to wither and
the yellow fields developed black patches. The villagers
were out in the fields all day and the doors of their houses
were shut. The dungudungas were loud at night. December came, and the mist lingered, even by day. The earth,
having poured out all its treasure, lay bare and quiet. Sukru
Jani counted the Tuesdays. The moonlit nights came and
then the dark nights, and still there were two more Tuesdays to come. It was difficult to find Tikra and Mandia
now. Every afternoon the space under the big tree in the
centre of the village was filled with dancers and the tinkling of ankle-bells could be heard on every side. Pale shadows flitted through the mist; no one knew who had gone
where. Many of the young people were drunk and heavy-
eyed with liquor brewed from the newly harvested rice.
Ripples of suppressed laughter told of bodies pressed
together in defiance of the December cold.

The older people sat round the fires in front of their
houses and talked. 'Yes, Nandibali, my son,' Sukru Jani
was saying, 'the new land has given us good crops, but
they won't last us the full year.'

'But this was only the first year,' Nandibali pointed out.
'The land was newly broken, and the manure did not have
time enough to mix with the soil. But wait, and you will
see what happens next year.'

'Next year things will be very different. Our case will
end soon. Next Tuesday our witness will be heard. The
land will come back to us. I don't know whether we
should keep the orange trees or cut them down.'

Nandibali said: 'It is not wise to think of these things too
early. If you float away now you'll find that the flood has
gone and left you dry. If Dharmu is on our side we are

bound to win; but the money-lender is so clever that it will not be easy to defeat him. Leave everything to Dharmu, and don't start making decisions in advance, or the god will be angry.'

Sukru Jani did not reply. He warmed his hands before the fire. The smoke and mist were see-sawing up and down. The night was cold but beautiful. He could not see anything distinctly; everything came and went.

'These young people have no faith,' he thought, 'especially Nandibali. It is unlucky to doubt everything; and they call it wisdom! How can they ever grow into men if they are afraid of everything?'

Through the mist came the sound of two Kondh flutes played together; the notes chased each other through the mist, met, locked, then tumbled down and separated; they grew tired and drowsy, then they spread their wings and sailed away into the moonlight, over the mist, and went no one knew where.

The dew falling on him always made him drowsy and pensive. Nothing was the same. The jungle was getting thinner every year; there was less and less rain; and the young men were becoming soft, like the soil in the coastal plains below.

'Whose fault is it that Mandia and Tikra are not yet married?' he thought. 'Can't they find brides for themselves? Must someone else go and capture brides for them?' he laughed to himself. 'Nandibali is more like the people of my generation: at least he is strong; but why should he imagine all kinds of unlucky things?'

Suddenly, he said to Nandibali: 'You are a young man, Nandibali; at your age one shouldn't be afraid of anything! We are certain to get the land back. And there'll be plenty

to do. We must decide about those orange trees right now!
I think we ought to leave a few trees in the middle, and we
can plant onions in between. The rest of the land can be
used for growing rice.'

Nandibali said: 'In that case the Sahukar will claim the
oranges when they are ready for picking, and there'll be
another fight.'

'You think we should cut all the trees down?' Sukru Jani
said. 'Perhaps you're right.'

He was thinking of something else. The sound of the
dance came to him from the square and he wondered how
the young people could still dance in that bitter cold.

'Have you spoken to all our witnesses?' he asked Nandibali. 'We must look after them properly, you know. See
that they have enough to drink and plenty of cheroots.'

'I'm told the Sahukar was trying to win them over to his
side, but had no luck,' Nandibali said.

'So that's why you're worried!' Sukru Jani laughed. 'It's
the Sahukar who should be worrying! He doesn't know the
people of this village. How can they betray me? Haven't
we lived together for generations? Still, I'll go and ask the
headman.'

He thought of Jili. How could she stick to the Sahukar at
a time like this, when he was trying to ruin them and take
their witnesses away? He remembered how helpful she had
been to him in the old days; she could work better than any
man.

Mandia returned a little later, reeling drunk.

'Have you heard, Mandia?' Sukru Jani said. 'The Sahukar has been trying to win our witnesses over!'

Mandia flared up. 'You don't know how to handle
him,' he shouted, 'leave him to me. I'm going to cut him

up into little bits and bury the pieces in that land! Don't try
to stop me, I tell you! I'll curse you if you do. I'll kill that
dog . . .'

He tottered away into the house.

'He's right, you know, even if he's drunk,' was Nandibali's comment.

'Certainly,' Sukru Jani said. 'He'll hack him to pieces inside our own house!'

Later that evening he thought of Jili again. Poor motherless girl! How she must be shivering in the cold! Surely
that miser of a Sahukar wasn't going to look after her
properly! She must be mad to stay with him.

'Why does a man go on living!' he thought. 'There's no
happiness anywhere!' He sighed. But he must live until the
land was recovered. After that – how happy one could be
wandering through the moonlight and the mist without a
body! There would be no hunger, no sorrow; only the
open sky and the moon.

Nandibali had gone to bed, and Sukru Jani sat alone.
The fire blazed like a funeral pyre, and every now and then
the logs crackled and burst with a noise like a pistol-shot.
This was the hour of night when the spirits of the dead
wandered about. Sukru Jani saw some shadows fly off a
tree and come towards him. The breeze blew in his face.
He felt as if a handful of ice-cold dew had been flung on his
chest. He went inside the house and lay down to sleep.

Suddenly it seemed very important that he should live.
He did not want to lose his children, his house and his land;
he did not want to die.

But he found his life lonely.

When he closed his eyes he saw the image of Sombari.
'Wait a little, Sombari,' he told her. 'You have waited

long; give me a little more time, let me attend to a few things.'

There were loud sounds of snoring in the house. Outside everything was quiet.

The fire had grown cold.

Chapter 111

Sukru Jani had to reach Koraput with his witnesses on the Tuesday, so he decided to leave his house on the previous Friday. That morning the house was swept clean and freshly plastered with mud, and a garland of mango leaves was hung over the door, for good luck. The tribal priest made a sacrifice at the crossing of the village paths. Crows and dogs were fed and then they were ready to start.

Sukru Jani had nine witnesses whose lands lay near the disputed land, and who knew all about his deal with the Sahukar. The headman and the Barik were also there. Sukru Jani had not found it easy to persuade them to accompany him to Koraput. There are only a few occasions when a villager becomes important enough to dictate terms to his neighbours: a marriage, a death or a court-case. He never allows such an opportunity to go to waste. Sukru Jani and his sons had to beg, implore and cajole their witnesses, and it was only the sight of money which finally made them agree.

At the end of the first day's journey the witnesses complained of exhaustion and hunger which could only be assuaged when a goat had been slaughtered and the meat washed down with a huge pot of liquor.

Next morning, they were about to start when it was found that none of them had any tobacco – and they could not possibly walk so far unless some was provided.

Sukru Jani called his sons and Nandibali aside and whispered: 'It is becoming more and more costly! And we still have to pay the Writer and the Pujari, and to arrange a feast for all the villagers when we have won the case.'

'Be quiet,' Nandibali warned him, 'don't let them hear you; if you displease them now, we shall lose our case.'

At heart, Sukru Jani did not grudge all these extravagances; he felt that this was an occasion to celebrate. He was leading a procession; the entire village was with him. He was going to get back his land. The money-lender could not touch him. It was a wonderful feeling.

For a long time they had not even heard anything of the money-lender. He had not come to the village again. 'He must have gone to meet his lawyer,' Sukru Jani thought. 'He must be preparing for the case on Tuesday; but who cares? Let him do what he likes!'

On the Saturday evening they reached a village on the outskirts of Koraput, where they camped for the night in the same lodging-house as before. There were many other people going to Koraput to attend the court. They had come from villages deep in the heart of the forest. Their cases were the usual ones concerning the payment of bride-price, the theft of maize or paddy from the fields, or disputes over land. Sukru Jani asked everyone if he had seen the Sahukar, but no one had. In the lodging-house they rehearsed what each of them had to say in court. The Writer had warned Sukru Jani that the Sahukar's lawyer would try to trap his witnesses, and that they should only answer his questions with one or two sentences: 'It is a lie!' or 'I know nothing.'

There was a bright moon. The village of Chindrigaon lay in a deep valley and from here Koraput town looked like an enormous ant-hill, and the houses like growths of fungus on it. In the distance, in a little village on the top of a hill, a fire was burning among the huts. There were other hillocks of different sizes surrounding the hill and the mist had spread over them. Sukru Jani thought of his own village, where at this time of year people kept watch over their rice fields all night long, and fires were lit against the cold.

Sunday and Monday they spent roaming the streets of Koraput. They did not see the Writer or the Pujari; and they were told that the court was closed on those days.

Tuesday arrived.

They were waiting outside the court long before it opened. They had no time to eat their mandia; they decided that they would cook a meal of rice after the business in court was over. People crowded into the court-room. The Writer and the Pujari were not there and Sukru Jani's face fell. The headman said: 'Don't worry; when your turn comes, your name wil be called out. The Writer will come in time.'

The court began its work amidst the usual noise and bustle. Names were called out, the people came and went. But Sukru Jani's name remained uncalled and the Writer was still missing.

Hours later, the magistrate rose from his chair and went out. The crowd inside the court-room dispersed. Sukru Jani walked to the peon of the court, bowed deeply and asked: 'When will our names be called, sir?'

The peon took them to the clerk of the court, to whom they repeated their question. He was writing something at his table and without raising his head he asked: 'Who has filed the case?'

'The name is Sukru Jani, sir,' the old man replied.

The clerk looked at the register of cases and read out: 'Sukru Jani versus Ramachandra Bisoi?' He looked at Sukru Jani and said: 'The date was fixed for the sixth day of this month. Why didn't you turn up? Your case has been dismissed as you were absent. You may go.'

Sukru Jani squatted on the floor at the feet of the clerk and wailed: 'Great lord, I shall die! That date is today. I was asked to come on this Tuesday.'

The peon said: 'Go and don't make a noise.' He drove them out of the court saying: 'Fool! You were sleeping all these days and suddenly remembered your case.'

Just then Mandia Jani saw the Writer some way off and shouted: 'There is the Writer?' They ran to meet him. He seemed to be going somewhere in a hurry; the Pujari was with him. 'How could our case be dismissed, sir?' Sukru Jani asked him.

'Your case?' the Writer replied. 'But we thought you and the Sahukar had settled everything peacefully and that is why you did not turn up on the date of hearing, which was on the sixth day of this month.'

'That's not true,' Sukru Jani cried.

'But that is what the Sahukar told us when he came on the date of the hearing. You never came, so your suit was dismissed. You still owe me five rupees and I have been waiting for you.'

Sukru Jani turned to the Pujari and said: 'Didn't you tell us, sir, that we should come here on the sixth Tuesday?'

He turned to the Writer and said: 'And you told us the same thing.'

The Writer and the Pujari shook their heads and said: 'The fellow is mad! We never said any such thing! We told him clearly the case would be heard on the sixth day of this month, which was a Tuesday, and now listen to him!'

The Parajas stood there in dismay. The court-room filled again and the magistrate returned, followed by a crowd of officials and policemen.

'Please tell me what we should do then,' Sukru Jani begged.

'There is nothing to be done,' the Pujari replied. 'Go home quietly; if you make a scene the magistrate will be angry and there will be real trouble for you.'

The Writer nodded his head in agreement.

'You did this to me!' Sukru Jani shouted. 'Both of you are against me; I saw you talking to the money-lender. My curse on you! May Dharmu be the judge!'

'Go, you idiot!' the Writer shouted back. 'If you make trouble, I'll drag you to the magistrate and then you'll see! What fools these people from the hills are! You explain something to them ten times, and they still don't understand. Then they come and blame you!'

Whereupon the other tribesmen present nodded their heads and said: 'It's true. We tribesmen cannot understand these things. We are fools. Why should you blame the Writer?'

And the headman, the Barik and the other villagers said. 'Yes, it is our fault.'

The Writer and the Pujari went away. Sukru Jani was weeping. Tikra and Nandibali supported him by the shoulders. 'Come, let's go,' they said.

'Let's go,' the Barik echoed. 'I'm hungry.'

On the w~y home they all kept saying that the Sahukar had tricked them, and that Dharmu would punish him. Sukru Jani was silent. He had nothing to say. From time to time he would stop and pull at his hair with both hands until the tears came into his eyes and flowed over. They would try to comfort him, and he would look at them dumbly, with a piteous expression on his face.

'Don't break down,' they repeated. 'The case is lost, but we can still go to the money-lender and appeal to him to give back your land.'

Mandia hardly seemed conscious of his surroundings. A torrent of abuse flowed from his lips, and he seemed mesmerized by his own invective.

'What a lot of money wasted!' Nandibali remarked to Tikra. 'I knew this would happen! What chance has a poor man against a rich man? And now the old man's back is broken – he'll never get over this. As for me, I'm in for a scolding from Bili.'

'My land is gone!' Sukru Jani moaned. 'Why should I go on living?'

The headman tried to console him: 'Don't say such things. I have given you land before and I can always find some more land for you.'

'We shall see who dares to take our land!' Mandia shouted. 'I won't give it up, even if my head is cut off. I always told you: "There is no need to start a case; we will cultivate the land and enjoy it. Let the money-lender complain to his father if he wishes to!" Well, we shall see now.'

But the others shook their hands and warned him: 'Don't be foolish. Do as your elders tell you. You have to accept what is written in your fate by Dharmu.'

'Fate!' Mandia shouted angrily. 'I don't believe in it! There is no justice! I don't want to hear about your Dharmu! Keep him to yourselves; we don't need these things. We are peasants and we've only one way of keeping ourselves alive – by tilling the soil. The case may be dead but the land is not dead; nor are we. Who can deny that the land is ours?' I shall have one last word with the Sahukar. Let him take his money and return the land; and if he does not agree, let him do what he likes! But I will *never* leave the land.'

Chapter 112

Man does not possess the soil; he is possessed by it. He can grip the soil in his fist, but it laughs, and waits; and one day he drops down, and the soil is enriched. Grass and mandia and rice grow out of him, and they too fall back into the soil. And so it goes on.

The soil was rising higher and higher inside Sukru Jani's battered body.

He was a hollow reed, drilled by his sixty years into a flute which could produce only one unhappy melody—the Bhairaviraga—which tells of everything having been lost.

The mist was fainter than for several preceding nights The moonlight shone through the leaves and even the grass was clearly lit up. A net of light and shade lay before him under the tamarind tree. The hills around him, everything, had the texture of a dream. His hut was dark, and inside him lay a dark sorrow; but the night bore no resemblance to him. He was like a black cloud intruding into the moonlight.

The sky had not fallen because he was unhappy! The drums were throbbing, the dance was on, and the hills had wrapped themselves up in white shawls and settled down to watch the fun.

He sat huddled outside his hut.

Tikra was out looking for a girl whom he had seen briefly under the salap tree, gazing at the moon; she had seen him too, but had slipped away, pretending otherwise. He had liked her face, and he wanted a word with her.

Mandia too was out somewhere.

Nandibali sat with a group in the centre of the village, still discussing the lawsuit.

That night Mandia came to the old man and said: 'Father, the Sahukar is at Kadamjholla. Let us go to him tomorrow; maybe he will listen to us!'

'Maybe,' Sukru Jani thought. But surely it was useless. The land was gone. His face became wet with tears. Until he fell asleep he kept on calling to Dharmu. The moonlight smiled.

Chapter 113

The Sahukar explained to Jili that Dharmu never makes an error, and that was why Sukru Jani had lost his suit.

'They were trying to rob you of your land,' he told her, 'but it didn't work. And now *I* should drag them to court for the money they owe me! That would be the right thing to do, but I'll do what *you* say. Shall we let the money go?'

Jili merely laughed.

Kadamjholla lay flooded with moonlight. The Kondh flutes filled the air. The Sahukar had arranged a feast for the Kondhs at their expense.

Jili was warm from the Sahukar's caresses. She felt the night was specially made for her. He had asked her to dress up, and she had worn her best sari and combed her hair and put flowers in it. She had drunk a little liquor to please him, and the winter night was as warm as spring. She felt light at heart.

But the Sahukar was restless, he hated to be tied down. Already he was tiring of Jili, and he had made up his mind not to pay the bride-price for her.

The night was lovely, but he felt a chill creeping into him through some chink in his being. There were patches of grey above his ears. He did not know how old he was; but his daughter was grown up and his son was old enough to drive the loaded cart to the market. His house was for them; he himself had always been a wanderer on the open road. He must get moving again.

He thought of the case he had just won. What long faces those Parajas must be wearing! For a moment he thought, almost with sympathy, of what the old man must have suffered. But when you looked after your own interests others were bound to get hurt; it couldn't be helped. If you stopped to pity them you would grow old at once.

Yes, the night was lovely. He heard a soft humming behind him. It must be Jili. Lovely girl, but she had to go. Not tomorrow, perhaps, but sooner or later he must send her away.

Chapter 114

In the darkness before sunrise Sukru Jani and his sons were making for Kadamjholla with feverish haste, ignoring the paths and taking short cuts across untrodden ground. From time to time they had to use the axes that Parajas always carry in the jungle. They entertained no serious hope that the Sahukar would listen to them; but perhaps if they fell at his feet and wept – perhaps, perhaps the stone would melt.

It had been Mandia's idea.

'The land was our bowl of rice, father. What shall we eat now?' he had said. Now the Sahukar would drag them back to slave for him; they would die gotis. In his rage he had wanted to take the land by force and plough it up. But this would only add to their troubles. It was better to go to the Sahukar and beg for mercy. And the early morning might find him in the right mood, refreshed by sleep. It was the best time for another reason also: there would be no one around – no one to witness the shame of their surrender. The words would come easier to them.

The darkness became less dense, and the forest awoke and stretched itself. They were still climbing the pass when morning broke, streaking the mist with crimson.

They descended the slope into the village and stood under the thatch-eaves of the Sahukar's house. Their throats were dry, they had lost their voices, they hardly knew what to say. They stood there with heads bowed, glancing occasionally at each other's faces.

A door opened, and the Sahukar stepped out. Without a

word, Mandia flung himself at his feet, followed by Sukru Jani and Tikra. Mandia cried: 'We are dead, we are dead, Sahukar! What has happened has happened; now take your money and give us back our land.' Sukru Jani wailed: 'Sahukar, you have enough money and land; give us back our bowl of rice, we beg you, and Dharmu will reward you!' And Tikra added: 'Look at our tears, Sahukar, and give us back our land.'

The Sahukar flew into a rage, kicking them away and roaring: 'Get up! Get out! I'm to give you the land back, am I? You rascals! Take me to court, would you? And what did the court decide? Are you going or shall I have you sent to jail?'

And the old man was sent reeling with another kick.

At this moment Jili came out, rubbing her sleepy eyes and arranging her clothes hurriedly. The old man saw her and shouted, 'Jili!'; and Mandia and Tikra too screamed 'Jili!'

The Sahukar twisted his lips into a crooked smile, and said: 'Yes, Jili! And isn't there another called Bili at home still? Bring her to me. I've taken the land; I've taken one sister; and I shall take the other too. I shall take your wives; I shall drive you from court to court through the length of the country. I shall make you sweat out your lives as gotis, and I shall rub your noses in the dust. If I don't, my name is not Ramachandra Bisoi!'

And raising his fists he shouted: 'You sons of whores, aren't you ashamed to come blubbering here like women? Go, go . . .'

Inside the heads of the Parajas something snapped. Their eyes glazed, and they trembled all over. Mandia Jani leapt forward with a roar like that of a wild beast.

'You've cheated us out of the land, Sahukar, but you won't enjoy it! You won't enjoy it.'

In a flash he raised his axe and brought it down on the Sahukar's head. Immediately the other two joined in. The Sahukar fell like an axed tree, and Mandia went on dealing blow after blow, shouting: 'You didn't enjoy the land! you didn't enjoy the land!'

Jili ran off, screaming wildly.

It was only when the blood spurted into their faces and eyes that they came to their senses. By this time their clothes were soaked with blood, the axes in their hands were dripping. They stared fixedly at the body for a few moments, mouths wide open. Then Tikra flung his axe away and began to howl.

Sukru Jani exclaimed: 'Oh!' Mandia looked at his father; and father and sons put their arms around each other and wept, their tears mingling with the blood. The scarlet sun rose higher through the mist; everything was red.

That afternoon, all three of them went, just as they were, to the police station at Lachhimpur and said: 'We have killed a man. Give us whatever punishment we deserve.'

And the Sub-Inspector, startled, said: 'Eh?'

THE END